G000277488

DEFENDING BRITAIN'S SKIES 1940–1945

DESPATCHES FROM THE FRONT
The Commanding Officers' Reports From the Field and At Sea.

DEFENDING BRITAIN'S SKIES 1940–1945

Introduced and compiled by
Martin Mace and John Grehan
With additional research by
Sara Mitchell

Pen & Sword
AVIATION

First published in Great Britain in 2014 by
Pen & Sword Aviation
an imprint of
Pen & Sword Books Ltd
47 Church Street
Barnsley
South Yorkshire
S70 2AS

Copyright © Martin Mace and John Grehan, 2014

ISBN 978 1 78346 207 0

The right of Martin Mace and John Grehan to be identified as Authors of
this Work has been asserted by them in accordance with the Copyright,
Designs and Patents Act 1988.

A CIP catalogue record for this book is available from the British Library.
All rights reserved. No part of this book may be reproduced or transmitted
in any form or by any means, electronic or mechanical including
photocopying, recording or by any information storage and retrieval
system, without permission from the Publisher in writing.

Printed and bound in England
By CPI Group (UK) Ltd, Croydon, CR0 4YY

Pen & Sword Books Ltd incorporates the Imprints of
Pen & Sword Aviation, Pen & Sword Family History,
Pen & Sword Maritime, Pen & Sword Military, Pen & Sword Discovery,
Pen & Sword Politics, Pen & Sword Atlas, Pen & Sword Archaeology,
Wharncliffe Local History, Wharncliffe True Crime, Wharncliffe Transport,
Pen & Sword Select, Pen & Sword Military Classics, Leo Cooper,
The Praetorian Press, Claymore Press, Remember When,
Seaforth Publishing and Frontline Publishing.

For a complete list of Pen & Sword titles please contact:
PEN & SWORD BOOKS LIMITED
47 Church Street, Barnsley, South Yorkshire, S70 2AS, England
E-mail: enquiries@pen-and-sword.co.uk
Website: www.pen-and-sword.co.uk

CONTENTS

CONTENTS

INTRODUCTION

The report by Sir Hugh Dowding on the Battle of Britain is the first of just three official despatches on the aerial defence of the United Kingdom during the Second World War. So significant had the Battle of Britain been seen at the time, and so ingrained had it become in the public psyche as symbolic of Britain's David and Goliath struggle against the might of Germany, it was a topic that had already been the subject of popular books before Dowding's despatch had been published. His despatch, he therefore concedes, would not offer anything particularly new or revealing to the reader, and would only be of historical interest. Dowding does himself an injustice in these remarks, as his report is full of detailed and careful analysis.

In his initial comments on the Battle of Britain, Dowding writes that the underlying object of the *Luftwaffe* was to bring Fighter Command continuously to battle, and to weaken its material resources and Intelligence facilities. Exactly when these operations began, and when they ended are far from certain dates, as Dowding points out. It is Dowding himself that chose 10 July as the start of the battle, a date which is now generally accepted, though he states that this is somewhat arbitrary as earlier attacks on convoys, which drew Fighter Command into action against the *Luftwaffe*, were all part of that process of weakening Britain's defensive fighter force.

That weakening of this force was something that Dowding had to fight to preserve during the Battle of France. Much of his despatch explains why he was so opposed to sending his squadrons into France. "I saw my resources slipping away like sand in an hour-glass," he wrote. Dowding was so anxious about the loss of hundreds of aircraft and pilots in France that he sought, and was granted, a personal interview with the War Cabinet. As is well-known, Dowding's arguments won the Cabinet over, despite the desperate appeals of the French for help. "I know what it must have cost the Cabinet to reach this decision," admitted Dowding, "but I am profoundly convinced that this was one of the great turning points of the war."

Dowding also gives considerable credit to the guns of the Air Defence System. He points out that on some nights as many as sixty per cent of the raiders approaching London from the south turned back after dropping their bombs in the open country or on the fringe of the Barrage.

Dowding provides a detailed explanation of how the Chain Home radar system worked and the methods by which the incoming aircraft were tracked and engaged. Interestingly, in this regard, the code word for height given to his fighters was 'Angels'. After this had been in use for some time, Dowding suspected that the Germans had worked out what this meant. He, therefore, introduced a false quantity into the code signal. Thus "Angels 18" no longer meant a height of 18,000 feet, but 21,000 feet. On more than one occasion German fighters were pounced upon from above because of this clever change.

Dowding refrains from providing a day by day, blow by blow account of the Battle of Britain, preferring to explain in general terms the methods adopted to defeat the *Luftwaffe*. These methods are fully explained in the kind of depth not normally provided in general histories of the Battle of Britain.

An understanding of the nature of the fighting in the Battle of Britain can only be gained through an appreciation of the various aircraft types and their capabilities, and this is provided by Dowding. In this regard it is interesting to note that he makes a point of challenging the stated top speed of the Hawker Hurricane. Its given maximum speed is generally declared to be around 335-340 mph, which Dowding says is over-rated. "I carried out a series of trials to obtain the absolute and comparative speeds of Hurricanes and Spitfires at optimum heights," he wrote. "Naturally the speeds of individual aircraft varied slightly, but the average speed of six Hurricanes came out at about 305 m.p.h."

He accepts that claims of enemy losses, which after the war were found to be highly inflated, were inaccurate but he believed that, at the time, they were "an honest approximation". By comparison, German claims, he says, were "ludicrous" and that "they know they were lying"!

Regardless of such opinions, Fighter Command won the Battle of Britain and the main reason for this, according to Dowding, was because if a German aircraft was brought down over Britain, those of its crew that were not killed were captured, whereas if a British machine was shot down and the pilot was not killed or badly wounded, he could return to his squadron and be back in the air by the time his squadron was scrambled again.

Though the general policy adopted in the publication of the Second World War despatches was that appendices would not be included in the published accounts, a number of Dowding's appendices were in fact retained and printed in *The London Gazette*. Why some were omitted and some included is not clear.

The second despatch in this compilation is that from General Sir Frederick A. Pile who was the General Officer Commanding-in-Chief, Anti-Aircraft Command, and covers the entire period of the war from 1939 to 1945.

Dowding, as we have noted, attributed his victory in the Battle of Britain to an undeniable logic, that, as the Germans were operating over enemy territory they were bound to lose more pilots than Fighter Command which was fighting on its own turf. Pile, however, gives a less prosaic reason for his success. The achievements of Anti-Aircraft Command, he insists, were due to the "excellence of the personnel". The personnel he refers to were the men of the Territorial Army. "The Territorial Army has always attracted men anxious to fit themselves to defend their country. These men," Pile proudly declares, "were the cream of the manhood of the country." One can only wonder what the other services thought of that statement.

However, in the early months of the war, Pile complained about the standard of the recruits he was being sent. It was originally intended that Pile would receive 20,000 of these wonderful Territorials every month but the war was three months old before he received the first batch. In the interim he was sent conscripts instead. Of these the best men were being given to the Army and he was compelled to complain at the way his command was being treated. Over time, though, Pile got the men (and later, of course, women) he wanted, and by May 1941, Anti-Aircraft Command numbered just under 300,000 of all ranks.

If Pile was generous in his appreciation of the merits of the ordinary men under his command, he positively lavished praise upon the hundreds of scientists he employed. These were recruited from all over the British Empire, and even included volunteers from the US before America actively joined in the fighting. "No tribute could be too high to pay to all these distinguished men," he wrote. "I believe it is true to say that thanks to their efforts Anti-Aircraft Command became the most technical and scientific Command in our own or any other army." Once again this is something others might challenge.

There is, though, no doubt that Anti-Aircraft Command was highly effective in defending Britain's skies and has probably not received sufficient credit for its achievements. In this light Pile's somewhat over-stated observations are understandable. What he does point out, and what has certainly not been widely understood, is that the men and women of Anti-Aircraft Command were on duty almost continuously. As Pile states, in the other services there was generally a period of intense action followed by a period of inactivity. This was not the case with Anti-Aircraft Command as its personnel were expected to turn out every night.

The scale of the operation under Pile's command is another aspect that has perhaps not been fully appreciated. There was for example, a continuous searchlight belt thirty miles deep which stretched from the Solent, east of London, north to the Humber and then north-west to the Tyne-Tees area. A further belt ran between the Forth and the Clyde. If any aircraft penetrated these belts, they would find that important cities had been made 'Gun Defended Areas', with searchlights to enable the heavy guns to fire by night. In addition to all this, light guns were deployed to counter low-level precision bombing for the protection of isolated points of importance, such as factories and airfields.

By the time of the V1 attacks, in June 1944, Anti-Aircraft Command had reached a level of sophistication such that it was able to quickly respond and effectively to counter these new weapons. According to Pile's despatch, of a total of 1,012 V1s plotted only 495 of them came within range of his guns and of those 495 only sixty-six got through the barrage to strike London.

Pile concludes his despatch in a by now predictable fashion – that of praising those under his command. "Finally," he wrote, "the Commanders and Staffs serving under me were worthy of the troops they led".

The next despatch is that submitted by Marshal of the Royal Air Force Sir Sholto Douglas which relates to the operations of Fighter Command from the time that Dowding was removed from office, in November 1940, until December 1941. Dowding had, to a great degree, seen off the threat of daylight bombing raids upon the United Kingdom, and the main problem faced by his successor was how to deal with the night attacks that began in earnest in September 1940 and continued at an intense level throughout the following eight months or so.

Radar was, of course, Fighter Command's most important tool for locating approaching enemy aircraft and much of Douglas' despatch details the various types available and their introduction and deployment. As the Germans used radio beams and similar devices to navigate to their targets, the disruption of these signals was also of great importance.

With the change of tactics by the *Luftwaffe* to night sorties, a corresponding change had to be made by Fighter Command. It soon became apparent that specialist squadrons would be needed. These would be specifically equipped with airborne radar and their pilots trained in night fighting. In December 1940, Douglas asked the Air Ministry for twenty such squadrons to be assembled as soon as possible. Of these he wanted twelve of the squadrons to be equipped with twin-engine fighters, more specifically the Bristol Beaufighter which was just becoming available.

By March 1941, A.I. radar-equipped twin-engine fighters accounted to half of the German aircraft shot down at night by Fighter Command. From then onwards, Douglas declares, the night fighter, rather than the A.A. gun, became the chief means of inflicting casualties on the night bomber.

Single-engine fighters, reliant upon purely visual detection, still played an important role in night defence, especially when large numbers of enemy aircraft were despatched. Once the bomber stream had been detected, Hurricanes and Spitfires could get amongst the mass of enemy bombers and inflict considerable damage.

Amongst the innovative schemes attempted by Douglas was that of deploying free-flying balloons carrying lethal charges in the path of German bombers approaching London. The intention was to use these on nights when the conditions were unsuitable for fighters; but it did not follow that whenever conditions were unsuitable for fighters they would be favourable for these balloons. The hope was that these balloons would crash into the German bombers and damage or destroy them. They were not a great success and the scheme was discontinued

Nevertheless, the combined effectiveness of the anti-aircraft barrage and the night fighters soon put an end to the so-called Blitz which, Douglas declared, failed to achieve any strategic purpose. "In eight months of intensive night raiding," he states, "the German bomber force did not succeed in breaking the spirit of the British people or preventing the expansion of our means of production and supply."

It is interesting to note that whilst Douglas recognises that the end of the night battles was a relief to most people in Britain, he personally felt a little disappointed. This was because the air defence systems, incorporating both that of the Anti-Aircraft Command and Fighter Command, had become so effective that the *Lufwaffe* was being rapidly destroyed. The enemy, he said, "had slipped out of our grasp."

Fighter Command was disbanded in 1943, being replaced by the Air Defence of Great Britain which was formed on 15 November 1943. It was placed under the command of Air Chief Marshal Sir Roderic Hill whose despatch is the last in this compilation. As Hill makes clear, the true purpose of his command was merely to establish a secure base for the offensive operations across the Channel. Even 11 Group, the one that had played the most active and crucial part in the defence of England during the Battle of Britain, was really under the direct control of the 2nd Tactical Air Force.

The defence of the whole of Great Britain was restricted to just ten day-fighter and eleven night-fighter squadrons so that the greatest possible effort could be concentrated on preparing for Operation *Overlord*. With the effectiveness of the *Luftwaffe* much reduced by 1944, the limited numbers available to Hill did not seem to be a problem; that was until the first V1s began to fall.

The defence against these weapons was, as we have seen, a combined effort with Pile's Anti-Aircraft Combined. It was found that the fighters were less effective than the anti-aircraft guns during poor visibility, but the reverse was the case in good visibility. So in clear weather no guns were allowed to fire, leaving the skies to the fighters, and in poor weather the aircraft stayed on the ground.

The greater part of Hill's despatch was devoted to defeating the V1s and V2s. With the restricted resources available to Hill, he was able to intercept many of the so-called Vengeance weapons. As Hill points out, during the ten months that they were operational, more than 10,000 flying bombs were directed at London, thereby squandering about a million and a half gallons of sorely-needed petrol and a productive effort which, according to Speer, would have been better employed in turning out 3,000 fighters.

In an interesting final assessment, Hill explains that the defence against the V1s was successful only because the RAF had air almost complete superiority in the air by that stage of the war. It had been a long and difficult journey from those dark days of 1940 but Dowding's legacy had finally been fulfilled.

*

The objective of this book is to reproduce the despatches from Dowding, Pile and Douglas as they first appeared to the general public some seventy years ago. They have not been modified, edited or interpreted in any way and are therefore the original and unique words of the commanding officers as they saw things at the time they were written. The only changes that we have made are with the footnotes which are placed at the end of each despatch rather than at the foot of the respective page. Any grammatical or spelling errors have been left uncorrected to retain the authenticity of the documents.

LIST OF ILLUSTRATIONS

1   Air Chief Marshal Sir Hugh C.T. Dowding, Commander-in-Chief of RAF Fighter Command during the Battle of Britain. (HMP)

2   The General Officer Commanding Anti-Aircraft Command, General Sir Frederick Alfred Pile. The formation of a body of anti-aircraft guns had been announced in 1938 but Anti-Aircraft Command was not formed until 1 April 1939 under General Sir Alan Brooke who then passed control to Sir General Sir Frederick Pile. Pile would remain in command until the end of the war. (Courtesy of Andy Saunders)

3   Air Chief Marshal Sir William Sholto Douglas pictured in February 1943 during his service as Air Officer Commander-in-Chief, Middle East Command. (Imperial War Museum; ME(RAF)7832)

4   Supermarine Spitfire Mk.IAs of 610 Squadron cruising above the British countryside during the Battle of Britain. The squadron was formed at RAF Hooton Park, Cheshire, on 10 February 1936 as a day bomber unit of the Auxiliary Air Force. On 1 January 1939, the Squadron was re-designated a fighter unit. On the outbreak of war it received Hawker Hurricanes, but by the end of September 1939 had exchanged these for Spitfires, becoming operational on 21 October. When the German offensive opened in May 1940, 610 Squadron moved to Biggin Hill. (ww2images)

5   Some of "The Few" are seen in this group shot of pilots of 249 Squadron taken at RAF North Weald during September 1940. From left to right are: Pilot Officer Percival R.F. Burton, Flight Lieutenant Robert Barton, Flight Lieutenant Albert Lewis DFC,

crashed into the ground at Cheeseman's Farm, Minster, Kent, on 5 February 1941. (HMP)

13   Firemen playing their hoses on dying embers in buildings along Queen Victoria Street after the last and heaviest major raid mounted by the *Luftwaffe* against the British capital during the Blitz. For six hours on the night of 10-11 May 1941, German aircraft dropped over 1,000 tons of bombs on London, claiming 1,486 lives, destroying 11,000 houses and damaging many important historical buildings. (HMP)

14   At 20.02 hours on 14 October 1940, a bomb dropped during a raid on London penetrated thirty-two feet underground and exploded just above the cross passage between the two platforms at Balham Underground Station. Above ground this double decker bus, travelling in blackout conditions, plunged into the crater created by the bomb. The dramatic spectacle of the trapped bus provided one of the iconic images of the Blitz. (HMP)

15   A Bristol Beaufighter night fighter. The Beaufighter came off the production line at almost exactly the same time as the first Airborne Intercept (AI) radar sets. With the four 20mm cannon mounted in the lower fuselage, the nose could accommodate the radar antennas, and the space in the fuselage enabled the AI equipment to be fitted easily. By early 1941, the Beaufighter was proving an effective counter to the *Luftwaffe*'s night raids (HMP)

16   Released to the press on 3 August 1944, this image shows a V-1 Flying Bomb diving down onto London. The buildings in the foreground are the Royal Courts of Justice (Law Courts) on the north side of the Strand. It is stated that this V-1 fell on Wild Street on 28 June 1944. (HMP)

DESPATCHES ON THE BATTLE OF BRITAIN

BY AIR CHIEF MARSHAL SIR HUGH C.T. DOWDING'S

The Air Ministry,
September, 1946.

THE BATTLE OF BRITAIN.

The following despatch was submitted to the Secretary of State for Air on August 20th, 1941, by Air Chief Marshal Sir Hugh C.T. Dowding, G.C.B., G.C.V.O., C.M.G., A.D.C.,

Air Officer Commanding-in-Chief, Fighter Command,
Royal Air Force.

PREAMBLE.

I. I have been instructed by the Air Council to write a Despatch on the Air Fighting of last Autumn, which has become known as the "Battle of Britain". The conditions are a little unusual because, firstly, the Battle ended many months ago, secondly, a popular account of the fighting has already been written and published, and, thirdly, recommendations for Mention in Despatches have already been submitted.

2. I have endeavoured, therefore, to write a report which will, I hope, be of Historical interest, and which will, in any case, contain the results of more than four years' experience of the Fighter Command in peace and war.

August 20, 1941.

THE BATTLE OF BRITAIN.

PART I.
PRELIMINARY.

3. In giving an account of the Battle of Britain it is perhaps advisable to begin by a definition of my conception of the meaning of the phrase. The Battle may be said to have started when the Germans had disposed of the French resistance in the Summer of 1940, and turned their attention to this country.

4. The essence of their Strategy was so to weaken our Fighter Defences that their Air Arm should be able to give adequate support to an attempted invasion of the British Isles. Experiences in Holland and Belgium had shown what they could do with armoured forces operating in conjunction with an Air Arm which had substantially achieved the command of the Air.

5. This air supremacy was doubly necessary to them in attacking England because the bulk of their troops and war material must necessarily be conveyed by sea, and, in order to achieve success, they must be capable of giving air protection to the passage and the landing of troops and material.

6. The destruction or paralysis of the Fighter Command was therefore an essential prerequisite to the invasion of these Islands.

7. Their immediate objectives might be Convoys, Radio-Location Stations, Fighter Aerodromes, Seaports, Aircraft Factories, or London itself. Always the underlying object was to bring the Fighter Command

continuously to battle, and to weaken its material resources and Intelligence facilities.

8. Long after the policy of "crashing through" with heavy bomber formations had been abandoned owing to the shattering losses incurred, the battle went on. Large fighter formations were sent over, a proportion of the fighters being adapted to carry bombs, in order that the attacks might not be ignorable.

9. This last phase was perhaps the most difficult to deal with tactically. It will be discussed in greater detail later on.

I0. Night attacks by Heavy Bombers were continuous throughout the operations, and, although they persisted and increased in intensity as Day Bombing became more and more expensive, they had an essentially different purpose, and the "Battle of Britain" may be said to have ended when the Fighter and Fighter-Bomber raids died down.

II. It is difficult to fix the exact date on which the "Battle of Britain" can be said to have begun. Operations of various kinds merged into one another almost insensibly, and there are grounds for choosing the date of the 8th August, on which was made the first attack in force against laid objectives in this country, as the beginning of the Battle.

I2. On the other hand, the heavy attacks made against our Channel convoys probably constituted, in fact, the beginning of the German offensive; because the weight and scale of the attack indicates that the primary object was rather to bring our Fighters to battle than to destroy the hulls and cargoes of the small ships engaged in the coastal trade. While we were fighting in Belgium and France, we suffered the disadvantage that even the temporary stoppage of an engine involved the loss of pilot and aircraft, whereas, in similar circumstances, the German pilot might be fighting again the same day, and his aircraft be airborne again in a matter of hours.

I3. In fighting over England these considerations were reversed, and the moral and material disadvantages of fighting over enemy country may well have determined the Germans to open the attack with a phase of fighting in which the advantages were more evenly balanced. I have therefore, somewhat arbitrarily, chosen the events of the I0th July as the opening of the Battle. Although many attacks had previously been made on convoys, and even on land objectives such as Portland, the I0th July saw the employment by the Germans of the first really big formation (70 aircraft) intended primarily to bring our Fighter Defence to battle on a large scale.

14. I had 59 squadrons in various stages of efficiency. A list of these units, with supplementary information, is given in Appendix A. Many of them were still suffering from the effects of the fighting in Holland and Flanders, at Dunkerque, and during the subsequent operations in France. Others were in process of formation and training. But, if the lessons of the Battle are to be correctly appreciated, due consideration must be given to the factors leading up to the situation existing when it began. Leaving out of account peace-time preparations and training, the Battle of Britain began for me in the Autumn of 1939.

15. The first major problem arose during the discussion of the question of sending Fighter Squadrons to France. The decisive factor was that of Supply. Our output at the beginning of the war was about 2 Hurricanes and 2 Spitfires per diem; and, although there were hopes of increasing Hurricane production, there was then no hope that Spitfire production would be materially increased for about a year. It is true that certain optimistic estimates had been made, but there were reasons to believe that these could not be implemented. At that time, we in England were out of range of German Fighters, and I had good hopes that unescorted bomb raids on this country could be met and defeated with a very small loss in Fighters; but there could be no illusions concerning the wastage which would occur if we came up against the German Fighters in France.

16. I therefore regarded with some apprehension the general policy of sending Home Defence Fighter Units to France; but, as it was clear that such an attitude was politically untenable, I wrote on the 16th September, 1939, a letter to the Air Ministry. In this letter I pointed out that the Air Staff Estimate of the number of Fighter Squadrons necessary for the defence of this country was 52, and that on the outbreak of war I had the equivalent of 34 (allowing for the fact that some Auxiliary Squadrons were only partially trained and equipped).

17. I wanted 12 new squadrons, but asked that 8 should be raised immediately, and made proposals for their location and employment. In a letter dated the 21st September the Air Ministry regretted that the most they could do towards meeting my requirements was to form 2

new squadrons and 2 operational training units. I was invited to a meeting of the Air Council on the 26th September,

18. On the 25th September I wrote expressing my disappointment and asking for a reconsideration. As a result of this letter, the Air Council Meeting, and a further meeting under the Chairmanship of the Deputy Chief of Air Staff, the Air Ministry wrote on the 9th October sanctioning the immediate formation of 8 new squadrons, though 6 of these could be formed initially only as half-squadrons owing to shortage of resources. This correspondence is too lengthy to reproduce here, but it deals also with my apprehensions concerning Hurricane wastage in France, which were realised in the Spring of 1940. It also dealt with an estimate worked out by the Air Ministry Organisation Staff that after 3 months of fighting we might expect the Fighter strength to have been reduced to 26 squadrons.

19. In October, 1939, the Air Ministry further reconsidered their policy, and ordered the formation of 10 additional Fighter Squadrons, 4 of which were destined for the Coastal Command.

20. In January, 1940, the Northern flank of our continuous Defence organisation was on the Forth, and the South-Western flank was at Tangmere in Sussex (with the exception of an isolated station at Filton for the local defence of Bristol and the mouth of the Severn). On the 2nd and 4th February I wrote two letters pointing out these limitations, and asking for an extension of Aerodrome facilities, Intelligence cover and communications.

21. On the 9th February I was told that a paper was in preparation, and that I would be given an opportunity to remark on the proposals at a later stage.

22. On the 16th March I received the paper referred to and forwarded my comments on the 23rd March.

23. On the 8th May I received a letter saying that a reply had been delayed. The proposals were now approved, and decisions would shortly be taken.

24. This delay was presumably unavoidable, but the result was that the organisation and development of the defences of the South and West of England were very incomplete when they were called upon to withstand the attacks which the German occupation of French aerodromes made possible.

25. The fighting in Norway has only an indirect bearing on this paper. Certain useful tactical lessons were gained, particularly with regard to deflection shooting, and I trust that the story of the epic fight of No. 263 Squadron under Squadron-Leader J.W. Donaldson, D.S.O., near Andalsnes, may not be lost to History.

26. The outcome, as it affects this account, was the virtual loss of 2 squadrons in the sinking of the Aircraft Carrier *Glorious* after the evacuation of Narvik.

27. Next came the invasion of Holland, and the call to send Fighters to the assistance of the Dutch. The distance to Rotterdam was about the extreme range of the single-seater Fighter, which therefore operated under the disadvantage of having a very brief potential combat-time, followed by the necessity of a long sea crossing on the homeward way. The Blenheims, of course, had the necessary endurance, but they had not been designed as fighters, and their use against day fighters proved costly in comparison with the limited success which they attained.

28. The Defiants were used here for the first time, and, although they proved very effective against unescorted bombers, they too suffered heavy casualties when they encountered fighters in strength. As the result of this experience I formed the opinion that the Blenheims should be kept exclusively for night fighting, if possible, while I retained an open mind about the Defiants pending some experience of short-range fighting.

29. Then began the fighting in Belgium and Northern France, and at once my fears about the incidence of wastage in this type of fighting began to be realised.

30. At the beginning of April, 1940, there were 6 Fighter Squadrons in France.

31. Then 4 more complete squadrons were sent when the fighting began.

32. Then on the 13th May 32 pilots and aircraft were sent – say the equivalent of 2 squadrons.

33. Almost immediately afterwards 8 Half-Squadrons were sent. This was done under the impression that the loss of 8 Half-Squadrons would affect me less than that of 4 entire Squadrons, because it was supposed that I should be able to rebuild on the nuclei left behind. But this assumption was incorrect because I had neither the time nor the

personnel available for purposes of reconstruction, and the remaining half-squadrons had to be amalgamated into Composite Units with a resulting disorganisation and loss of efficiency. At this time, too, I was ordered to withdraw trained pilots from squadrons and to send them overseas as reinforcements.

34. I had now lost the equivalent of I6 Squadrons, and in addition 4 Squadrons were sent to fight in France during the day and to return to English bases in the evening.

35. Other pilots were withdrawn from the Command through the system by which the Air Ministry dealt direct with Groups on questions of Personnel.

36. It must be remembered that during this period the Home Defence Squadrons were not idle, but that Hurricane Squadrons were participating in the fighting to a considerable extent, 4 Squadrons daily left S.E. England with orders to carry out an offensive patrol, to land and refuel in France or Belgium, and to carry out a second sortie before returning to England.

37. Hitherto I had succeeded generally in keeping the Spitfire Squadrons out of the Continental fighting. The reason for this, as stated above, was that the supply situation was so bad that they could not have maintained their existence in face of the Aircraft Casualty Rate experienced in France: between the 8th May and the I8th May 250 Hurricanes were lost.

38. When the Dunkerque fighting began, however, I could no longer maintain this policy, and the Spitfires had to take their share in the fighting.

39. When the Dunkerque evacuation was complete I had only 3 Day-Fighting Squadrons which had not been engaged in Continental fighting, and I2 Squadrons were in the line for the second time after having been withdrawn to rest and re-form.

40. All this time, it must be remembered, the attack on this Country had not begun; with a few accidental exceptions no bomb had been dropped on our soil. I was responsible for the Air Defence of Great Britain, and I saw my resources slipping away like sand in an hour-glass. The pressure for more and more assistance to France was relentless and inexorable. In the latter part of May, I940, I sought and obtained permission to appear in person before the War Cabinet and to

state my case. I was accorded a courteous and sympathetic hearing, and to my inexpressible relief my arguments prevailed and it was decided to send no more Fighter Reinforcements to France except to cover the final evacuation.

4I. I know what it must have cost the Cabinet to reach this decision, but I am profoundly convinced that this was one of the great turning points of the war.

42. Another decision, of perhaps equal importance, was taken at about this time. I refer to the appointment of Lord Beaverbrook to the post of Minister of Aircraft Production. The effect of this appointment can only be described as magical, and thereafter the Supply situation improved to such a degree that the heavy aircraft wastage which was later incurred during the "Battle of Britain" ceased to be the primary danger, its place being taken by the difficulty of producing trained fighter pilots in adequate numbers.

43. After the Evacuation from Dunkerque the pressure on the Fighter Command became less intense, but it by no means disappeared. Hard fighting took place along the coast from Calais to Le Havre to cover the successive evacuations from that coast. Then the centre of gravity shifted to Cherbourg and its neighbourhood, and the "Battle of Britain" followed on without any appreciable opportunity to rest and re-form the units which had borne the brunt of the fighting.

44. The above considerations should be kept in mind when Appendix A (Order of Battle on the 8th July, I940) is being studied.

45. The Guns and Searchlights available for the Air Defence of Great Britain were arranged as shown on the map which constitutes Appendix B.

46. The fall of Belgium and France had increased the danger to the South and West of England, and had necessitated a considerable modification of the original arrangements when bombing attacks could start only from German soil.

47. The distribution of Army Units was, as a matter of fact, in a condition of perpetual change to meet new situations as they arose, and I must pay a very sincere tribute to the flexibility of the Army organisation, and to the tact, patience and loyalty of the Commander-in-Chief of the Anti-Aircraft Command, Lt. Gen. Sir Frederick A. Pile,

Bart., K.C.B., D.S.O., M.C., which enabled these constant changes to be made without disorganisation.

48. In theory the Commander-in-Chief, Fighter Command, was the authority responsible for settling the dispositions of all guns allotted to the Air Defence of Great Britain; but this was little more than a convenient fiction. The number of guns available was so inadequate for the defence of all the vulnerable targets in the country, and the interests concerned were so diverse and powerful, that it was not to be supposed that an individual member of any one Service would be left to exercise such a prerogative uninterruptedly. A disproportionate amount of my time was taken up in discussions on gun distribution, and each decision was at once greeted with a fresh agitation, until finally I had to ask that all proposals should be discussed by a small Committee on which all interests were represented, and I normally accepted the recommendations of this Committee during quiet periods. During active operations I consulted General Pile, and we acted according to our judgment.

One rather important lesson emerged from our experience, viz., that the general fire-control of all guns in the Air Defence System should be vested in the Air Defence authorities. I do not, of course, mean that, if an invasion had taken place, the guns co-operating with the troops in the Field should have been subordinated to any A.A. Defence Commander, but the existence of "free-lance" guns[1], the positions and even the existence of which were unknown to me, was an appreciable handicap, especially at night. It was impossible to acquaint them with the approach of enemy raiders, or of the fact that our own aircraft were working in the vicinity.

49. When the night attacks on London began to be really serious, General Pile, in consultation with myself, decided to send heavy reinforcements. Within 24 hours the defences to the South and South-East of London were approximately doubled, and the great increase in the volume of fire was immediately noticed and had a very good effect on public morale. The physical effect in the shape of raiders destroyed was by no means negligible, but the main effect was never generally known. The track of every raid was, of course, shown on various operations tables, and on some nights as many as 60 per cent. of the

raiders approaching London from the South turned back after dropping their bombs in the open country or on the fringe of the Barrage.

50. The A.A. Guns at Dover enjoyed unusual opportunities for practice, with the result that their crews became acknowledged experts in the art of Anti-Aircraft Gunnery. Their skill, however, was attained through the circumstance that they and the Dover Balloon Barrage were continuously the objectives of German attack; they manned their guns continuously night and day, and I must pay a high tribute to their morale, enthusiasm and efficiency.

A report from the 6th A.A. Division, which was busily and typically employed, is included at Appendices C, C.A, C.B. and C.C.

5I. A short Appendix (C.D) is added showing the number of rounds fired per aircraft destroyed, for the whole Anti-Aircraft Command.

52. On the map which constitutes Appendix A.A. are shown the boundaries of Groups and Sectors, and also the positions of the Balloon Barrages, together with an indication of the front covered by Radio Location Stations and the area covered by the Observer Corps.

53. The Balloon Barrages had, at this stage, had little opportunity of justifying their existence, except perhaps at Rosyth and Scapa Flow, since bombing attacks against land objectives in Britain had not yet begun. It was thought, however, (and later experience confirmed this opinion), that the heavy cost of their installation and maintenance, and their drain on man-power, were on the whole justified. It is true that their material results, in terms of enemy aircraft destroyed, were not impressive, they suffered staggering casualties in electric storms, and had brought down a number of our own aircraft; on the other hand, they exercise a very salutary moral effect upon the Germans and to a great extent protected the vital objectives, which they surrounded, against low-altitude attacks and dive-bombing.

54. This is not the place to give an account of the romantic discovery and development of Radio Location. It may be explained, however, that the backbone of the system consisted of a series of large "chain" stations at intervals averaging about 30 miles. These gave warning, by means of reflected electrical echoes, of the presence of aircraft within the radius of their effective action, which attained to nearly 200 miles in the most favourable circumstances. The average effective radius was

about 80 miles, but they had the serious limitation that they failed altogether to give indications of aircraft flying below I,000 feet.

55. To overcome this disability, which was particularly hampering to operations against low-flying minelayers, smaller units called "C.H.L. Stations" were included in the protective line.

56. These had a restricted range (about 30 miles), and were incapable of giving heights with any degree of accuracy; they were, however, extremely accurate in azimuth, and constituted an essential feature of the Defensive and Warning Systems.

57. The Radio Location system was growing so fast and had to meet so many calls from overseas that the training of the technical personnel and the maintenance of the elaborate scientific apparatus presented great difficulties. In spite of these handicaps, however, the system operated effectively, and it is not too much to say that the warnings which it gave could have been obtained by no other means and constituted a vital factor in the Air Defence of Great Britain.

58. The functions of the Observer Corps (since granted the "Royal" prefix) are too well known to require description here. Suffice it to say that this loyal and public-spirited body of men had maintained their watch with admirable efficiency since the beginning of the war and throughout a winter of exceptional severity. It is important to note that, at this time, they constituted the sole means of tracking enemy raids once they had crossed the coast line. Later experience was to show that "sound plots," which were all that could be given for night raiders, and aircraft flying above clouds or at extreme altitudes, were not adequate for purposes of accurate interception; but their work throughout was quite invaluable. Without it the Air Raid Warning systems could not have been operated, and Inland Interceptions would rarely have been made.

59. The credit for building up and developing the Observer Corps in recent years is due largely to its Commandant, Air Commodore A.D. Warrington Morris; C.M.G., O.B.E.

60. The Air Raid Warning System was operated centrally from Fighter Command Headquarters (with a small exception in the Orkneys and Shetlands).

6I. The country was divided into about I30 "Warning Districts," the boundaries of which were determined by the lay-out of the public telephone system. These districts were shown on a map in my Operations Room, and the tracks of all enemy raids, whether over the land or sea, were plotted by means of counters deposited and removed as necessary by a number of "Plotters."

62. The counters were of three colours, according to the 5-minute period in which they were placed on the table. This was necessary to facilitate their removal at the end of I5 minutes, and so to obviate the confusion caused by "stale plots."

63. Three telephone operators were in continuous communication with the Trunk Exchanges in London, Liverpool and Glasgow, and when a raid was within 20 minutes' flying distance of a warning district the Air Raid Warning officer would send a message, as, for instance: "I0. Norwich. Yellow." The London operator would transmit this to the London Trunk Exchange, and the London operator would immediately retransmit it to Norwich, where other operators would pass it on to approved recipients in the Warning District. This was a preliminary caution for the information of Police, Fire Stations, &c., and involved no public warning.

64. About 5 minutes later, if the said District were still threatened, a "Red Warning" would be given. This was the signal for the Sirens to sound. A "Green" signal indicated "Raiders Passed," and the Sirens sounded the "All Clear."

65. At night, when it became essential to maintain exposed lights in Dockyards, Railway Sidings and Factories up to the last minute, so as to obviate unnecessary loss of working time, a "Purple" warning was introduced. This was a signal for the extinction of exposed lights, but it did not connote a public warning.

66. There were also subsidiary warnings, transmitted by a fourth operator, to close down Radio Stations which might assist the enemy's navigation by enabling him to use wireless Direction Finding.

67. The credit for working out this system in conjunction with the Home Office is due largely to Air Vice-Marshal A.D. Cunningham, C.B.E.

68. The Fighter Command was divided into Groups and Sectors in accordance with the arrangement shown in Appendix AA. Only Nos. II, I2 and I3 Groups were fully organised at the beginning of the Battle. Each Group and Sector Headquarters had an Operations Table

generally similar to that already described at Command Headquarters, but covering an appropriately smaller area. The British Isles and neighbouring seas were covered by an imaginary "grid" which was used by all concerned for plotting purposes. An expression consisting of one letter and four digits gave the position of a point with an accuracy of I square kilometre.

69. Plots from which tracks could be built up were received first from the Radio Location Station, and later from the Observer Corps (and to a small extent from Searchlight Detachments) after a raid had crossed the coast.

70. All Radio Location plots came to a "Filter Room" table at Command Headquarters (next door to the room in which the Operations Table was situated), and, after surplus information had been eliminated, tracks were passed by direct telephone line simultaneously to my Operations Table and to those of Groups and Sectors concerned.

7I. Observer Corps plots, on the other hand, went first to Observer Group Centres (where plotting tables were also installed) and thence to Sector and Fighter Group Operations tables. The tracks were then "told" to my Operations Room from the Group Tables.

72. In order to avoid waste of flying effort and false Air Raid Warnings it was obviously very necessary to differentiate between friendly and enemy formations, and this was the most difficult as well as the most important task of my Filter Room. Liaison Officers from Bomber and Coastal Commands were permanently on duty, and they were in possession of all available information concerning the operations of our own Bombers and Coastal patrols. During I940 an electrical device became generally available which modified the echo received by the Radio Location System from our own aircraft in a characteristic manner. This was of the greatest value.

73. The credit for working out the complicated details of the Filter Room belongs largely to Wing Commander (now Group Captain) R.G. Hart, C.B.E.

74. It appeared to me quite impossible to centralise Tactical control at Command Headquarters, and even Group Commanders would be too busy during heavy fighting to concern themselves with details of Interception.

75. The system was that the Command should be responsible for the

identification of approaching formations and for the allotment of enemy raids to Groups where any doubt existed. Group Commanders decided which Sector should meet any specified raid and the strength of the Fighter force which should be employed. Sector Commanders detailed the Fighter Units to be employed, and operated the machinery of Interception.

76. Various states of preparedness were laid down, *e.g.,* Released, Available (20 minutes), Readiness (5 minutes), and stand-by (2 minutes), and Sectors reported all changes to Group Headquarters, where an up-to-date picture of the state of affairs was recorded by lights on the walls of the Operations Room. Various liaison officers from the Observer Corps, guns and searchlights were maintained in Group and Sector Operations Rooms.

77. It will be seen that the Sector Commander had on his table the best available information as to the position and track of an enemy formation; but, in order to effect an accurate interception, it was necessary that he should also know the position and track of his own Fighters.

78. This was recorded by means of R/T D/F (Radio Telephony Direction Finding). R/T signals were transmitted automatically for I5 seconds out of each minute by selected Fighter aircraft and were picked up by two or three D/F stations installed in Sectors for the purpose. The readings were passed by direct telephone lines to Sector Headquarters, and a mechanical plotting device gave an almost instantaneous plot of the Fighter's position.

79. In the more recently organised Sectors these D/F stations had not been installed, and it was necessary to keep track of the Fighters by giving them precise orders as to speed and direction, and plotting their tracks by Dead Reckoning. This method was adequate only if the force and direction of the wind at various altitudes could be correctly estimated.

80. The Sector Commander could thus see on his operations tables the positions and courses of enemy formations and of his own Fighters, and was enabled so to direct the latter as to make interceptions with the former in a good percentage of occasions by day. Interception depended, of course, on the Fighters being able to see the enemy, and, although the system worked adequately against enemy formations in

daylight, the degree of accuracy obtainable was insufficient to effect interception against night raiders not illuminated by Searchlights, or against individual aircraft using cloud cover by day.

81. Orders were given to pilots in their aircraft by means of a very simple code which could be easily memorised. For instance "Scramble" meant Take off. "Orbit" meant Circle. "Vector 230" meant Fly on a course of 230 Degrees.

82. I realised that the enemy might pick up the signals and interpret them, but any elaborate code was out of the question if it included reference to some written list in the air.

83. As a matter of fact the enemy did pick up and interpret the signals in some cases, but not much harm was done, except when they were able to discover the height at which a formation was ordered to operate, and the time when it was ordered to leave its patrol line and land.

84. "Pancake" was the signal for the latter operation, and I therefore introduced several synonyms, the significance of which was not obvious to the enemy.

85. The code word for height was "Angels," followed by the number of thousands of feet; when it appeared probable that the enemy were taking advantage of this information I introduced a false quantity into the code signal. Thus "Angels 18" really meant Fly at 21,000 and not 18,000. On more than one occasion German Fighter formations arriving to dive on one of our patrols were themselves attacked from above.

86. The system as a whole had been built up by successive steps over a period of about four years, and I was not dissatisfied with the way in which it stood the test of war.

87. The steps taken to devise a system of night Interception are described later in this Despatch.

88. I must now give a brief account of the characteristics of the aircraft commonly employed on both sides. As regards the Fighter types available in the Command, the bulk of the force consisted of Hurricanes and Spitfires; the former were beginning to be outmoded by their German counterparts. They were comparatively slow and their performance and manoeuvrability were somewhat inadequate at altitudes above 20,000 ft. The Spitfires were equal or superior to anything which the Germans possessed at the beginning of the Battle.

89. The Hurricanes and Spitfires had bulletproof windscreens and

front armour between the top of the engine and the windscreen. They also had rear armour directly behind the pilot, which was previously prepared and fitted as soon as we began to meet the German Fighters. The early adoption of armour gave us an initial advantage over the Germans, but they were quick to imitate our methods. While German aircraft remained unarmoured, I think it is now generally agreed that the single-seater multi-gun fighter with fixed guns was the most efficient type which could have been produced for day fighting. With the advent of armour some change in armament and/or tactics became necessary, and the subject is discussed in more detail in Appendix F.

90. The Defiant, after some striking initial successes, proved to be too expensive in use against Fighters and was relegated to night work and to the attack of unescorted Bombers.

9I. The Blenheim was also unsuitable for day-time combat with Fighters, owing to its low speed and lack of manoeuvrability. It had been relegated to night duties for these reasons, and because adequate space was available in its fuselage for an extra operator and the scientific apparatus which was necessary for the development of a new night-interception technique. The cockpit had not been designed for night flying and the night view was extremely bad. Its already low performance had been further reduced by certain external fittings which were essential for the operation of the Radio Detecting apparatus.

92. The Beaufighter was looked on as a Blenheim replacement in which most of the above disadvantages would be overcome. Its speed promised to be adequate and its armament consisted of 4 20-mm. Cannons instead of the 5 .303-inch Brownings of the Blenheim. There was thus hope that decisive fire could be brought to bear in the short period during which visual contact could be expected to be maintained at night.

93. Like the Blenheim, it had not been designed as a Night Fighter (it was an adaptation of the Beaufort Torpedo Bomber), and the night view from the cockpit was bad; but Air Vice-Marshal Sir Q. Brand, K.B.E., D.S.O., M.C., D.F.C., a veteran night fighter of the previous war, had designed a new cockpit lay-out, which did not, unfortunately, materialise during my tenure of the Fighter Command. The output of Beaufighters was also very low.

94. Another type which was pressed into service as a Night Fighter

was the Douglas D.B.7 (now the Havoc). It had low fire power and comparatively poor performance with its original engines. Its chief advantage lay in its tricycle undercarriage, which proved very popular for landings in bad visibility. Only one Squadron of these was in being when I left the Command.

95. One Squadron of Gladiators was still in use in the Command. As explained above, the organisation of No. I0 Group was not complete, and there was no large aerodrome close enough to Plymouth to allow of direct protection being given to that town and to the Dockyard at Devonport. A squadron of Gladiators was therefore located at a small aerodrome called Roborough in the immediate vicinity. The Gladiators, though slow by modern standards, were very manoeuvrable, and had given good results in Norway by deflection shooting in the defence of fixed objectives, where the Bombers could not avoid the Gladiators if they were to reach their targets.

96. Some American single-seater aircraft were in Great Britain, but the types then available were deficient in performance and fire power and were not employed to any material extent.

97. The Whirlwind raised high hopes in some quarters. It claimed a very high top speed and carried 4 Cannon Guns. It had, however, a totally inadequate service ceiling (about 25,000 ft.) and a poor performance at that altitude. It also suffered from a continuous series of teething troubles, and the single Squadron equipped with this type was never fit for operations in my time.

98. It is very difficult to give any kind of concise description of the types of Enemy Aircraft used during the Battle. The Germans, while adhering to broad standard types, were continually modifying and improving them by fitting more powerful engines and altering the armament. The original Messerschmitt I09, for instance, had a performance comparable with that of the Hurricane, but the latest type could compete with the Spitfire, and had a better ceiling. Some of them had 4 machine guns and others had 2 machine guns and 2 cannons. Some of them were fitted to carry bombs and some were not.

99. The Messerschmitt I10 was a twin-engined fighter designed primarily for escorting Bombers and used also as a Fighter-Bomber. It was somewhat faster than the Hurricane, but naturally much less manoeuvrable than the single-engined types. Its usual armament was

2 fixed cannons and 4 machine guns firing forward, and one free machine gun firing to the rear. Our pilots regarded it as a less formidable opponent than the later types of M.E. I09.

I00. The Heinkel II3 Fighter made its appearance in limited numbers during the Battle. It was a single seater, generally resembling the M.E. 109. Its main attributes were high performance and ceiling, so that it was generally used in the highest of the several layers in which attacking formations were usually built up.

I0I. The Junkers 87 was a single-engined Dive-Bomber. It had a low performance (top speed well under 250 m.p.h.). It had 2 fixed machine guns firing forward and one free gun firing to the rear. When it was able to operate undisturbed by Fighters it was the Germans' most efficient Bomber against land or sea targets owing to the great accuracy with which it dropped its bombs; but when it was caught by fighters it was nothing short of a death-trap, and formations of J.U. 87's were practically annihilated on several occasions.

I02. The Heinkel III and the various types of Dornier (I7, I7Z and 2I5) constituted the main element of the German striking force. They were twin-engined aircraft and were generally similar, although the former was slightly the larger. Their speed was something over 250 m.p.h., and then armament consisted normally (but not always) of 4 free machine guns firing backwards and one firing forwards. Their radius of action varied with tankage and bomb load, but, if necessary, all objectives in England and Northern Ireland could be reached from aerodromes in France.

I03. The Junkers 88 was the most modern of the German Bombers. It also was a twin-engined type with a performance of about 290 m.p.h. Its armament was generally similar to that of the H.E. III and the Dorniers and it had a slightly longer range. It could be used on occasions as a Dive-Bomber and, though probably somewhat less accurate than the J.U. 87, was much less vulnerable owing to its superior performance and armament.

I04. Before beginning an account of the Battle, I must refer briefly to the publication entitled *The Battle of Britain,* issued by the Air Ministry. This, if I may say so, is an admirable account of the Battle for public consumption, and I am indebted to it, as well as to the book *Fighter Command,* by Wing Commander A.B. Austin, for help in the compilation of this Despatch. There is very little which I should have wished to alter, even if circumstances had permitted my seeing it before publication (I was absent in America at the time), but there are two points to which I should like to draw attention:-

I05. In the diagram on page 7 the speed of the Hurricane is seriously over-rated at 335 m.p.h. I carried out a series of trials to obtain the absolute and comparative speeds of Hurricanes and Spitfires at optimum heights. Naturally the speeds of individual aircraft varied slightly, but the average speed of six Hurricanes came out at about 305 m.p.h.

I06. The second point is of greater importance. I quote from page 33: "What the Luftwaffe failed to do was to destroy the Fighter Squadrons of the Royal Air Force, *which were, indeed, stronger at the end of the battle than at the beginning.*" (The italics are mine.)

I07. This statement, even if intended only for popular consumption, tends to lead to an attitude of complacency which may be very dangerous in the future. Whatever the study of paper returns may have shown, the fact is that the situation was critical in the extreme. Pilots had to be withdrawn from the Bomber and Coastal Commands and from the Fleet Air Arm and flung into the Battle after hasty preparation. The majority of the squadrons had been reduced to the status of training units, and were fit only for operations against unescorted bombers. The remainder were battling daily against heavy odds.

I08. The indomitable courage of the Fighter Pilots and the skill of their Leaders brought us through the crises, and the morale of the Germans eventually cracked because of the stupendous losses which they sustained.

I09. Any attempt to describe the events of the Battle day by day would make this Despatch unduly long and would prevent the reader from obtaining a comprehensive picture of the events. I have therefore decided to show the main features of each day's fighting in an Appendix on which our own and the Germans' aircraft casualties will be shown graphically. I shall then be able to deal with the progress of the Battle by phases, thus avoiding the tedious and confusing method of day-to-day description. The information is given in Appendix D.

II0. As regards our casualties, we generally issued statements to the effect that we lost "x" aircraft from which "y" pilots were saved. This did not of course mean that "y" pilots were ready immediately to continue the Battle. Many of them were suffering from wounds, burns or other injuries which precluded their return to active flying temporarily or permanently.

III. It might also be assumed that all German crews who were in aircraft brought down during the Battle, were permanently lost to the Luftwaffe because the fighting took place on our side of the Channel. Such an assumption would not be literally true, because the Germans succeeded in rescuing a proportion of their crews from the sea by means of rescue boats, floats and aircraft which will be later described.

II2. The decisive features of the Battle were the Ratio of Casualties incurred by ourselves and the Germans, and the Ratio of Casualties to the numbers actively employed on both sides. Appendix D has been drawn up with these points in mind.

II3. I must disclaim any exact accuracy in the estimates of Enemy losses. All that I can say is that the utmost care was taken to arrive at the closest possible approximation. Special intelligence officers examined pilots individually after their combats, and the figures claimed are only those recorded as "Certain." If we allow for a percentage of over-statement, and the fact that two or more Fighters were sometimes firing at the same enemy aircraft without being aware of the fact, this can fairly be balanced by the certainty that a proportion of aircraft reported as "Probably Destroyed" or "Damaged" failed to return to their bases. The figures, then, are put forward as an honest approximation. Judging by results, they are perhaps not far out.

II4. The German claims were, of course, ludicrous; they may have been deceived about our casualties, but they know they were lying about their own.

II5. I remember being cross-examined in August by the Secretary of State for Air about the discrepancy. He was anxious about the effect on the American people of the wide divergence between the claims of the two sides. I replied that the Americans would soon find out the truth; if the Germans' figures were accurate they would be in London in a week, otherwise they would not.

II6. Our estimate of German casualties, then, may be taken as reasonably accurate for practical purposes; but our estimates of the strength in which attacks were made is based on much less reliable evidence. The Radio-Location system could give only a very approximate estimate of numbers and was sometimes in error by three or four hundred per cent. This is no reflection on the System, which was not designed or intended to be accurate in the estimation of considerable numbers; moreover, several stations were suffering from the effects of severe bombing attacks. As the average height of operations increased, the Observer Corps became less and less able to make accurate estimates of numbers, and, in fact, formations were often quite invisible from the ground.

II7. Even the numerical estimates made by pilots who encountered large formations in the air are likely to be guesswork in many instances. Opportunities for deliberate counting of enemy aircraft were the exception rather than the rule.

II8. Although Secret Intelligence sources supplemented the information available, it is possible that on days of heavy fighting complete formations may have escaped recorded observation altogether.

II9. This is unfortunate, because it is obviously of the greatest importance to determine the relative strengths of the Attack and the Defence, and to know the ratio of losses to aircraft employed which may be expected to bring an attack to a standstill in a given time. History will doubtless elucidate the uncertainty, but perhaps not in time for the information to be of use in the present war.

I20. My personal opinion is that, on days of slight activity, our estimates are reasonably accurate, but that they probably err on the low side on days of heavy fighting when many and large formations were employed.

I2I. As has been explained above, few squadrons were fresh and intact when the Battle began. No sufficient respite has been granted since the conclusion of the Dunkerque fighting to rest the Squadrons which had not left the Fighter Command, and to rebuild those which had undergone the ordeal of fighting from aerodromes in Northern France. These last had been driven from aerodrome to aerodrome, able only to aim at self-preservation from almost continuous attack by Bombers and Fighters; they were desperately weary and had lost the greater part of their equipment, since aircraft which were unserviceable only from slight defects had to be abandoned.

PART II.
THE BATTLE.

I22. The Battle may be said to have divided itself broadly into 4 Phases: First, the attack on convoys and Coastal objectives, such as Ports, Coastal Aerodromes and Radio Location Stations. Second, the attack of Inland Fighter Aerodromes. Third, the attack on London. And fourth, the Fighter-Bomber stage, where the target was of importance quite subsidiary to the main object of drawing our Fighters into the air and engaging them in circumstances as disadvantageous to us as possible. These phases indicated only general tendencies; they overlapped and were not mutually exclusive.

I23. It has been estimated that the Germans sent over, on an average throughout the Battle, four Fighters to each Bomber or Fighter-Bomber, but any such estimate must be very rough.

I24. I must emphasise, throughout, the extreme versatility of the German methods both in the timing and direction of their attacks, and in the tactical formations and methods employed.

I25. They enjoyed the great advantage of having a wide front from which attacks could be delivered. First a blow would be delivered from Calais, perhaps against London; then after a carefully-timed interval, when II Group Fighters might be expected to be at the end of their petrol endurance, a heavy attack would be made on Southampton and Portland. Other attacks, after being built up to formidable dimensions, would prove to be only feints, and the Bombers would turn away before reaching coast of England, only to return again in half an hour, when the Fighters, sent up to intercept them, were landing.

I26. Time-honoured methods of escort were at first employed. A strong Fighter formation would fly a mile or so behind and above the Bombers. When the Germans found that our Fighters could deliver a well-timed attack on the Bombers before the Fighters could intervene, or when our Fighters attacked from ahead or below, each move was met by a counter-move on the part of the Germans, so that, in September, Fighter escorts were flying inside the Bomber formation, others were below, and a series of Fighters stretched upwards to 30,000 feet or more.

I27. One Squadron Leader described his impressions of the

appearance of one of these raids; he said it was like looking up the escalator at Piccadilly Circus.

128. I must pay a very sincere tribute to the Air Officer Commanding No. II Group, Air Vice-Marshal K.R. Park, C.B., M.C., D.F.C., for the way in which he adjusted his tactics and interception methods to meet each new development as it occurred.

129. Tactical control was, as has already been stated, devolved to the Groups; but tactical methods were normally laid down by Command Headquarters. During periods of intense fighting, however, there was no time for consultation, and Air Vice-Marshal Park acted from day to day on his own initiative. We discussed matters as opportunity offered.

130. He has reported on the tactical aspects of the Battle in two very interesting documents, which are, however, too long to reproduce here.

131. A close liaison was kept between Nos. I0 and II and I2 Groups. It sometimes happened that, in the heaviest attacks, practically all II Group Fighters would be in the air. II Group would then ask I2 Group to send a formation from Duxford to patrol over the aerodromes immediately East of London so that these might not be attacked when defenceless.

132. Mutual help was also arranged between Nos. I0 and II Groups. When Portsmouth was attacked, for instance, No. I0 would help No. II Group, and *vice versa* when the attack was on Portland or some Convoy to the West of the Isle of Wight.

133. The amount of physical damage done to Convoys during the first phase was not excessive. About five ships (I think) were actually sunk by bombing, others were damaged, and Convoys were scattered on occasion. It was, of course, much easier to protect the Convoys if they kept as close as possible to the English Coast, but one Convoy at least was routed so as to pass close to Cherbourg, and suffered accordingly. Later, it was arranged that Convoys should traverse the most dangerous and exposed stretches by night, and Convoys steaming in daylight either had direct protection by Fighter escorts, or else had escorts at "Readiness" prepared to leave the ground directly danger threatened.

134. Three of the Radio Location Stations in the South of England suffered rather severe damage and casualties. No Station was permanently put out of action, and the worst damage was repaired in

about a month, though the Station was working at reduced efficiency in about half that time. The operating personnel, and particularly the women, behaved with great courage under threat of attack and actual bombardment.

I35. As regards aerodromes, Manston was the worst sufferer at this stage. It, Hawkinge and Lympne were the three advanced grounds on which we relied for filling up tanks when a maximum range was required for operations over France. They were so heavily attacked with bombs and machine guns that they were temporarily abandoned. This is not to say that they could not have been used if the need had been urgent, but, for interception at or about our own coastline, aerodromes and satellites farther inland were quite effective.

I36. Heavy damage was done to buildings, but these were mostly non-essential, because aircraft were kept dispersed in the open, and the number of men and women employed was not large in comparison with the number at a Station which was the Headquarters of a Sector.

I37. Works personnel, permanent and temporary, and detachments of Royal Engineers were employed in filling up the craters on the aerodromes. Experience at this stage showed that neither the personnel nor the material provided were adequate to effect repairs with the necessary speed, and the strength and mobility of the repair parties was increased. Stocks of "hard-core" rubble had been collected at Fighter aerodromes before the war.

I38. It may be convenient here to continue the subject of damage to Fighter Stations other than those attacked in the first Phase.

I39. Casualties to personnel were slight, except in cases where a direct hit was made on a shelter trench. The trenches commonly in use were lined with concrete and were roofed and covered with earth; but they gave no protection against a direct hit, and, in the nature of things, they had to be within a short distance of the hangars and offices.

I40. Only non-essential personnel took cover; aircraft crews and the staff of the Operations Room remained at their posts. The morale of the men and women of ground crews and staffs was high and remained so throughout.

I4I. At Kenley and at Biggin Hill direct hits were sustained on shelter trenches, at the latter place by a bomb of 500 kilog. or more. The trench and its 40 occupants were annihilated.

142. Wooden hangars were generally set on fire by a bombing attack, and everything in them destroyed.

143. Steel, brick and concrete hangars, on the other hand, stood up well against attack, though, of course, acres of glass were broken. Hangars were generally empty or nearly so, and those aircraft which were destroyed in hangars were generally under repair or major inspection which made it necessary to work under cover.

144. It must, nevertheless, be definitely recorded that the damage done to Fighter aerodromes, and to their communications and ground organisation, was serious, and has been generally under-estimated. Luckily, the Germans did not realise the success of their efforts, and shifted their objectives before the cumulative effect of the damage had become apparent to them.

145. Damage to aerodrome surface was not a major difficulty. It was possible for the Germans to put one or two aerodromes like Manston and Hawkinge out of action for a time, but we had so many satellite aerodromes and landing grounds available that it was quite impossible for the Germans to damage seriously a number of aerodromes sufficient to cause more than temporary inconvenience.

146. This is an important point, because, in mobile warfare, Fighter aerodromes cannot be hastily improvised in broken country, and the number of aerodromes actually or potentially available is a primary factor in the "Appreciation of a Situation".

147. Sector Operations Rooms were protected by high earth embankments, so that they were immune from everything except a direct hit, and, as a matter of fact, no direct hit by a heavy bomb was obtained on any Operations Room. Communications were, however, considerably interrupted, and I must here pay a tribute to the foresight of Air Vice-Marshal E.L. Gossage, C.B., C.V.O., D.S.O., M.C., who commanded No. II Group during the first eight months of the war. At his suggestion "Stand-by" Operations Rooms were constructed at a distance of two or three miles from Sector Headquarters, and a move was made to these when serious attacks on Fighter Aerodromes began. They were somewhat inconvenient make-shifts, and some loss of efficiency in Interception resulted from their use. Work was put in hand immediately on more permanent and fully-equipped Operations Rooms conveniently remote from Sector Headquarters; these though in no way

bomb-proof, were outside the radius of anything aimed at the Sector Aerodrome, and owed their immunity to inconspicuousness. Most of these were finished by October 1940.

148. Aerodrome Defence against parachute troops, or threat of more serious ground attack, was an important and a difficult problem, because Home Defence troops were few and were needed on the Beaches, and the majority of troops rescued from Dunkerque were disorganised and unarmed. The Commander-in-Chief, Home Forces, did, however, make troops available in small numbers for the more important aerodromes and armoured vehicles were extemporised. The difficulty was enhanced by a comparatively recent decision of the Air Ministry to disarm the rank and file of the Royal Air Force. The decision was reversed, but it was some time before rifles could be provided and men trained in their use.

149. The slender resources of the Anti-Aircraft Command were strained to provide guns for the defence of the most important Fighter and Bomber Aerodromes. High Altitude and Bofors guns were provided up to the limit considered practicable, and the effort was reinforced by the use of Royal Air Force detachments with Lewis guns and some hundreds of 20-mm. Cannon which were not immediately required for use in Aircraft.

150. A type of small Rocket was also installed at many aerodromes. These were arranged in lines along the perimeter, and could be fired up to a height of something under 1,000 feet in the face of low-flying attack. They carried a small bomb on the end of a wire. Some limited success was claimed during a low flying attack at Kenley, and they probably had some moral effect when their existence became known to the Enemy. They were, of course, capable of physical effect only against very low horizontal attacks.

151. The main safeguard for Aircraft against air attack was Dispersal. Some experiments on Salisbury Plain in the Summer of 1938 had shown that dispersal alone, without any form of splinter-proof protection, afforded a reasonable safeguard against the forms of attack practised by our own Bomber Command at the time. Thirty unserviceable Fighters were disposed in a rough ring of about 1,000 yards diameter, and the Bomber Command attacked them for the inside of a week with every missile between a 500-pound bomb and an

incendiary bullet, and without any kind of opposition. The result was substantially:- 3 destroyed, I damaged beyond repair, II seriously damaged but repairable, and the rest slightly damaged or untouched.

I52. I therefore asked that small splinter-proof pens for single aircraft should be provided at all Fighter Aerodromes. This was not approved, but I was offered pens for groups of three. I had to agree to this, because it was linked up with the provision of all weather runways which I had been insistently demanding for two years, and it was imperatively necessary that work on the runways should not be held up by further discussion about pens. I think that the 3-aircraft pens were too big. They had a large open face to the front and a concrete area, of the size of two tennis courts, which made an ideal surface for the bursting of direct-action bombs. Eventually, splinter-proof partitions were made inside the pens, and till then some aircraft were parked in the open. Losses at dispersal points were not serious; the worst in my recollection was 5 aircraft destroyed or seriously damaged in one attack. Small portable tents were provided which could be erected over the centre portion of an aeroplane, leaving the tail and wing-tips exposed. These protected the most important parts and enabled ground crews to work in bad weather.

I53. About this time an improvised Repair System was organised and worked well. With the hearty co-operation of the Ministry of Aircraft Production it was decided that Units should be relieved of all extensive repairs and overhauls, both because of their preoccupation in the Battle and because of the danger of further damage being done by enemy action to aircraft under repair. Broadly speaking, any aircraft capable of returning to its base was capable of another 15 minutes' straight flight to a Repair Depot: aircraft incapable of flight were sent by road. Small repairs, such as the patching of bullet holes, were done by the Unit. Two such Repair Depots were improvised about 30 miles to the west of London, and this undoubtedly prevented an accumulation of unserviceable aircraft at Fighter Stations.

I54. It was also about this time that the final decision was made to relegate the Defiant to night operations. It had two serious disabilities; firstly, the brain flying the aeroplane was not the brain firing the guns: the guns could not fire within I6 Degrees of the line of flight of the aeroplane and the gunner was distracted from his task by having to direct the pilot through the Communication Set. Secondly, the guns could not be fired below the horizontal, and it was therefore necessary to keep below the enemy. When beset by superior numbers of Fighters the best course to pursue was to form a descending spiral, so that one or more Defiants should always be in a position to bring effective fire to bear. Such tactics were, however, essentially defensive, and the formation sometimes got broken up before they could be adopted. In practice, the Defiants suffered such heavy losses that it was necessary to relegate them to night fighting, or to the attack of unescorted Bombers.

155. The above remarks have carried me beyond the first phase of the Battle and into the second; but I find it impossible to adhere to a description of the fighting phase by phase. The Enemy's Strategical, as well as his Tactical moves had to be met from day to day as they occurred, and I give an account of my problems and the lessons to be derived from them roughly in the order of their incidence. The detailed sequence of events is sufficiently indicated in the Diagram at Appendix "D".

156. Throughout the Battle, of course, fighting continually occurred over the sea, and German aircraft, damaged over England, had to return across the Straits of Dover or the English Channel. Far more German than British crews fell into the sea. The Germans therefore developed an elaborate system of sea-rescue. Their Bombers had inflatable rubber dinghies, and various other rescue devices were adopted. Crews were provided with bags of a chemical known as fluorescine, a small quantity of which stained a large area of water a vivid green. Floating refuges with provisions and wireless sets were anchored off the French coast. "E Boats" and rescue launches were extensively employed, and white-painted float-planes, marked with the Red Cross, were used even in the midst of battle. We had to make it known to the Germans that we could not countenance the use of the Red Cross in this manner. They were engaged in rescuing combatants and taking them back to fight again, and they were also in a position, if granted immunity, to make valuable reconnaisance reports. In spite of this, surviving crews of these aircraft appeared to be surprised and aggrieved at being shot down.

157. Our own arrangements were less elaborate. Life-saving jackets were painted a conspicuous yellow, and later the fluorescine device

was copied. Patrol aircraft (not under the Red Cross) looked out for immersed crews, and a chain of rescue launches with special communications was installed round the coast. Our own shipping, too, was often on the spot, and many pilots were rescued by Naval or Merchant vessels.

I58. This is perhaps a convenient opportunity to say a word about the ethics of shooting at aircraft crews who have "baled out" in parachutes.

I59. Germans descending over England are prospective Prisoners of War, and, as such, should be immune. On the other hand, British pilots descending over England are still potential Combatants.

I60. Much indignation was caused by the fact that German pilots sometimes fired on our descending airmen (although, in my opinion, they were perfectly entitled to do so), but I am glad to say that in many cases they refrained and sometimes greeted a helpless adversary with a cheerful wave of the hand.

I6I. Many of the targets attacked during the first two phases of the Battle were of little military importance, and had but slight effect on our War Effort. Exceptions to this were day-attacks carried out on the Spitfire works at Southampton and the sheds at Brooklands where some of our Hurricanes were assembled and tested. Both these attacks had some effect on output, which would have been serious but for the anticipatory measures taken by Lord Beaverbrook.

I62. About this time one Canadian, two Polish and one Czech squadrons became fit for Operations.

I63. A squadron of Canadian pilots of the Royal Air Force (No. 242) had been in existence for some months, and was one of the squadrons which went to France in June to cover the evacuation from the West Coast. On its return it became one of the foremost fighting Squadrons in the Command, under the leadership of the very gallant Squadron Leader (now Wing Commander) D.R.S. Bader, D.S.O., D.F.C. No. I (Canadian) Squadron, now also came into the line and acquitted itself with great distinction.

I64. I must confess that I had been a little doubtful of the effect which their experience in their own countries and in France might have had upon the Polish and Czech pilots, but my doubts were soon laid to rest, because all three Squadrons swung in the fight with a dash and enthusiasm which is beyond praise. They were inspired by a burning hatred for the Germans which made them very deadly opponents. The first Polish Squadron (No. 303) in No. II Group, during the course of a month, shot down more Germans than any British unit in the same period. Other Poles and Czechs were used in small numbers in British Squadrons, and fought very gallantly, but the language was a difficulty, and they were probably most efficiently employed in their own National units. Other foreign pilots were employed in British Squadrons, but not in appreciable numbers. The American "Eagle" Squadron was in process of formation during the Battle.

165. The Auxiliary Squadrons were by this time practically indistinguishable from Regulars. It will be remembered that the Scottish Auxiliaries were responsible for the first Air success of the War in the Firth of Forth. To set off against the discontinuity of their training in peace time they had the great advantage of permanency of personnel, and the Flight Commanders at the outbreak of the War were senior and experienced. At the same time, this very permanence led to the average age of the pilots being rather high for intensive fighting, which exercises a strain which the average man of 30 cannot support indefinitely. This point has now ceased to be of importance because of fresh postings. It is mentioned only because it is a factor to be kept in mind in peace time. No praise can be too high for the Auxiliaries, both as regards their keenness and efficiency in peace time and their fighting record in war.

166. I may perhaps mention the question of the Long Range Guns which were mounted along the coast of France near Cap Grisnez. They were within range of our coastal aerodromes, which they occasionally subjected to a desultory shelling. Their main targets, however, were Dover and the Convoys passing through the Straits. So far as I am aware, neither they nor the guns which we installed as counter measures, had any great influence on the air fighting, but they did of course make it impossible for any of our warships to approach the French coast in clear weather, and might have had an important effect if it had been possible for the Germans to launch an invading army.

167. About the end of the second phase, the problems of keeping units up to strength and of relieving them when exhausted began to assume formidable proportions. It was no new experience, because the

drain of units and pilots to France, coupled with the Dunkerque fighting, had created similar problems in the Spring.

168. The comparative relaxation in the intensity of the fighting in June and July had afforded a little respite, but units had only partially recovered and were neither fresh nor up to strength when the fighting again became intense.

169. When Squadrons became exhausted, obviously the most satisfactory way of reinforcement was by means of moving complete units, and this was done when time allowed. Serviceable aircraft were transferred by air, and Operational Aircraft Crews (about 35 men per Squadron) were transferred by Civil Aircraft put at my disposal for the moves. The remainder of the personnel travelled by train or motor transport according to circumstances. Some of the distances involved were considerable, as for instance when a Squadron from Wick had to be brought down in the London Area.

170. The First-line strength of a Squadron was 16 aircraft, of which not more than 12 were intended to be operationally available at any one time. The other 4 would normally be undergoing Inspection or Overhaul. In addition to this there was a small reserve of three to five aircraft per Squadron available on the station.

171. There was a limit to the number of trained pilots which could be kept on the strength of a Squadron even in times of operational passivity, because not more than about 25 could be kept in full practice in Flying Duties.

172. A fresh squadron coming into an active Sector would generally bring with them 16 aircraft and about 20 trained pilots. They would normally fight until they were no longer capable of putting more than 9 aircraft into the air, and then they had to be relieved. This process occupied different periods according to the luck and skill of the unit. The normal period was a month to six weeks, but some units had to be replaced after a week or 10 days.

173. Air Vice-Marshal Park found that the heaviest casualties were often incurred by newly-arrived Squadrons owing to their non-familiarity with the latest developments of air fighting.

174. It soon became impossible to maintain the to-and-fro progress of complete unit personnel from end to end of the country, and the first limitation to efficiency which had to be accepted was the retention of

the majority of personnel at Sector Stations and the transfer only of flying personnel and aircraft crews. This limitation was regrettable because it meant that officers and men were strange to one another, but worse was to come.

I75. By the beginning of September the incidence of casualties became so serious that a fresh squadron would become depleted and exhausted before any of the resting and reforming squadrons was ready to take its place. Fighter pilots were no longer being produced in numbers sufficient to fill the gaps in the fighting ranks. Transfers were made from the Fleet Air Arm and from the Bomber and Coastal Commands, but these pilots naturally required a short flying course on Hurricanes or Spitfires and some instruction in Formation Flying, Fighter Tactics and Interception procedure.

I76. I considered, but discarded, the advisability of combining pairs of weak units into single Squadrons at full strength, for several reasons, one of which was the difficulty of recovery when a lull should come. Another was that ground personnel would be wasted, and a third was that the rate at which the strength of the Command was decreasing would be obvious.

I77. I decided to form 3 Categories of Squadron:-

(*a*) The units of II Group and on its immediate flanks, which were bearing the brunt of the fighting.

(*b*) A few outside units to be maintained at operational strength and to be available as Unit Reliefs in cases where this was unavoidable.

(*c*) The remaining Squadrons of the Command, which would be stripped of their operational pilots, for the benefit of the A Squadrons, down to a level of 5 or 6. These C Squadrons could devote their main energies to the training of new pilots, and, although they would not be fit to meet German Fighters, they would be quite capable of defending their Sectors against unescorted Bombers, which would be all that they would be likely to encounter.

I78. The necessity for resorting to such measures as this indicates the strain which had been put on the Fighter Command and the Pilot

Training organisations by the casualties which the Command had suffered in this decisive Battle.

179. In the early stages of the fight Mr. Winston Churchill spoke with affectionate raillery of me and my "Chicks". He could have said nothing to make me more proud; every Chick was needed before the end.

180. I trust that I may be permitted to record my appreciation of the help given me by the support and confidence of the Prime Minister at a difficult and critical time.

181. In the early days of the War the question of the provision of Operational Training Units (or Group Pools, as they were called at that time) was under discussion. It was referred to in the correspondence which I have mentioned in paragraph 17 of this Despatch. At that time I was so gravely in need of additional Fighter Squadrons that I was willing to do without Group Pools altogether while we were still at long range from the German Fighters.

182. The functions of these Group Pools, or O.T.Us., was to accept pilots direct from Flying Training Schools or non-fighter units of the Royal Air Force and train them in the handling of Fighter types, formation flying, fighting tactics, and R/T control and interception methods. I realised that the Fighters in France could not undertake this work and must have a Group Pool allotted primarily to meet their requirements, but I felt that, so long as we at Home were out of touch with German Fighters, I would prefer to put all available resources into new Squadrons and to undertake in Service Squadrons the final training of pilots coming from Flying Training Schools, provided that they had done some formation flying and night flying, and had fired their guns in the air.

183. Of course, when intensive fighting began, final training of pilots in Squadrons could no longer be given efficiently, and at the time of the Battle three O.T.Us. were in existence. It was found that three weeks was about the minimum period which was of practical value, but that a longer course, up to six weeks, was desirable when circumstances permitted.

184. During the Battle the output from the O.T.Us. was quite inadequate to meet the casualty rate, and it was not even possible to

supply from the Flying Training Schools the necessary intake to the O.T.Us.

185. The lack of flexibility of the Training system, therefore, proved to be the "bottleneck" and was the cause of the progressively deteriorating situation of the Fighter Command up till the end of September. This statement is in no sense a criticism of the Flying Training Command. The problem, as I state it here, can have no ideal solution and some compromise must be adopted.

186. Assuming that in periods of maximum quiescence the Fighter Squadrons of the Royal Air Force require an intake of x pilots per week, in periods of intense activity they require about ten times the number.

187. It is necessary to start the flying training of a pilot about a year before he is ready to engage Enemy Fighters, and therefore the training authorities should be warned, a year ahead, of the incidence of active periods. This is obviously impossible. If they try to be ready for all eventualities by catering for a continuous output to meet a high casualty rate, the result is that, during quiet periods, pilots are turned out at such a rate that they cannot be absorbed, or even given enough flying to prevent their forgetting what they have been taught. If, on the other hand, they cater for the normal wastage rate, Fighter Squadrons are starved of reinforcements when they are most vitally needed.

188. The fundamental principle which must be realised is that Fighter needs, when they, arise, are not comparative with those of other Commands, but absolute. An adequate and efficient Fighter force ensures the Security of the Base, without which continuous operations are impossible.

189. If the Fighter defence had failed in the Autumn of 1940, England would have been invaded. The paralysis of their fighters in the Spring was an important factor in the collapse of the French resistance. Later, the unavoidable withdrawal of the Fighters from Crete rendered continued resistance impossible.

190. Day Bomber and Army Co-operation aircraft can operate when their own Fighters are predominant, but are driven out of the sky when the Enemy Fighters have a free hand.

191. I submit some suggestions by which the apparently insuperable difficulties of the problem may be reduced.

(*a*) Start by aiming at a Fighter output well above that needed in quiescent periods.

(*b*) Ensure that at Flying Training Schools, pupils earmarked for other duties may be rapidly switched over to Fighter training.

(*c*) Organise the O.T.Us. with a "Normal" and an "Emergency" Syllabus, the latter lasting for three weeks and the former twice as long.

(*d*) Fill up the Service Fighter Squadrons to a strength of 25 pilots, or whatever the C.-in-C. considers to be the maximum which can be kept in flying and operational practice.

(*e*) Form Reservoirs, either at O.T.Us, or in special units where surplus pilots may maintain the flying and operational standard which they have reached.

(*f*) When the initiative lies in our hands (as, for instance, when we are planning to deliver an offensive some time ahead), the intake of Flying Training Schools should be adjusted to cater for the additional stress which can be foreseen.

(*g*) (And this applies principally to overseas theatres of war where rapid reinforcement is impossible.) Let the Day Bomber and Army Co-operation Squadrons have a number of Fighters on which they can fly and train as opportunity offers. This is a revolutionary suggestion, but it is made in all seriousness. If their Fighters are overwhelmed the Day Bomber and Army Cooperation units will not be able to operate at all. No very high standard of training should be attempted, especially in Radio controlled Interception methods: but the intervention of these units as Fighters, working in pairs or small formations, might well prove to be the decisive factor in a critical situation.

192. It will be observed that, at the end of the second Phase of the Battle, the power of reinforcing by complete units had substantially disappeared. We still possessed an effective reserve of trained pilots,

but they could be made available only by stripping the Squadrons which were not engaged in the South and South-East of England.

193. The effective strength of the Command was running down, though the fact was not known to the public, nor, I hoped, to the Germans. They for their part must certainly be feeling the effect of their heavy losses, but there was very little indication of any loss of morale, so far as could be seen from a daily scrutiny of the examinations of Prisoners of War. Our own pilots were fighting with unabated gallantry and determination.

194. The confidence of the German High Command probably received something of a shock about this time. The sustained resistance which they were meeting in South-East England probably led them to believe that Fighter Squadrons had been withdrawn, wholly or in part, from the North in order to meet the attack. On the 15th August, therefore, two large raids were sent, one to Yorkshire and one to Newcastle. They were escorted by Fighters. The distance was too great for Me. 109s, but not for Me. 110s.

195. If the assumption was that our Fighters had been withdrawn from the North, the contrary was soon apparent, and the bombers received such a drubbing that the experiment was not repeated. I think that this incident probably had a very depressing influence on the outlook of the German High Command.

196. As I have said, our own pilots were fighting with the utmost gallantry and determination, but the mass raids on London, which were the main feature of the third phase of the Battle, involved a tremendous strain on units which could no longer be relieved as such. Some Squadrons were flying 50 and 60 hours per diem.

197. Many of the pilots were getting very tired. An order was in existence that all pilots should have 24 hours' leave every week, during which they should be encouraged to leave their station and get some exercise and change of atmosphere: this was issued as an order so that the pilots should be compelled to avail themselves of the opportunity to get the necessary rest and relaxation. I think it was generally obeyed, but I fear that the instinct of duty sometimes over-rode the sense of discipline. Other measures were also taken to provide rest and relaxation at Stations, and sometimes to find billets for pilots where they could sleep away from their Aerodromes.

198. During this third phase the problem arose, in an acute form, of the strength of Fighter formations which we should employ. When time was the essence of the problem, two squadrons were generally used by A.V.M. Park in No. II Group. He had the responsibility of meeting attacks as far to the Eastward as possible, and the building up of a four-squadron formation involved the use of a rendezvous for aircraft from two or more aerodromes. This led to delay and lack of flexibility in leadership.

199. On the other hand, when No. I2 Group was asked to send down protective formations to guard the aerodromes on the Eastern fringe of London, it was often possible to build up big formations, and these had great success on some occasions, though by no means always.

200. Because a similar situation may well arise in future, I think that it is desirable to enter into some detail in this connection.

20I. I may preface my remarks by stating that I am personally in favour of using Fighter formations in the greatest strength of which circumstances will permit, and, in the Dunkerque fighting, where we could choose our time and build up our formations on the outward journey, I habitually employed four-Squadron formations as a preferable alternative to using two-Squadron formations at more frequent intervals; but, during the attacks on London, the available strength of Fighters did not admit of this policy, nor was time available.

202. I quote from Air Vice-Marshal Park's report:-

"The general plan adopted was to engage the enemy high-fighter screen with pairs of Spitfire Squadrons from Hornchurch and Biggin Hill half-way between London and the coast, and so enable Hurricane Squadrons from London Sectors to attack bomber formations and their close escort before they reached the line of fighter aerodromes East and South of London. The remaining Squadrons from London Sectors that could not be despatched in time to intercept the first wave of the attack by climbing in pairs formed a third and inner screen by patrolling along the lines of aerodromes East and South of London. The fighter Squadrons from Debden, Tangmere, and sometimes Northolt, were employed in wings of three or in pairs to form a screen South-East of

London to intercept the third wave of the attack coming
inland, also to mop up retreating formations of the earlier
waves. The Spitfire Squadrons were redisposed so as to
concentrate three Squadrons at each of Hornchurch and
Biggin Hill. The primary rôle of these Squadrons was to
engage and drive back the enemy high-fighter screen, and so
protect the Hurricane Squadrons, whose task was to attack
close escorts and then the bomber formations, all of which
flew at much lower altitude."

203. I think that, if the policy of big formations had been attempted at
this time in No. II Group, many more Bombers would have reached
their objectives without opposition.

204. Air Vice-Marshal Park also quotes the results of the ten large
formations ordered from Duxford into No. II Group in the last half of
October, when the Germans were employing Fighter-types only. Nine
of these sorties made no interception, and the tenth destroyed one Me.
I09.

205. The most critical stage of the Battle occurred in the third phase.
On the I5th September the Germans delivered their maximum effort,
when our Guns and Fighters together accounted for I85 aircraft. Heavy
pressure was kept up till the 27th September, but, by the end of the
month, it became apparent that the Germans could no longer face the
Bomber wastage which they had sustained, and the operations entered
upon their fourth phase, in which a proportion of enemy Fighters
themselves acted as Bombers.

206. This plan, although the actual damage caused by bombs was
comparatively trivial, was aimed primarily at a further whittling down
of our Fighter strength, and, of all the methods adopted by the Germans,
it was the most difficult to counter. Apart from the previous difficulty
of determining which formations meant business, and which were
feints, we had to discover which formations carried bombs and which
did not.

207. To meet this difficulty, Air Vice-Marshal Park devised the plan
of using single Spitfires, flying at maximum height, to act as
Reconnaissance aircraft and to report their observations immediately
by R/T.

208. A special Flight was organised for this purpose, and it was later recommended that the Spitfires should be employed in pairs, for reasons of security, and that the Flight should become a Squadron. A special R/T receiving set was erected at Group Headquarters so that reports might be obtained without any delay in transmission from the Sector receiving station. There is reason to believe that the Germans also adopted a system of using high-flying H.E. II3s as Scouts. Their information concerning our movements was transmitted to the ground and relayed to their Bombers in the air.

209. In the fourth phase, the apparent ratio of losses in our favour dropped appreciably. I say "apparent" because, in fighting at extreme altitudes, fighters often could not see their victims crash, and the percentage reported as Certainly Destroyed was unfairly depressed. Our own casualties, nevertheless, were such that the C. Category squadrons, which I was hoping to build up to operational strength again, remained in their condition of semi-effectiveness.

2I0. Serious as were our difficulties, however, those of the enemy were worse, and by the end of October the Germans abandoned their attempts to wear down the Fighter Command, and the country was delivered from the threat of immediate invasion.

2II. The Order of Battle at the beginning of November is shown at Appendix E. Categories of Squadrons (A, B. or C, *vide* paragraph I77) are indicated.

2I2. Increasingly throughout the Battle had the importance of a high "ceiling" been manifested. It is by no means necessary that every Fighter shall have its best performance at stratospheric heights; any such policy would result in a loss of performance at lower altitude, and we must never lose sight of the basic principle that the Fighter exists for the purpose of shooting down Bombers, and that its encounters with other Fighters are incidental to this process.

2I3. There are, nevertheless, arguments for giving to a percentage of Fighters a ceiling (determinable by specific physiological tests) above which no enemy can climb without the use of Pressure Cabins. Just as the "Weather Gauge" was often the determining factor in the tactics of sailing ships, so the "Height Gauge" was often crucial in air combat. Exhaust-driver turbo-superchargers have certain advantages over gear-driven blowers at great height, and should be considered for adoption in spite of their disadvantages.

2I4. It must be remembered also that the initiative always rests with the Bomber, who can select at will the height at which he will make his attack. We must be prepared, therefore, for the appearance of the pressure-cabin Bomber, flying at a height unattainable by any non-pressurised Fighter. (I should perhaps explain that there is a height, about 43,000 feet, above which the administration of any quantity of oxygen at atmospheric pressure becomes ineffective because it cannot be inhaled and a pressure cabin or a pressure suit becomes essential.) Of course, a pressure-cabin Bomber is inefficient and vulnerable, because it is difficult to operate free guns from a pressure cabin, and pressure leakage from holes made in the walls of the cabin will prostrate the crew. The threat from pressurised Bombers is therefore serious only if we have no Fighters to meet them, and for this reason we should always possess a limited number of pressurised Fighters.

2I5. Various other lessons were learned from the experience of fighting at extreme altitudes. One very tiresome feature was that a considerable proportion of ultra-high-flying raids was missed by the Intelligence systems, or reported so late that time was not available to climb and intercept. This made it necessary to employ standing patrols just below oxygen height (about I6,000 feet). These patrols climbed to intercept at extreme height when ordered to do so. This cut at the roots of the Fighter Command system, which was designed to ensure economy of effort by keeping aircraft on the ground except when required to make an interception.

2I6. Another lesson was that the system of using an "Above Guard" should be retained even when an attack was initiated from extreme altitude.

2I7. Flying and fighting-fatigue increases with altitude, and the comfort of the pilot requires unremitting attention. Cockpit heating and the meticulous pursuit and elimination of air leaks are of great importance. Attention should also be paid to the elimination of icing on cockpit hoods (which are apt to freeze immovably) and on the inside and outside of windscreens.

2I8. A serious handicap, which I have not hitherto mentioned, was the fact that the change over from "High Frequency" to "Very High

Frequency" Radio Telephony was still in progress. The V.H.F. was an immense improvement on the H.F., both in range and clarity of speech; but the change over, which had started nearly a year before, was held up by the slow output of equipment. This meant that much work had to be done on aircraft Radio equipment during the Battle, and Squadrons equipped with V.H.F. could not communicate with H.F. Ground Stations, and *vice versa.*

2I9. Some of our worst losses occurred through defective leadership on the part of a unit commander, who might lead his pilots into a trap or be caught while climbing by an enemy formation approaching "out of the sun." During periods of intense activity promotions to the command of Fighter squadrons should be made on the recommendation of Group Commanders from amongst Flight Commanders experienced in the methods of the moment. If and when it is necessary to post a Squadron Leader (how ever gallant and experienced) from outside the Command, he should humbly start as an ordinary member of the formation until he has gained experience. Only exceptionally should officers over 26 years of age be posted to command Fighter Squadrons.

220. The experience of the Battle made me a little doubtful if the organisation of a squadron into 2 Flights, each of 2 Sections of 3 aircraft, was ideal. It was, of course, undesirable to make any sweeping change during the Battle, and I relinquished my Command shortly after its termination; but the weakness lay in the Section of 3 when it became necessary to break up a formation in a "Dog Fight." The organisation should allow for a break up into pairs, in which one pilot looks after the tail of his companion. A Squadron might be divided into 3 Flights of 4 (which would limit the employment of half-Squadrons), or it might consist of 2 Flights of 8, each comprising 2 Sections of 4. This latter suggestion would upset standard arrangements for accommodation.

22I. The matter is not one which can be settled without consultation with various authorities and Branches of the Air Ministry. I therefore merely raise the point without making any definite recommendation.

222. A great deal of discussion took place before and in the early stages of the war as to the best method of "harmonisation" of the guns of an 8-gun Fighter: that is to say the direction, in relation to the longitudinal axis of the aircraft, in which each gun should be pointed in order to get the best results.

223. There were three schools of thought:-

One maintained that the lines of fire should be dispersed so
that the largest possible "beaten zone" might be formed and
one gun (but not more than one) would always be on the
target.

The second held that the guns should be left parallel and so
would always cover an elongated zone corresponding with the
vulnerable parts of a Bomber (Engines, Tanks and Fuselage).

The third demanded concentration of the fire of all guns at a
point.

224. Arguments were produced in favour of all three methods of
harmonisation, but in practice it was found that concentration of fire
gave the best results. Guns were harmonised so that their lines of fire
converged on a point 250 yards distant: fire was therefore effective up
to about 500 yards, where the lines of fire had opened out again to their
original intervals after crossing at the point of concentration.

225. It was very desirable to get data as to the actual ranges at which
fire effect had been obtained. The Reflector Sight contained a rough
range-finder which the range of an aircraft of known span could be
determined if it was approached from astern, but, in spite of this, pilots,
in the heat of action, generally underestimated the ranges at which they
fired.

226. Cinema guns, invaluable for training purposes, were used in
combat also; and many striking pictures were obtained, from which
valuable lessons were learned.

227. The types of ammunition used in the guns varied during the
course of the Battle. It was necessary to include some incendiary
ammunition, but the type originally available gave a distinct smoke-
tracer effect. Now tracer ammunition in fixed guns at any but very short
range gives very misleading indications, and I wished pilots to use their
sights properly and not to rely on tracer indications. (The above
remarks do not apply at night, nor to free guns, where tracer is essential
for one of the methods taught for aiming.)

228. During the Battle "de Wilde" ammunition became available in
increasing quantities. This was an incendiary ammunition without any
flame or smoke trace, and it was extremely popular with pilots, who

attributed to it almost magical properties. 8-gun Fighters, of course, were always liable to be sent up at night, and it was therefore desirable to retain some of the older types of incendiary bullets. These were preferred to the "tracer" proper, which gave too bright a flame at night.

229. A typical arrangement, therefore, was:-

Old-type incendiary in the 2 outer guns,

de Wilde in one gun while supplies were limited,

Armour piercing in 2 guns, and ball in the other 3.

230. A discussion on the offensive and defensive equipment of aircraft will be found in Appendix F. It will be of interest to all concerned with the Design of Technical Equipment of Aircraft.

PART III.
NIGHT INTERCEPTION.

23I. No story of the Battle would be complete without some account of the Night operations. It is true that they constituted only a subsidiary activity in comparison with the main German objective of fighting us to a standstill by day so that Air Superiority might be attained as a preliminary to Invasion. The night attacks did little directly to affect the efficiency of the Day Fighting Squadrons, though they had certain indirect effects. Although actual casualties were insignificant, disturbance and loss of sleep were caused; damage was done to factories where aircraft engines and accessories were produced; and the stress of continuous operations, day and night, imposed a very heavy strain on Formation Commanders and Staff officers, and upon the personnel of all Operations Rooms.

232. I had long been apprehensive of the effect of Night attacks, when they should begin, and of the efficacy of our defensive measures.

233. We relied on daytime interception methods, and on the Searchlights to illuminate and hold the Bombers. If they were capable of doing this, all would be well, since the distance at which an illuminated Bomber can be seen by night is comparable with the range of visibility by daylight.

234. The first night attack worthy of the name was made early in

June and the results were encouraging. Aircraft were well picked up and held by the Searchlights and 6 were shot down. The attack was, however, made at comparatively low altitudes (8,000-12,000 ft.) and the Germans, profiting by this lesson, resorted thereafter to greater heights at which the Searchlights were practically ineffective. In close consultation with myself, General Pile tried every conceivable method of operation, but without material success.

235. About this time Radio Location instruments were fitted in Blenheims and it became necessary to develop at high pressure a system of operation which should enable Night Fighters to make interceptions even against unilluminated targets.

236. The difficulty of this task will be realised when it is considered that it became necessary to put the Fighter within one or two hundred yards of the Enemy, and on the same course, instead of the four or five miles which were adequate against an illuminated target.

237. It may be asked why the Searchlights were so comparatively impotent when they had afforded an accessory to successful defence at the end of the last war. The answer lies partly in the height factor already discussed, and partly in the greatly increased speed of the Bomber, which was about three times that obtaining in 1914. The sound locator, on which Searchlights mainly relied at this time, naturally registered the apparent position of the source of sound and lagged behind the target to the extent of the time taken by sound to travel from the target to the Sound Locator. When the speed of the target is low it is comparatively easy to allow for this lag, but at the speeds of modern bombers the angular distance which must be allowed for in searching is so great that the Searchlights were generally defeated.

238. The first thing which appeared obvious to me was that a "sound Plot" track transmitted from the Observer Corps with a variable and unpredictable "lag" was good enough only for Air Raid Warning purposes and was much too inaccurate to be of use for controlled interception at night: height indications also were little better than guesswork. The Radio Location apparatus (known as A.I.) fitted in twin-engined fighters had a maximum range of 2 or 3 miles, but it was limited by the height at which the Fighter was flying. If, for instance, the Fighter was flying at 10,000 feet, ground echoes were reflected from

all ranges greater than this, and an aircraft echo from 10,500 feet would be indistinguishable among the ground echoes.

239. The minimum range of the A.I. was also restricted at this time to about 1,000 feet. Below this distance the aircraft echo was swamped by instrumental disturbance. Continuous and intensive development work was in progress to minimise these limitations.

240. No Radio Location apparatus was available at this time for inland tracking, and I turned for help to the Army, which had developed for use with guns a Radio Location apparatus known as the G.L. Set. Within a limited range (about 40,000 feet) this set could give very accurate position plots, and, moreover, could read height to within plus or minus 1,000 feet at average ranges.

241. Although these sets were few in number and were urgently required for their original purpose of gun control, General Pile realised the urgency of our need and made available about 10 sets for an experiment in the Kenley Sector on the usual line of approach of London Raiders, which commonly made their landfall near Beachy Head.

242. The G.L. sets were installed at Searchlight Posts, and direct telephone communication was arranged with the Kenley Sector Operations Room. Here a large blackboard was installed, and the G.L. plots were shown at intervals of about 30 seconds and with a greater accuracy in height than had before been possible by any means.

243. The track of the pursuing fighter was determined by means of the R/T Direction Finding Stations.

244. Major A.B. Russell, O.B.E., T.A.R.O., co-operated in the development of this system in the Kenley Sector. His practical knowledge and tireless enthusiasm were of the greatest value.

245. Promising results were obtained almost from the first and numerous instances occurred where echoes were obtained on the A.I. sets in the aircraft. Practical results were, however, disappointing, partly because the A.I. apparatus proved to be unexpectedly capricious in azimuth, and partly because the Blenheim was slower than many of the German Bombers and was deficient in fire-power. Many Germans escaped after an initial A.I. "pickup" and even after visual contact had been effected.

246. The A.I. apparatus was then fitted into the Beaufighters, which

were just beginning to appear in Service. The machines and their engines suffered from "teething trouble" to an unusual degree, and the adaption of A.I. to a new type was accompanied by certain difficulties. In addition, they were operating from a wet aerodrome at Redhill, and the development of delicate electrical apparatus, combined with a new type of aircraft and engine, with rudimentary maintenance facilities, was a matter of the greatest difficulty. In nine cases out of ten something would go wrong with the aeroplane or with the A.I. set or with the R/T Direction Finding apparatus or with the Communication system before an interception could be made. No. 2I9 Squadron, under Squadron Leader J.H. Little, were engaged in this work and operated with great energy and enthusiasm under extremely adverse and difficult conditions.

247. It would, of course, have been desirable to carry out all this development work by day when faults would have been much more easily detected and remedied, but the low rate of Aircraft Serviceability precluded Day-and-Night work, and London was being bombed almost every night, so that I could not afford to neglect the chance of getting practical results. These, though disappointing, were not entirely negligible; several Bombers were shot down in this area during the experimental period, and many discovered that they were pursued and turned back before reaching their objectives. Night Fighting Development work was also going on at the same time at the Fighter Interception Unit at Tangmere in Sussex.

248. A supplementary use was found for the A.I. by the installation of A.I. "Beacons" in the vicinity of Night Flying Aerodromes. These afforded a valuable Navigational aid for "Homing" in cases where any defect occurred in the R/T D/F system.

249. Shortly before I left the Command a new piece of Radio-Location apparatus became available in the shape of the "G.C.I." set with the Plan Position Indicator. This was an Inland-Reading Set which showed the position of all aircraft within its range on a fluorescent screen as the aerial was rotated.

250. The main advantages of this set were that it had a longer range than the G.L. set and it was possible to track the Bomber and the Fighter by the same apparatus instead of following one with the G.L. and the other by R/T D/F. Moreover it was found that in some

circumstances the accuracy of the R/T D/F method was inadequate for night interceptions.

25I. On the other hand, the accuracy of height readings by the G.C.I., apparatus was less than that obtainable with the G.L. I understand that this has now been improved.

252. Whatever the exact technical method of plotting positions and tracks of aircraft, the object was to place the Fighter behind the Bomber, and in such a position that the echo of the latter would show in the Fighter's A.I. set. The Fighter then tried to overtake the Bomber until it became visible to the naked eye.

253. At that time only multi-seaters could be fitted with A.I., and therefore, concurrently with the Night Interception experiments, methods were tried of using the Searchlights as pointers for Night Fighters, even if the target were out of range of the Searchlight Beam. Experiments were made with the Searchlights in "clumps" to increase their illuminating power and the visibility of their beams to Fighters at a distance.

254. A small Radio-Location set was designed to fit to the Searchlight itself, so as to get over the time-lag which was such an insuperable obstacle to the use of Sound Locators. It is probable that if Searchlights can substitute the speed of light for that of sound they may take on a new lease of useful life.

255. The disadvantage of relying entirely on Radio-controlled methods of Night Interception is that "saturation point" is quickly reached, and when mass raids are in progress only a limited number of fighters can be operated. Results obtained in the Spring of I94I show that Day Fighters can obtain important results in conditions of good visibility, especially if attention is paid to all methods of improving the night vision of pilots.

256. During the Battle the "Intruder" system was initiated on a small scale. Night fighters without A.I. were sent across to France in an attempt to catch Bombers while taking off from, or landing at, their aerodromes; or to intercept them at points where they habitually crossed the French Coast.

257. I had to leave the Development of Night Interception at a very interesting stage; but it is perhaps not too much to say that, although much remained to be done, the back of the problem had been broken.

The experiments had, of course, been carried out in a small area, and raiders which avoided the area could be intercepted only by previously existing methods; but the possibilities had been demonstrated and could be applied on a larger scale as soon as the necessary apparatus was provided.

258. The method is, of course, also applicable to the day interception of raiders making use of cloud cover, which have hitherto proved extremely elusive; and it is not too much to hope, that the eventual development of very high-frequency A.I. may enable accurate fire to be opened against unseen targets, so that not even the darkest night nor the densest cloud will serve as a protection to the Raider.

259. The day may come when every Single-Seater Fighter is fitted with A.I., but this is not yet feasible. What can be done is to fit all Searchlights with Radio-Location apparatus so that every Searchlight Beam is a reliable pointer towards an enemy, even if the range is too great for direct illumination.[2] If then the Fighter can be informed in addition of the height of the Raider, Day Fighters will be able to join usefully and economically in night operations on dark nights.

APPENDIX "C."

6TH A.A. DIVISION, JULY-OCTOBER 1940.

(*Note.* – This report relates only to 6th A.A. Division. It does not cover the operations of A.A. Command as a whole.)

Glossary of Abbreviations.

H.A.A.	Heavy Anti-Aircraft.
L.A.A.	Light Anti-Aircraft.
G.O.R.	Gun Operations Room.
A.A.L.M.G.	Anti-Aircraft Light Machine-Gun.
V.I.E.	Visual Indicator Equipment.
G.P.O.	Gun Position Officer.
G.L.	Radio Location Set for Gun Laying.
V.P.	Vulnerable Point.
F.A.S.	Forward Area Sight.
S.O.R.	Sector Operator's Room.
G.D.A.	Gun Defended Area.

I. Layout of A.A. Defences.

(*a*) The area covered by 6th A.A. Division coincided with the R.A.F. sectors Debden, North Weald, Hornchurch, Biggin Hill and Kenley (i.e., the major part of No. II Fighter Group, R.A.F.). Thus the coastal boundary extended from Lowestoft (exclusive) in the North to Worthing (exclusive) in the South; the internal boundary marching with that of the Metropolitan area.

(*b*) Distribution of A.A. defences was briefly as follows:-

(i) H.A.A. Guns.

The Divisional area contained four main "gun defended areas" at Harwich, Thames and Medway North (guns emplaced along the North bank of the Thames Estuary), Thames and Medway South (guns emplaced along the South bank of the Thames Estuary and defending Chatham and Rochester) and Dover (including Folkestone). In addition, H.A.A. guns were deployed for the defence of certain aerodromes.

Each "gun defended area" was based on a Gun Operations Room: at Felixstowe, Vange, Chatham and Dover respectively. This G.O.R. was connected directly to II Fighter Group Operations Room at Uxbridge, from which it received plots of enemy raids, which were in turn passed down to all gun sites.

The armament of each H.A.A. site consisted of the following: 4 (sometimes 2) 4.5, 3.7 or 3-inch guns with predictor. Appendix "A" shows the H.A.A. defences as at the beginning of August 1940 and the end of October 1940.

(ii) L.A.A. Guns.

45 Vulnerable Points in the Divisional area were defended by L.A.A. guns. These V.Ps. consisted of Air Ministry Experimental Stations, Fighter Aerodromes, Dockyards, Oil Depots, Magazines, Industrial Undertakings and Factories.

Armament consisted of the following guns: 40-mm. Bofors (with Predictor No. 3 and Forward Area Sights), 3-inch, 20 cwt. (Case I), A.A.L.M.G. and 20-mm. Hispano. Appendix "B" shows the V.Ps. with their armament as in August and October 1940.

Searchlights were deployed in single light stations at approximately 6,000 yards spacing throughout the area, but with a closer spacing in certain instances along the coast and in "gun defended areas" where the distance between lights was approximately 3,500 yards.

These lights were deployed on a brigade basis following R.A.F. sectors, and each light was connected by direct telephone line and/or R.T. set No. I7 to Battery Headquarters via troop H.Q. and thence to an army telephone board at the R.A.F. Sector Operations Room.

The equipment of a Searchlight site consisted of the following:-

90-cm. Projector with, in most cases, Sound Locator Mk. III. In some instances sites were equipped with Sound Locators Mk. VIII or Mk. IX. During the late Summer and Autumn the number of Mk. VIII and Mk. IX Sound Locators gradually increased, and V.I.E. equipment and I50-cm. Projectors were introduced. Each Searchlight site was equipped with one A.A.L.M.G. for use against low-flying aircraft and for ground defence.

2. Enemy Tactics.

(a) High Level Bombing Attacks.

These took place generally *between heights of 16,000/20,000 feet. Bombers approached their targets in close protective formations until running up to the line of bomb release, when formation was changed to Line Astern (if there was a definite objective to the attack). Attacks frequently occurred in waves, each wave flying at approximately the same height and on the same course. On engagement by H.A A. guns, avoiding action was taken in three stages:-*

Stage I. – The bombers gained height steadily and maintained course and formation.

Stage 2. – Formations opened out widely and maintained course.

Stage 3. – Under heavy fire, formations split and bombers scattered widely on different courses. It was after this stage had been reached that the best opportunity was provided for fighters to engage.

(*b*) Low Level and Dive Bombing Attacks.

In the latter stages of the enemy air offensive numerous instances of low level and dive bombing attacks occurred, in particular against fighter aerodromes (Manston, Hawkinge, Lympne, Kenley).

L.A.A. and H.A.A. employed in dealing with these forms of attack met with varying success, but in cases where no planes were brought down the effect of fire from the A.A. defence almost invariably disconcerted the dive bomber so that few bombs were dropped with accuracy.

Considerable efforts were made by Me. I09's and Ju. 87's to destroy the balloon barrage at Dover, and, though at times they partially succeeded, excellent targets were provided for the Dover H.A.A. and L.A.A. guns.

3. Part played by H.A.A. Guns.

Targets of all types presented themselves to H.A.A. sites, ranging from solid bomber formation to single cloud hopping or dive bombers, balloon strafers or hedge hoppers, all of which were successfully engaged by appropriate method of fire.

The action of the defence achieved success in the following ways:-

(*a*) The actual destruction or disablement of enemy aircraft (see Appendix "C").

(*b*) The breaking up of formations, thus enabling the R.A.F. to press home attacks on smaller groups of bombers.

(*c*) Destroying the accuracy of their bombing by forcing the enemy aircraft to take avoiding action.

(*d*) By pointing out to patrolling fighters the whereabouts of enemy formations by means of shell bursts.

The following methods of fire were in operation at this period:-

(*a*) Seen Targets.

(i) Each gun site was allotted a zone of priority and

responsibility for opening fire on a target rested with the G.P.O.

(ii) Targets could be engaged by day if identified as hostile beyond reasonable doubt or if a hostile act was committed. By night, failure to give recognition signals was an additional proviso.

(iii) It was the responsibility of the G.P.O. to cease fire when fighters closed to the attack.

(*b*) Unseen Targets.

Unseen firing at this time was in its infancy and considerable initiative was displayed in evolving methods for engaging targets unseen by day or by night.

The following methods were employed:-

(i) Geographic Barrages.

Many forms of barrage were used by different G.D.As. but all were based on obtaining concentrations at a point, on a line, or over an area, through which the enemy aircraft must fly.

Suitable barrages for lines of approach and heights were worked out beforehand. Approach of enemy aircraft was observed by G.L. and, by co-ordination at G.O.Rs., the fire from each site could be controlled to bring a maximum concentration of shell bursts at the required point.

(ii) Precision Engagements.

Method A. – Due to poor visibility or wrong speed settings searchlight intersections were often made without actual illumination of the aircraft. By obtaining slant range from G.L. and following the intersection on the Predictor, sufficient data were available to enable shells to burst at or near the intersection.

Method B. – This provided for engagement without searchlight intersections. Continuous bearings and slant ranges from the

G.L. were fed into the Predictor and engagement of target undertaken on the data thus provided. For sites which were not equipped with G.L. the appropriate information was passed down from G.O.R.

It will be appreciated that procedure varied with different Gun Zones, according to circumstances and the equipment available. It should be remembered that all engagements of unseen targets were subject to the express permission of the Group Controller at Uxbridge, so that danger of engaging friendly aircraft was obviated.

(c) *Anti-Dive-Bombing Barrage.*

Special barrages against dive bombers were organised round the following V.Ps.: Harwich Harbour, Thameshaven Oil Installations, Tilbury Docks, Chatham Dockyard, Sheerness Dockyard, Dover Harbour, Purfleet Oil and Ammunition Depots.

This barrage could be employed at any time at the discretion of the G.P.O. when he considered that other and more accurate methods were unlikely to be effective. The barrage was designed for a height of 3,000 feet and assumed a dive angle of 60°. It was based on a barrage circle round each gun site which was divided into 4 quadrants in which the barrages were placed.

The maximum effort from H.A.A. guns was required from the 19th August to the 5th October, during which time the crews had little rest, continuous 24 hours manning being required at Dover, a "duty gun station" system being worked in all areas.

Evidence is available to show how time and time again enemy bombers would not face up to the heavy and accurate fire put up by gun stations. Particularly worthy of mention are two attacks on Hornchurch aerodrome when on both occasions fighters were on the ground for refuelling. A.A. fire broke up the formation and prevented *any damage to the station* buildings and aircraft on the ground.

4. Part played by L.A.A. Guns.

The targets which offered themselves to L.A.A. guns were in the main small numbers engaged in dive bombing or low level attacks on V.Ps. Opportunity usually only offered fleeting targets, and quickness of thought and action was essential to make fullest use of the targets which presented themselves.

Success against targets by L.A.A. guns was achieved in the following ways:-

(*a*) The destruction or disablement of enemy aircraft (See Appendix "C").

(*b*) The prevention of accurate bombing causing the bombers to pull out of their dive earlier than they intended.

Methods of firing employed by L.A.A. guns as follows:-

(i) Bofors.

Fire was directed either by No. 3 Predictor or by Forward area Sights; some Bofors were not equipped with the Predictor when the latter method only could be used.

The Predictor equipped guns require a I30 Volt A.C. electric supply which was provided either from engine-driven generators or from the mains. Shooting with the Predictor achieved very great accuracy and the results and destruction of aircraft and the average ammunition expenditure proved the efficiency of this equipment (see Appendix "C"). The F.A.S. method permitted quick engagements of targets although without the accuracy afforded by the Predictor.

(ii) 3-inch 20-cwt. Guns (Case I).

Some V.Ps. were equipped with the 3-inch 20-cwt. gun without Predictor which was fired from deflection sights; shrapnel was normally used. H.E., however, was used for targets at greater height.

(iii) A.A.L.M.G.

Lewis Guns on A.A. mountings proved extremely effective in attacking low-flying enemy aircraft. These guns were mounted in single, double or quadruple mountings and were fired by the Hosepipe method using tracer ammunition.

(iv) Hispano 20-mm. Equipment.

A few of these weapons only were deployed and, owing to shortage of ammunition and lack of tracer, were not found very effective.

5. Part Played by Searchlights.

(a) Day.

Owing to the close spacing of Searchlight sites they formed a valuable source of intelligence and rapid reports were able to be made upwards of casualties to friendly and enemy aircraft, pilots descending by parachute and other incidents of importance. In addition, they have been able to provide valuable reports of isolated enemy aircraft, trace of which had been lost by the Observer Corps.

The value of the A.A.L.M.G. with which each site was equipped cannot be too highly stressed, and during the 4 months under review no less than 23 enemy aircraft were destroyed, confirmed, by A.A.L.M.G. at Searchlight sites (this includes a few in which A.A.L.M.G. at H.A.A. sites also shared). Prisoner of War reports showed that it was not generally known by the German Air Force pilots that Searchlight sites were equipped with A.A. defence.

(b) Night.

Tactical employment of Searchlights at night was by either:-

(i) 3-beam rule, in which 3 sites only engaged the target; or

(ii) by the Master-beam system, in which one Master beam per three sites exposed and was followed by the remaining two beams acting under the orders of the Master beam.

The decision to engage was the responsibility of the Detachment Commander, and no direct tactical control was exercised from Battery Headquarters.

In the early stages of the Battle of Britain night activity was on a small scale and Searchlights had few raids to engage. Some illuminations were effected, but throughout it was difficult, by ground observations, to assess the actual numbers. Frequently illuminations were reported by sites not engaging the targets. The difficulty of illumination was increased as the number of night raids increased, owing to the difficulty of sites selecting the same target.

There is evidence to show that Searchlight activity, whilst being difficult to measure, forced enemy aircraft to fly at a greater height than they would otherwise have done. Bombs were frequently dropped when enemy aircraft were illuminated, which were possibly intended to discourage Searchlights from exposing. Evasive tactics by the enemy consisted of changing height and speed continuously to avoid being illuminated rather than a violent evasive action upon illumination.

6. *G.L. Equipment.*

At the beginning of August experiments had just been completed to determine whether G.L. equipment could satisfactorily be used as a Ships detector. Apart from the results of this experiment three other facts emerged:-

(*a*) The G.L. principle was of considerable value when used in conjunction with Searchlights.

(*b*) That G.L. sets sited in an anti-ship rôle, *i.e.,* on the top of a cliff, were of considerable value in detecting low-flying aircraft.

(*c*) It showed the value of small R.D.F. detectors within the main R.A.F. chain, in plotting enemy aircraft direct to sectors.

At the beginning of the Battle of Britain, 2I G.L. sets were in use by 6th A.A. Division, and by October this number had been increased by another I4.

(i) G.L. at Gun Stations.

The main function of these equipments was to provide data for Unseen target engagements as described above. One other function of these sets is worth special mention.

Two sets were specially sited on the cliffs at Dover to pick up targets at low level. These sets were able to register aircraft taking off from the aerodromes immediately behind Calais, thereby obtaining information considerably earlier than could be provided by the main R.D.F. station on the coast. This information was reported back to Oxbridge Operations Room by a priority code message which indicated the approximate number of aircraft which had taken off and their position. This report was received some 5/6 minutes before it could be received through the usual R.D.F. channels, and therefore enabled the Controller to order his Fighters off the ground correspondingly earlier than would otherwise have been the case.

This system, which was also adopted somewhat further along the coast in the neighbourhood of Beachy Head, was of all the more value as the enemy were heavily bombing the R.D.F. stations, which were consequently sometimes out of action.

(ii) G.L. Stations with Searchlights.

During the latter stages of the offensive, when the night raids on London commenced, it was realised that the G.L. would be of considerable assistance to Night Fighters. An "elevation" attachment to the equipment was produced and this enabled height to be obtained, which in conjunction with a plotting scheme at S.O.R., enabled Searchlight beams to be directed more accurately on a target to assist night fighters. The results obtained from this were not completely satisfactory, but they showed the way to the development of the present system.

(iii) *Mine-Laying Aircraft.*

It was found that the experiments conducted in the ship-detector rôle could be very satisfactorily applied to detecting mine-laying aircraft which flew in at a height too low to be picked up by the C.H. Stations.

It enabled accurate tracks of these aircraft to be kept which were afterwards passed to the Naval Authorities, who were then able to sweep up the mines which had been laid by these aircraft.

7. *Statistics.*

Careful records have been kept of ammunition expenditure and enemy aircraft shot down, and details are shown in Appendix "C." The following points are worthy of note:-

(*a*) The total enemy aircraft Destroyed, Confirmed Category I by 6th A.A. Division during the months July-October I940, inclusive, was 22I; of this total I04 were destroyed on seven days, thus:-

15	August,	1940	15
18	"	"	22
24	"	"	10
31	"	"	20
2	September,	I940	13
7	"	"	14
15	"	"	10
	"	"	104

(*b*) A considerable number of enemy aircraft were claimed as Probably Destroyed and Damaged.

(*c*) The total amount of H.A.A. expended was 75,000 rounds.

(*d*) The total amount of Bofors ammunition expended was 9,4I7 rounds.

8. *Ground Defence*

Preparations were made by all A.A. defences to assume a secondary ground defence rôle; Bofors were provided with A/T ammunition, and sited to cover approaches to aerodromes, V.Ps., &c. Certain 3.7 inch guns suitably sited were given an anti-ship rôle, and preparations were made for barrages to be put on certain beaches. Under the immediate threat of invasion in May 1940, mobile columns of A.A. troops were formed, but these troops reverted to their A.A. rôle before the Battle of Britain began.

9. *Lessons Learnt.*

(*a*) The outstanding lesson learnt from this intensive air attack was undoubtedly the soundness and suitability of the organisation and arrangements of the control and direction of the anti-aircraft defences. These measures devised in peace time and perfected during the earlier and quieter period of hostilities, stood the severe test with amazing resilience and adaptability. No major alterations in the system were indicated or, indeed, were made subsequent to these operations.[3] The way in which the activities of the anti-aircraft linked in and were capable of co-ordination with the major partners in the venture – R.A.F. Fighter Command, No. II Fighter Group, and sector commands – is perhaps worthy of special note.

(*b*) Other lessons learnt are by comparison of minor import. Chief among them was the great vulnerability of aircraft if caught by accurate H.A.A. fire when in close formation. A good instance of this occurred in an action on the 8th September, when a geschwader of 15 Do. 17s, flying in formation at 15,000 feet, approached a gun site South of River Thames. The opening salvo from the four 3.7-inch guns brought down the three leading aircraft, the remaining machines turning back in disorder, scattering their bombs on the countryside in their flight to the coast.

The value of H.A.A. fire as a means of breaking up bomber squadrons to enable them to be more easily dealt with by our fighters was demonstrated on numerous occasions in the Thames Estuary.

The importance of A.A. shell bursts as a "pointer" to fighters, even though the guns cannot themselves effectively engage the enemy, was also frequently demonstrated.

(*c*) A somewhat negative lesson was the inability of A.A. guns, however well served, to completely deny an area to penetration by determined air attack. Evidence, however, was overwhelming that accurate fire, apart from causing casualties, did impair the enemy's aim, and thus avoid, or at least mitigate, the damage to precise targets.

(*d*) A rather unexpected result was the high proportion (about 10 per cent.) of planes brought down by A.A.L.M.G. fire. It is doubtful, however, whether with the increased armour now carried by enemy aircraft this lesson still obtains.

(*e*) The value of training in recognition was repeatedly emphasised throughout these operations. Fortunately, very few instances of friendly aircraft being engaged occurred. Apart from the accuracy of the information as to movement of aircraft furnished to gun sites, this was no doubt due to a reasonable standard in recognition having been attained.

It was, and still is, continually brought home to the A.A. gunner that, before all else, he must not engage a friendly aircraft. With this thought firmly impressed on the G.P.O., some instances of late engagement or failure to engage perforce occurred. In some cases, had the standard of training been higher, to enable the earlier recognition of a machine as "hostile beyond reasonable doubt," the number of machines destroyed would have been increased.

Chelmsford, August 2, 1941.

APPENDIX "C.A."

H.A.A. GUN DEFENDED AREAS AND ARMAMENT.

G.D.A	August 1940.			October 1940.		
	4·5-in.	3·7-in.	3-in.	4·5-in.	3·7-in.	3-in.
Harwich	-	I5	8	-	8	7
T. and M. North	32	8	I2	24	4	I2
T. and M. South	32	32	I4	28	20	I0
Dover and Manston	-	I2	I6	-	I2	I6
Wattisham	-	-	4	-	-	4
Biggin Hill	-	-	4	-	-	4
Kenley	-	-	-	-	-	2
North Weald	-	+ 4	4+2	-	-	4

APPENDIX "C.B."

L.A.A., V.P's AND ARMAMENT.

V.P.	August 1940. 40-mm	A.A.L.M.G. (No. of Barrels).	Hisp-ano.	3-in., Case I.	Misc.	October 1940. 40-mm.	A.A.L.M.G.	Hisp-ano.	3-in., Case I.	Misc.
Aerodromes.										
Debden	4	3	–	–	–	4	17	–	–	–
Wattisham	–	12	–	–	–	4	8	–	–	–
Biggin Hill	3	2	–	–	–	6	3	–	–	–
Manston	4	4	–	–	–	4	4	–	–	–
West Malling	2	10	–	–	–	4	10	–	–	–
Croydon	–	12	–	–	–	4	8	–	–	–
Kenley	4	8	–	2	–	4	10	–	3	–
Redhill	–	–	–	–	–	3	–	–	–	–
Gravesend	4	4	–	–	–	4	–	–	–	–
Shorts (Rochester)	–	–	–	–	–	4	8	3	–	–
Detling	–	–	–	–	–	2	12	2	–	–
Eastchurch	–	–	–	–	–	2	10	–	–	–
Hawkinge	4	4	–	–	–	4	4	–	–	–
Lympne	–	–	–	–	–	–	2	–	–	–
North Weald	3	12	–	–	–	5	8	–	–	–
Martlesham	4	10	–	–	–	4	11	–	–	–
Rochford	2	8	–	–	–	4	12	–	–	–
Hornchurch	3	7	–	–	–	5	–	–	–	–
Stapleford Abbotts	–	–	–	–	–	2	–	–	–	–

V.P.	August 1940.					October 1940.				
	40-mm.	A.A.L.M.G. (No. of Barrels).	Hisp-ano.	3-in., Case I.	Misc.	40-mm.	A.A.L.M.G.	Hisp-ano.	3-in., Case I.	Misc.
A.M.E. Stations.										
Darsham	2	7	–	–	–	2	8	–	–	–
Dunkirk	3	6	–	–	–	3	7	–	–	–
Rye	3	6	–	–	–	3	11	–	–	–
Pevensey	3	6	–	–	–	3	21	–	–	–
Bawdsey	–	–	–	–	–	3	3	–	–	–
Great Bromley	–	–	–	–	–	3	11	–	–	–
Canewdon	3	4	–	–	–	3	12	–	–	–
Industrial and Oil.										
Crayford	–	8	–	–	–	3	30	3	1	–
Dartford	–	–	–	–	–	1	20	4	–	–
Northfleet	–	–	–	–	–	–	16	–	–	–
Grain (Barges)	2	4	–	–	–	2	34	2	1	–
Chelmsford	–	8	–	–	–	2	21	–	–	–
Murex (Rainham)	–	20	–	–	–	–	20	–	–	–
Purfleet	–	14	–	2	–	–	16	–	2	–
Canvey	–	12	–	2	–	–	12	–	1	–
Thameshaven	–	4	–	4	–	–	–	–	3	–
Shellhaven	–	8	–	3	–	–	8	–	1	–

V.P.	August 1940.					October 1940.				
	40-mm.	A.A.L.M.G. (No. of Barrels).	Hisp-ano.	3-in., Case I.	Misc.	40-mm.	A.A.L.M.G.	Hisp-ano.	3-in., Case I.	Misc.
Naval.										
Chatham	-	-	-	-	-		24	4	3	-
Chattenden	-	-	-	-	-		28	-	-	-
Sheerness	-	-	-	-	-		22	5	-	-
Landguard	-	-	-	-	-		15	-	1	-
Wrabness	-	-	-	-	-		23	-	-	-
Parkeston Quay	-	-	-	4	-		10	-	-	-
Dover	5	9	-	4	-		16	4	-	4 A/T
Tilbury	-	14	-	-	1—2-pdr		18	-	-	-
Southend Pier	-	-	-	-	-		-	-	-	1—2-pdr.

APPENDIX "C.C."

I. – AMMUNITION EXPENDITURE AND CLAIMS, CATEGORY I.

	Total Ammunition Expended	Enemy Aircraft Destroyed	Average Rounds per E/A
H.A.A. (seen targets)	48,155	161	298
H.A.A. (barrage and unseen fire)	26,869	11	2,444
L.A.A. Bofors only	9,417	47	200
A.A.L.M.G. (at S.L. and H.A.F. sites)	Not recorded	23	——

NOTES :-

(i) The above table gives records from September 3, 1939 to November 3, 1940.

(ii) The total enemy aircraft destroyed during the months inclusive July-October was 221.

(iii) The following ammunition was expended from September 3, 1939 to June 30, 1940:-

      H.A.A 2,995

      L.A.A. (Bofors) 1,919

(iv) All the enemy aircraft destroyed by L.A.A. (47) have been credited to Bofors for the purpose of the average; in practice, Lewis guns had a considerable share in several of these as well as in two cases, Hispano (2,94I rounds) and 3-in. Case I (I94 rounds).

(v) Bofors average may be still further sub-divided thus:-

With Predictor.................I79 (3,I87 rounds)
With F.A.S. ....232 (6,230 rounds)

II. – TABLE SHOWING TYPES OF AIRCRAFT DESTROYED JULY-OCTOBER I940.

Type.	*No.*
HE. III	30
Do. I7	39
Do. 2I5	I4
Ju. 87	I5
Ju. 88	I9
Me. I09	80
ME. II0	I5
Unidentified	9
	22I

III.

Destroyed by day	203
Destroyed by night	I8
	22I

APPENDIX "C.D."

AMMUNITION EXPENDITURE AND ENEMY AIRCRAFT DESTROYED THROUGHOUT ANTI-AIRCRAFT COMMAND FOR JULY, AUGUST AND SEPTEMBER I940.

July I940 –

Day[4] ....}344 rds. Per aircraft.
Night ....}(26 a/c = 8,935 rds.)

August I940 –

Day[4] ....}232 rds. per aircraft.
Night ....}(I67 a/c = 38,764 rds.)

September I940 –

Day[5] ....}I,798 rds. per aircraft.
Night ....}(I44 a/c = 258,808 rds.)

APPENDIX "E."

FIGHTER COMMAND

Order of Battle, November 3, 1940.

No. 9 GROUP.

Squadron.	War Station.	Type of Aircraft.	Category.
3I2 (Czech)	Speke	Hurricane	C
6II	Ternhill	Spitfire	C
29 (½)	Ternhill	Blenheim	Night-Flying

No. 10 GROUP.

79	Pembrey	Hurricane	C
87 (½)	Bibury	Hurricane	B
504	Filton	Hurricane	C
609	Middle Wallop	Spitfire	A
604	Middle Wallop	Blenheim	Night-Flying
238	Middle Wallop	Hurricane	A
56	Boscombe Down	Hurricane	A
I52	Warmwell	Spitfire	A
60I	Exeter	Hurricane	C
87(½)	Exeter	Hurricane	B
234	St. Eval	Spitfire	C
247(½)	Roborough	Gladiator	C

APPENDIX II GROUP.

25	Debden	Blenheim and Beaufighter	Night-Flying
73	Castle Camp	Hurricane	Night-Flying
I7	Martlesham	Hurricane	A

229	Northolt	Hurricane	A
6I5	Northolt	Hurricane	A
302 (Polish)	Northolt	Hurricane	A
257	North Weald	Hurricane	A
249	North Weald	Hurricane	A
46	Stapleford	Hurricane	A
264	Hornchurch	Defiant	Night-Flying
4I	Hornchurch	Spitfire	A
603	Hornchurch	Spitfire	A
222	Rochford	Spitfire	A
I4I	Gravesend	Defiant	Night-Flying
74	Biggin Hill	Spitfire	A
92	Biggin Hill	Spitfire	A
66	West Malling	Spitfire	A
42I (½)	West Malling	Hurricane	Reconnaissance
605	Croydon	Hurricane	A
253	Kenley	Hurricane	A
50I	Kenley	Hurricane	A
2I9	Redhill	Blenheim and Beaufighter	Night-Flying
I45	Tangmere	Hurricane	A
2I3	Tangmere	Hurricane	Night-Flying
422 (½)	Tangmere	Hurricane	Night-Flying
602	West Hampnett	Spitfire	A
23	Ford	Blenheim	Night-Flying

No. I2 GROUP.

Squadron.	War Station.	Type of Aircraft.	Category.
303 (Polish)	Leconfield	Hurricane	C
6I6	Kirton-in-Lindsey	Spitfire	C
85	Kirton-in-Lindsey	Hurricane	C
I5I	Digby	Hurricane	C
I	Wittering	Hurricane	C
266	Wittering	Spitfire	C
29 (½)	Wittering	Blenheim	Night-Flying
72	Coltishall	Spitfire	C
64	Coltishall	Spitfire	C
242	Duxford	Hurricane	A
3I0 (Czech)	Duxford	Hurricane	A
I9	Duxford	Spitfire	A

No. I3 GROUP.

607	Turnhouse	Hurricane	C
65	Turnhouse	Spitfire	B
232 (½)	Drem	Hurricane	C
263 (½)	Drem	Hurricane	C
I (Canadian)	Prestwick	Hurricane	C
32	Acklington	Hurricane	C
6I0	Acklington	Spitfire	C
600 (½)	Acklington	Blenheim Night-Flying	
43	Usworth	Hurricane	C
54	Catterick	Spitfire	C
600 (½)	Catterick	Blenheim Night-Flying	
245	Aldergrove	Hurricane	C

No. I4 GROUP.

3	Castletown	Hurricane	C
III (½)	Dyce	Hurricane	C
III (½)	Montrose	Hurricane	C

NON-OPERATIONAL SQUADRONS.

Group.	Squadron.	Station.	Type of Aircraft.
9 Group	308 (Polish)	Baginton	Hurricane
I2 Group	306 (Polish)	Church Fenton	Hurricane
	307 (Polish)	Kirton-in-Lindsey	Defiant
	7I (Eagle)	Church Fenton	Buffalo
I3 Group	263 (½)	Drem	Whirlwind

NOTE – Two "B" Squadrons, Nos. 74 and 145, had already been thrown onto battle, leaving only two available at the end.

APPENDIX "F."

NOTE ON THE OFFENSIVE AND DEFENSIVE EQUIPMENT OF AIRCRAFT.

I. The general principle of developing the maximum possible fire power, which is accepted in all Armies and Navies, must presumably be applicable to Fighter Aircraft, provided that this can be done without unduly sacrificing Performance and Endurance.

2. The 8-gun fighter may be said to exemplify this principle, and at the beginning of the war its results were decisive against German Bombers, which were unarmoured at that time.

3. Our Fighter pilots were protected against the return fire of Bombers by their engines, and by bullet-proof glass and armour, for their heads and chests respectively.

4. Furthermore, at this time the return fire from German Bombers was negligible. They had concentrated on Performance as the principle means of evasion (a false lesson drawn from the low speed of the Fighters used in the Spanish War) and the few guns which they carried were manually controlled, and so badly mounted that they were practically useless. These facts, in combination with the fire power and armour protection of our own Fighters, made the latter virtually immune to the fire of unescorted Bombers, and their casualties in Home Defence fighting up to the Spring of I940 were quite negligible.

5. The German Bombers had good self-sealing tanks, and this was perhaps the only important particular in which they were ahead of us. In our development work we had demanded that tanks should be "Crash Proof" as well as self-sealing, and the drastic conditions, which

our experimental tanks had to meet had made them unduly heavy and cumbrous.

6. So far as our Fighters were concerned, the wing tanks in the Hurricane were removed and covered with a fabric known as "Linatex" which had fairly good self-sealing characteristics. The reserve tank in the fuselage was left uncovered, as it was difficult of access and it was thought that it would be substantially protected by the armour which had been fitted. During the Battle, however, a great number of Hurricanes were set on fire by incendiary bullets or cannon shells, and their pilots were badly burned by a sheet of flame which filled the cockpit before they could escape by parachute.

7. The reserve tanks were therefore covered with Linatex as a matter of the highest priority, and a metal bulkhead was fitted in front of the pilot to exclude the rush of flame from the cockpit.

8. The Germans soon began to fit fuselage armour to protect their pilots and crews, but for some unexplained reason neither side had fitted armour behind the engines of their Bombers. The back of the engine is much more vulnerable to rifle-calibre bullets than the front, owing to the mass of ancillary equipment which is there installed. While the back of the engine lies open to attack, the rifle-calibre machine gun remains a useful weapon, and the fact is a fortunate one for us.

9. The application of armour to Bombers did not, of course, come as a surprise to us, and its implications had long been discussed.

10. Excluding devices such as hanging wires, exploding pilotless aircraft, etc., I have always thought that the courses open to the Fighter, when rifle-calibre machine-gun fire from astern becomes ineffective, may be summarised as follows:-

(A) Deliver fire from ahead or from a flank.

(B) Pierce the armour.

(C) Attack the fuel tanks with incendiary ammunition.

(D) Destroy the structure of the aircraft by means of direct hits from explosive shells.

(E) Use large shells with Time and Percussion fuzes.

Discussing these in order:-

I1. – (A) Fire from ahead or from a flank is effective but difficult to deliver accurately at modern speeds. Fire from ahead proved very effective on occasions during the Battle, but relative speeds are so high that the time available for shooting is very short, and Fighters generally find themselves in a position to deliver such an attack more by accident than by design.

I2. Beam attack is very difficult to deliver accurately, owing to the amount of deflection which had to be allowed. The deflection ring on a Fighter's sight allows for an enemy speed of I00 m.p.h., and therefore a full diameter outside the ring must sometimes be allowed.

I3. The method is effective against formations, when the aircraft hit is not always the one aimed at, and certainly the Gladiators in Norway developed this technique with great success. On the whole, however, Fighters which were constrained to this method of attack would have a very limited usefulness.

I4. – (B) The simplest reaction for the Fighter is to pierce the armour, but it entails the use of bigger calibres. It must be remembered also that it is not sufficient merely to pierce the armour, but the bullet must have sufficient remaining velocity to do lethal damage thereafter. High velocities, in addition to bigger calibres, are therefore necessary.

I5. The .5-inch gun appeared, at first sight, to be the natural successor to the .303 inch, but experiments showed that the type available to us in the Autumn of I940 was practically defeated by the 8-mm. armour carried in the M.E. I09. It was true that the bullet would pierce 20-mm. or more of armour in the open, but it was found that the minute deceleration and deflection of the axis of the bullet, caused by its passage through the structure of the fuselage, exercised a very important diminution on its subsequent penetrative powers.

I6. Experiments carried out with .5-inch guns of higher velocity in America have given encouraging results, and it is not at present possible to dogmatise on the subject. It would, however, be foolish to adopt a gun which could be defeated by a slight thickening of the armour carried by the Bomber and the aim should be to defeat the thickest armour which it is practically possible for the enemy to carry.

I7. We have at present no gun of a calibre between .5-inch and 20-mm. (.8 inch). The latter was originally adopted by the French because it was of about the right size to fire an explosive shell through an airscrew of a Hispano Suiza engine, and was adopted by us from them. If, therefore, it proves to be of the best weight and calibre for an armour piercing, that is due to accident rather than design.

I8. A study of available data might lead one to suppose that a calibre of about I5-mm. would be the ideal, and I understand that this size has recently been adopted by the Germans; but we cannot now start designing a new gun for this war, and we must choose between the .5-inch and the 20-mm. We shall soon get reliable data from American Fighter types in action. They have faith in the .5-inch gun.

I9. The Armament of the Royal Air Force is not its strongest point, and in my opinion we should do our own Design and Experimental work, and satisfy our requirements without being dependent on Woolwich and Shoeburyness.

20. – (C) Incendiary ammunition may be fired from guns of any calibre and Bomber tanks have been set on fire by .303 inch ammunition. The bigger the bullet, however, the bigger the hole, and a small bullet stands a good chance of being quenched before it can take effect. In any case, the fuel tanks of a Bomber constitute so small a proportion of the whole target that they cannot be made the sole objective of attack; and it seems that the adoption of a large-calibre gun and the use of a proportion of incendiary ammunition therein will afford a satisfactory compromise.

2I – (D) It was assumed by the French that the 20-mm. shell would be effective against the structure of modern aircraft. I do not know what trials they carried out, but the tests done by us at Shoeburyness and Orfordness indicate that the effect of a 20-mm. shell exploding instantaneously on the surface of an aircraft is almost negligible, except in a small percentage of lucky strikes. The normal effect is that a hole of about 6-inch diameter is blown in the surface, and that the effect at any distance is nil, since the shell is blown almost into dust. Occasionally the fuze penetrates and does some damage, but this is slight in comparison with the total weight of the shell. Even the big 37-mm. shell, though it may be spectacular damage, will not often bring a Bomber down with a single hit. Greater damage is done if the fuze is given a slight delay action, so that it bursts inside the covering of the aircraft, but small delay action fuzes are unreliable in operation and difficult to manufacture, and, on the whole, it seems doubtful if explosive shells are as efficient as armour-piercing and incendiary projectiles, especially as they will not penetrate armour. Another point must be remembered, viz., that a drum of explosive shells is a very dangerous item of cargo: if one is struck and detonated by a bullet it is not unlikely that they will all go off and blow the aeroplane to pieces.

22. – (E) The use of large shells (comparable to Anti-Aircraft types) from Fighter aircraft is practically prohibited by considerations of weight if a gun is used. The gun itself must be heavy and the structure must be strengthened to withstand the shock of recoil. The walls and base of the shell also have to be made uneconomically heavy to withstand the discharge. All these difficulties, however, can be overcome if the Rocket principle is used. It is true that a Rocket can be discharged only in the direct line of flight, but that is no particular handicap to a Fighter. It can have a light firing tube, there is no recoil, and the shell can be designed for optimum fragmentation effect. (I have been told that a 3-inch Rocket shell develops the same explosive and fragmentation effect as a 4.5-inch Anti-Aircraft gun shell). It also starts with an advantage over the terrestrial rocket in that it has an initial velocity of about 300 m.p.h. through the air, which gives it enhanced accuracy. For this weapon a "Proximity Fuze" would be ideal, but, pending the development of this, there is no reason why the Rocket should not be used with a Time and Percussion Fuze used in conjunction with a range-finder in the Aircraft.

23. This item was put on the programme about 7 years ago, and I think it a great pity that it was allowed to drop. True, unexpected difficulties may be encountered, and nothing may come of the project, but it is an important experiment, and our knowledge of what is and is not possible will not be complete until it has been tried.

24. I think that our decision to adopt the 20-mm. gun is probably the wisest which we could have taken, but to carry increased load efficiently something bigger than the Hurricane or Spitfire is needed. The Typhoon with 2,000 h.p. should be ideal when it has been given an adequate ceiling.

25. In the meantime the Hurricane must be somewhat overloaded with 4 Cannons, and mixed armament (2 Cannons and 4 Brownings) in the Spitfire is merely a compromise necessitated by loading

conditions. Might not the high-velocity American .5-inch gun prove a suitable armament for the small fighter?

26. As regards ammunition for the 20-mm. gun, the so-called "solid" bullet was merely a cheap steel bullet produced by the French for practice purposes. Its mass and velocity have enabled it hitherto to smash through armour to which it has been opposed, but an improved design will probably be needed before long; doubtless the matter is receiving attention. I understand that the incendiary bullet – the equivalent of the de Wilde .303-inch – has been giving good results.

27. One other attribute of a naked steel bullet must not be overlooked, viz., its incendiary effect when it strikes a ferrous structure. During ground trials a Blenheim was set on fire by the second hit from a "solid" bullet. Unfortunately, German aircraft do not normally contain much iron or steel.

28. If we look into the not too distant future, I think we shall find that an additional and quite different reason may arise for the adoption of the high-velocity gun with a comparatively heavy projectile. I refer to the increasing intensity and effect of return fire from Bombers.

29. Our Fighters are protected to a very large degree from the return fire of Bombers which they attack from astern, so long as they have to sustain the impact only of rifle-calibre bullets.

30. The situation will be quite different, however, if turrets with .5-inch guns are commonly used in Bombers. The Bomber has the comparative advantage over the pursuing Fighter of firing "down-wind" (one may get a clear idea of the situation by imagining both aircraft to be anchored in space, with a 300-m.p.h. wind blowing from the Bomber to the Fighter). The result is likely to be that effective armouring of Fighters against return fire will be impossible, and fighting ranges in good visibility may be considerably lengthened. In such circumstances high velocity, flat trajectory and a heavy projectile will attain increasing importance; attention will also have to be paid to accurate methods of sighting, and allowance for gravity drop.

Footnotes

1 These guns belonged to Field Force Units. As such units were, of necessity, highly mobile; their exact location was not always known to Fighter Command. Nor, after a recent move, were they always included in the telephone system.

2 As a result of the experience gained during this period, all searchlight equipments have since been fitted with Radar control. This, combined with intensified training, has made them, since 1941, extremely accurate.

3 This statement applies only to the higher organisation, and must not be taken to mean that no improvements were made in the control and direction of A.A. gunnery.

4 Mainly by day, little night activity.

5 Including considerable night activity and large expenditure of ammunition by night.

2

THE ANTI-AIRCRAFT DEFENCE OF THE UNITED KINGDOM.

BY GENERAL
SIR FREDERICK A PILE

The War Office, December, 1947.

FROM 28TH JULY, 1939, TO 15TH APRIL, 1945.

The following despatch was submitted to the Secretary of State for War on the 21st October, 1946, by GENERAL SIR FREDERICK A. PILE, Bt., G.C.B., D.S.O., M.C., General Officer Commanding-in-Chief, Anti-Aircraft Command.

PART I.
PREAMBLE.

1. I have been commanded by the Army Council to submit a report on the Anti-Aircraft defence of the United Kingdom during the war and have the honour to present my despatch herewith.

2. For convenience the report has been divided into two parts and in this first part I propose to deal with events from the outbreak of war until May, 1941.

SECTION I
General

3. In September, 1939, the Anti-Aircraft defences of the country were organised in a Command Headquarters, seven Divisional Headquarters, a varying number of Brigades in each Division and a number of gun and searchlight units in each Brigade.

4. Anti-Aircraft Command Headquarters was situated at Stanmore, adjacent to the Headquarters of Fighter Command, R.A.F., and with them was jointly responsible for the Air

Defence of Great Britain, the A.O.C.-in-C. Fighter Command being in operational command.

A system of responsibility such as this obviously entailed the closest liaison and willing co-operation on both sides. I wish to put on record that the relations between my Headquarters and Fighter Command Headquarters were always most cordial.

5. The areas allotted to each of the seven Divisions were as follows:-

Ist – The Metropolitan area of London.
2nd – Northern East Anglia, the East Midlands and Humber.
3rd – Scotland and Northern Ireland.
4th – North-west England, the West Midlands and North
    Wales.
5th – South Wales, south-west and southern England.
6th – South-east England and southern East Anglia.
7th – North-east England.

An additional organisation, directly controlled for operations from my Headquarters, was responsible for the defence of the Orkneys and Shetlands. It is essential to emphasise that A.A. Divisions were in no way comparable to Divisions in the Field Army, being of no fixed size and at times being up to four times as large and covering many thousand square miles of country.

6. The failure of our first overseas campaign in Norway confirmed my opinion of the paramount importance of the Anti-Air craft defences; if we could obtain, mastery in the air, there would be no invasion; if we could not, no expeditionary force could be launched from the

United Kingdom. I therefore pressed for and secured a large expansion of our Anti-Aircraft defences during 1940.

7. At the end of 1940 I felt it essential to propose a considerable re-organisation in order to relieve the burden on the existing Command and Divisions and also to achieve closer coordination of boundaries with Fighter Command. Five new Divisions were created as follows:-

8th – covering the south coast as far east as Bournemouth.
9th – South Wales.
10th – Humber.
11th – the West Midlands and central Wales.
12th – Clyde and Northern Ireland.

In addition, to ease the supervision of this organisation, three AA Corps were created:

1. AA Corps in the South (1, 5, 6, 8 and 9 Divisions) corresponding with 10 and 11 Groups R.A.F.
2. AA Corps in the Midlands (2, 4, 10 and 11 Divisions) corresponding with 9 and 12 Groups R.A.F.
3. AA Corps in the North (3, 7, and 12 Divisions) corresponding with 13 and 14 Groups R.A.F.

8. When I was appointed to the command of the Anti-Aircraft defences on 28th July, 1939, I was faced with the most grave shortage of equipment. At the outbreak of war the total number of Heavy Anti-Aircraft guns under my command was 695, many of which were of old and obsolescent types and a number of which were only on loan from the Royal Navy. The approved and recommended total at this time was 2,232.

The position with Light Anti-Aircraft guns was even worse, there being only 253 out of an approved total of 1,200, some of which again had been borrowed from the Royal Navy. Of the best Light Anti-Aircraft gun, the 40-mm. Bofors, there were only 76.

Searchlights were in a somewhat better position, as there were 2,700 equipments out of an approved total of 4,128 and a recommended total of 4,700.

9. The increase in equipments throughout the period under review may conveniently be noted here.

At the end of 1939 there were 850 Heavy guns, 510 Light guns and 3,361 Searchlights.

At the beginning of July, 1940, when air attacks on the United Kingdom began in earnest, there were 1,200 Heavy guns, 549 Light guns and 3,932 Searchlights.

By May, 1941, there were 1,691 Heavy guns, 940 Light guns, and Searchlights had reached a total of 4,532 early in 1941 but owing to shortage of manpower the number of equipments in action had to be reduced before May, 1941.

10. The Anti-Aircraft defences at the outbreak of war were entirely manned by units of the Territorial Army. Their total strength at the time they were mobilised was 106,690.

While the training of a Territorial Army in peace time bristles with difficulties, the Territorial system has many advantages which far outweigh the disadvantages.

The Territorial Army has always attracted men anxious to fit themselves to defend their country. These men were the cream of the manhood of the country. In the Command it is no exaggeration to say that the success which it achieved was due in great part to the excellence of the personnel and without some similar voluntary organisation in the future I do not see how the Anti-Aircraft defences of this country can be adequately manned except at prohibitive cost.

11. As a result of the introduction of conscription early in 1939 it was intended to allot 20,000 militia every three months to help man the defences. In actual fact, war began three months before the arrival of the first allotment. By July, 1940, the total manpower in Anti-Aircraft Command was 157,319 and in May, 1941, just over 300,000.

12. It very soon became evident that the quality of the conscripts allotted to the Command was inferior and that I was not receiving such a good selection of the Army intake as other arms. This was due to restrictions as to age and medical fitness on the men to be posted to Arms liable to serve overseas, and I later had occasion to protest against a process of allocation of manpower which involved the posting of the best type of recruits to other Arms at the expense of A.A. Command.

13. Throughout the period covered by this part of my despatch, and indeed throughout the war, I was constantly faced with manpower problems. The shortage of manpower and the large demands made on

the Command to supply personnel and units for the Field Army (in all I70 gun or searchlight regiments went overseas) led first of all to the introduction of Mixed Units and later to the Home Guard manning anti-aircraft equipment. It led also to drastic reductions in the number of searchlight units.

I4. The deployment of the anti-aircraft defences at the outbreak of a war is a very delicate matter. The possibility of an immediate and paralysing attack from the air means that they must be ready at a very early stage, before the normal process of mobilization has been developed. They have a big responsibility at that time for the protection of the national economy upon which the whole war effort must depend.

I5. The various means by which the troops might be called up before official mobilization took place in such a way as not to damage further any strained international relations were investigated. The B.B.C. was obviously out of the question and might in any case be off the air at the time it was needed; the telephone service would undoubtedly be overloaded; letters or telegrams provided no confirmation of delivery of the message and I finally concluded that messages by hand to key men, through whom the order would be spread downward to all who were involved, provided the only satisfactory solution. It so happened that when mobilization was required the defences were already manned in part and had been as a precaution since 28th April, I939, with the result that the problem in the end was not fully presented.

I6. When war began without any major air attack the first task was to improve the standard of training throughout Anti-Aircraft Command. Training in an anti-aircraft rôle requires progressive development. First, the individual has to be trained for his particular task on the equipment; next, the detachment has to be trained to work as a team and finally, the various detachments have to learn to co-ordinate their efforts as a tactical whole.

I7. While I have already placed on record the splendid service which the Territorial units rendered in the early months of the war, their training, limited as it had been both by lack of equipment and the little time they had been able to spend on it, fell far short of that required for war. Some units, forcibly converted to a searchlight rôle, were found to contain some men unsuitable for the work and others who preferred their original rôle. The targets with which they had had to practise had been very slow and had taken no evasive action. Attempts to secure more up-to-date aircraft from the Air Ministry were largely nullified because of the R.A.F.'s own shortage of planes. Practice by night was handicapped by the fact that all planes were ordered to fly with navigation lights, thus making exercises unrealistic. It is my opinion, an opinion not necessarily endorsed by the other military or air authorities, that it is essential that the Army should be independent of other services in the matter of providing for air co-operation in the training of Anti-Aircraft units.

18. The state of training of the Militia when they arrived was considerably lower than that of the Territorial Army.

19. The only training establishment at the outbreak of war was the School of Anti-Aircraft Defence, which proved totally inadequate for training more than a limited number of officers and N.C.Os. as instructors. To supplement this, Divisional Schools were formed in each of the seven areas into which the country was then divided. Many Brigades and even Regiments founded unofficial schools of their own, where equipment and methods had to be improvised. Owing to the wide dispersal of Anti-Aircraft detachments throughout the country these schools were able to fulfil a need which could not otherwise have been met.

20. The flow of Militia into the Command continued after the battle had been joined and in the first three months of the battle no less than 70,000 recruits received their first training in an anti-aircraft rôle on gunsites which were for the most part in constant action against the enemy.

21. While it was clear that our training was woefully deficient it was also obvious that the successful engagement of enemy planes required the highest technical excellence in equipment.

I was most fortunate in having the help of Professor A.V. Hill who obtained for the Command some of the finest scientists in the land. These scientists were indefatigable in their efforts to improve our equipment and training. They were recruited from all over the British Empire; and even before America came into the war many of her scientists had volunteered to work on our gun sites. No tribute could be too high to pay to all these distinguished men. Although we had many hundreds eventually serving in the Command we never had enough; but I believe it is true to say that thanks to their efforts Anti-Aircraft Command became the most technical and scientific Command in our own or any other army.

22. The problem of scientific training became acute with the introduction of radio-location – or radar as it was later called. A radio school was formed at Petersham at which selected specialist officers and civilian scientists were trained on the equipment. It was arranged that they would subsequently live and work on gunsites and give the Artillery officers the assistance and advice of which they must otherwise inevitably have been deprived. The work of these young men, many straight from the universities, was invaluable.

23. Mention must also be made of the formation of the Operational Research Group of Anti-Aircraft Command; an invaluable organization consisting of scientists and military liaison officers, whose study of operational problems was of such value that their activities were later extended to embrace all forms of military warfare. This body was then re-named Army Operational Research Group.

24. For the greater part of the period under review the administration of many of the ancillary services rested with Home Commands, who were responsible for the Anti-Aircraft services within their respective areas. On many occasions I had to protest most strongly against this division of control, since I was hampered in my attempts to obtain full efficiency as long as I had no control over many aspects of the life of the troops under my command. In addition, difficulties arose because Home Command boundaries differed from those of Anti-Aircraft Corps and Divisions. In the early part of 1941 full control of most services was vested in me. This decision greatly eased our difficulties.

25. Before I proceed to the details of the battle against the Luftwaffe it is necessary to outline briefly the plans for the disposition of the various forms of defence.

26. It was envisaged that the enemy's main objectives would include aircraft factories, cities, and particularly London and the main purpose of the defences was to prevent their reaching these objectives. The area around the cities and between them and the coast was, therefore, made an Air Fighting Zone in which our fighter aircraft would operate, assisted at night by searchlights. To this end there was a continuous searchlight belt 30 miles deep which stretched from the Solent, east of

London, north to the Humber and then north-west to the Tyne-Tees area. A further belt ran between the Forth and the Clyde.

To deal with aircraft which nevertheless penetrated this defence, the important cities were made Gun Defended Areas, with searchlights to enable the Heavy guns to fire by night.

For the protection of isolated points of importance, such as factories and airfields, Light guns were deployed against low level precision bombing.

As more equipment became available more cities were defended and the defences of others increased. Searchlight cover was extended to the greater part of the country.

Each Gun Defended Area had its Gun Operations Room, which was a nerve-centre of the defences and could be used either to pass information to the guns or actually to control the fire.

In each R.A.F. Sector in the Air Fighting Zone the Sector Operations Room was fitted for transmission of information or orders to the searchlights.

27. I felt it necessary to express alarm at the comparative immobility of our defences and particularly of Heavy guns, but since static guns were much more rapidly produced than mobile guns, I was forced to accept them. Consequently I was handicapped whenever it became necessary to move guns from one area to another.

It was not possible to have sufficient equipment or manpower to defend every town which might be attacked nor could even the most mobile defences be moved sufficiently fast to beat any given point as quickly as the enemy aircraft. The value of mobile defences lies in the fact that the air battle, like any other battle, has a pattern which the enemy tries to carry out. When such a pattern is evident (e.g. the attacks on our ports; "Baedeker" raids etc.) defences can be organised rapidly to meet it.

SECTION II.
The Day Raider.

28. All the equipment available during the first year of war had been designed for shooting at seen targets. Except in cloudy weather it was,

therefore, generally suitable for dealing with attacks by day and it was by day that the first attacks were made.

The principle used was the following: a predictor fitted with telescopes was laid on and followed the target, a height calculated by a height finder was set into it and the predictor mechanism automatically calculated where the target would be at the time the shell burst in the sky and by means of electric pointers enabled the gun to be aimed at that point.

There were, however, limitations to this equipment. Predictors were not designed to accept heights over 25,000 feet and as the enemy developed his tactics he flew more frequently at greater heights; further, there was a limit to the speed at which the predictor could traverse so that close targets often moved across the sky too fast to be followed. Except in very clear weather the "pick up" was too late to ensure adequate time to bring effective fire to bear.

29. Reference has already been made to the shortage of equipment in the early part of the war. The responsibility for allocating what equipment there was rested primarily with the A.O.C.-in-C. Fighter Command, who invariably consulted me in the matter. The demands for defence were, however, so various and the interests involved so powerful that we were continually faced with fresh agitations for defences. In order to deal with these requests a sub-committee of the Chiefs of Staff Committee known as the C.O.S. AA Committee was formed. The three services were represented on this committee and the Minister of Home Security was also on it.

30. Another effect of the shortage was that none of the units was fully equipped with the weapons it was intended they should have and though other types of weapons were brought in to fill the gap, complications arose because units frequently had to operate two, three or more types of equipment simultaneously.

3I. The Heavy guns included the 4.5-inch of which I had 355 by June, I940, when day raiders began to be serious. Secondly, there was the 3.7-inch on either a mobile or a static mounting, and this gun became the mainstay of heavy anti-aircraft armament throughout the war and in my opinion was the finest all purposes gun produced by any country during the war. Unfortunately it was never mounted in a tank.

In June, 1940, I had 306 mobile and 313 static 3.7-inch guns and finally I had 226 obsolescent 3-inch guns.

Light anti-aircraft guns at the same date comprised the following:- 273 40-mm Bofors, which was the chief Light weapon; 136 obsolescent 3-inch guns adapted for low level shooting; 140 miscellaneous types of 2-pounder guns on loan from the Royal Navy; and 38 20-mm Hispano cannons.

32. The first raids were made in October, 1939, upon the Forth and upon Scapa Flow. Though the guns were successful in destroying some of the raiders, it was at once apparent that peacetime training and the existing equipment was insufficient to deal entirely successfully with wartime targets, which continually dived and turned and flew at comparatively high speeds. Steps were taken to have alterations designed and made to meet the needs of the situation, but nearly two years elapsed before these were actually produced.

Until June, 1940, enemy activity consisted mainly of sporadic minelaying or reconnaissance flights, often by single planes, and of small scale attacks upon convoys and the northern bases of the Home Fleet.

33. I do not propose to discuss on what exact date the Battle of Britain began, but what is certain is that in the second half of June, 1940, there was a marked increase in activity by the German air forces over and around the United Kingdom.

34. With the limited resources at my disposal it was impossible to give the country the degree of protection required at this time and the main weight of the attacks during the daylight Battle of Britain was borne by Fighter Command. Nevertheless it is only right to draw attention to the important part played by the guns during this battle, a part which the R.A.F. have never minimised; and inded of the large daily totals of enemy aircraft destroyed in the battle, at times twenty, and on one occasion thirty, fell to the guns.

When the enemy began to come over in large formations the Heavy guns frequently laid the foundation of the Fighter successes by breaking up the formations with their fire, thereby rendering them vulnerable, while the presence of small groups of enemy aircraft or individual planes, which might otherwise have escaped the attention of fighter pilots, was indicated to them by bursts of anti-aircraft fire in the sky.

Light guns filled a rôle for which there could be no alternative weapon, particularly in the defence of airfields. Experience abroad had already demonstrated, and future experience was to confirm, that airfields lacking anti-aircraft defence were unable to continue in action against a sustained attack. Only guns, and lots of them, can defend an aircraft during the vulnerable moments when it is taking-off or landing.

35. The Battle of Britain may conveniently be divided into four phases although these sometimes overlapped. During the second half of the battle there were attacks by night as well as by day, but I propose to defer discussion of the night raids until later in this despatch. The first phase of the battle consisted largely of attacks on convoys in the Channel and on south coast ports. The heaviest engagements occurred between Harwich and Lyme Bay, although places as far on either flank as the Orkneys and Cardiff received some attention. So long as the enemy confined his attacks to shipping, the guns of A.A. Command could take no part in the battle and it fell to Fighter Command, who were able by their radar to observe concentrations of aircraft in the Calais region, to endeavour to deal with them. When ports were attacked the guns were in action: and at Portsmouth, Portland and in particular Dover, heavy engagements were frequent and several enemy aircraft were destroyed. It was at this time that Dover began to be "Hellfire Corner" for German pilots.

36. The second phase opened on August 12th, 1940, when the enemy began to attack the coastal airfields. Reference has already been made to the importance of anti-aircraft defence for airfields and, though many raiders were shot down in these attacks, considerable damage to the airfields was in fact done and many were temporarily put out of commission. Especially in the early attacks of this phase the standard of training in the Light anti-aircraft gun detachments was insufficiently high and later, when frequent practice had led to improvement, the limited number of guns proved a handicap. The damage however, to the airfields would generally have been still more serious and of more permanent a character without the presence of the few guns which could be spared.

37. The policy of filling the gaps in the heavier equipment with Lewis light machine-guns was amply justified during this second phase. On 18th August, 1940, ten aircraft were destroyed by these

weapons alone, and it was a fortunate chance of war that German aircraft were lightly armoured at the time when equipment was short and that heavier armour was only fitted when the defences had more weapons capable of penetrating it.

38. The third phase of the battle, directed against inland airfields, opened on 24th August, 1940. The Light anti-aircraft defences continued to show improved results and, because many of the attacks were delivered against the outskirts of the London area, the heavy guns in the Thames Estuary were able to take part in the battle. This was the densest concentration of Heavy guns which the Germans had so far encountered and, though only a limited number of planes was destroyed, formations were consistently broken up before they reached their objectives.

39. On 7th September, 1940, the fourth phase of the battle began with a heavy raid on London. During the preceding phases we had received constant demands for guns to defend other places, not only on the south coast but in industrial areas which were beginning to feel the weight of night attacks. We had, therefore, reluctantly drained London of its defences until no more than 92 Heavy guns remained. As soon as it became apparent that London was to be the target, I had to draw back into the capital as many guns as I could reasonably manage and within 48 hours the total had increased to 203.

40. The attack on London was made both by night and by day, and of the initial inefficacy of the night defences I shall have something to say later. By day, though it was impossible for the R.A.F. to prevent the Germans reaching the capital and though when they were there it was too late to prevent them bombing the city, the guns destroyed a considerable number in many of the formations. It was significant too that the most spectacular success which the enemy achieved by day, namely the firing of the dock area on 7th September, 1940, occurred when the gun defences were numerically at their lowest ebb. The increase in the number of guns at once reduced the amount of damage which the enemy was able to inflict; his formations were more effectively broken and the successes of the fighter aircraft continued to mount. On 15th September, 1940, due largely to the R.A.F., the enemy effort was so decisively beaten that though attacks continued by day until 30th September, 1940, it was undoubtedly then that the

turning-point of the battle against the day raider had been reached.

41. I have dealt only briefly with this battle because it was primarily a battle between air forces.

From 10th July, 1940, the day which most authorities have accepted as the opening day of the battle, until 30th September, 1940, the guns of Anti-Aircraft Command destroyed by day 296 enemy aircraft and damaged or probably destroyed a further 74.

42. During October, 1940, the enemy reserved his bombers almost exclusively for night operations but he continued for a time to attack the country by day with fighter-bombers. For the most part these attacks did not penetrate far inland and were often delivered on unprotected coastal towns. Militarily the attacks had little significance, except in so far as they were designed to wear down our fighter forces and with the existing resources it was impossible to provide gun defences for these coastal towns without denuding vital factories of protection.

SECTION III.
The Night Raider.

43. I come now to that form of air attack which, in the early days, before a successful night fighter technique had been developed, was essentially a gun battle; I refer to the night raids. I have already mentioned that practically all equipment had been designed for visual shooting at seen targets, and this applied to shooting by night as well as to shooting by day.

44. The equipment which was available in the first year of the war had been designed some years previously at a time when the possibility of targets taking violent evasive action at high speeds had been insufficiently realised. It had been hoped that if raiding took place at night the searchlights would be able by means of sound-locators to find their targets, illuminate them and continue the illumination without difficulty. This would enable the guns to use their normal visual methods of engagement and the fighters outside the Gun Defended Areas to make their interceptions and attacks.

45. Even before the war it was obvious however that the likelihood of night raiding had been increased by the improvement in navigational

methods and the greater reliability of aircraft engines and also that, even without evasive action by the enemy, cloud would seriously handicap all forms of night defence. Visually controlled searchlights appeared to be of doubtful value to the guns.

46. There appeared to be no satisfactory solution to this problem until the invention of radar and, as the delivery of the first radar sets for guns was not due until 1940, some alternative means of dealing with unseen targets had to be found. The only available equipment was the sound-locator.

Pre-war experience had shown that under good conditions and within certain ranges sound-locators could pick up and follow single slow-flying targets and that, by making due allowance for the fact that sound travels comparatively slowly, searchlights could be directed at the actual position of the target.

47. The use of sound-locators with the guns involved the additional complication that the guns had to be directed not at the actual position but at that position where the aircraft might be expected to be by the time the shell burst in the sky. What had to be done, therefore, was to track the target by sound-locator for some time in order to establish its course, then to pass information to the guns on which a future position could be calculated, take the necessary steps to aim the guns and set the fuzes. In all, this meant allowing an interval of anything up to a full minute between the calculation of the target's future position by a sound-locator and the arrival of the shell at its destination. During this interval the air-craft might be expected to fly between four and six miles.

Moreover, in calculating the future position, it had to be assumed that the aircraft would continue to fly on a constant course at a constant height and at a constant speed, the likelihood of which was small after the first signs of interference by the ground defences.

48. The plan which was evolved for the defence of London was known as the Fixed Azimuth System. Two lines of sound-locators spaced at 2-mile internals were sited at right-angles to the Thames Estuary on the eastern flanks of London and another similar system was laid out on the western side.

Each sound-locator was directly linked to the London Gun Operations Room and it was expected that the two nearest locators in the outer line would on the approach of an enemy aircraft be able almost simultaneously to report a bearing and an angle of sight from which the Operations Room could determine the position and height of the plane by calculating the intersection. Similar information from two locators in the inner line would supply direction and speed.

The Operations Room could then fix a "future position" at which the target would be engaged. This position would be passed in code back to the guns who would make the necessary adjustments to suit their own situation and fire on a given order.

49. In the cities of the provinces the problem was less acute because the smaller size of the target limited the area in the sky in which the enemy could operate successfully. Consequently in many places it was possible to work out geographical barrages which could be fired on an order from the local Gun Operations Room and guns were sited accordingly.

50. Sporadic night raids against this country began during the Summer of I940. In early August they began to intensify and on 8th/9th August provincial cities were attacked by raiders endeavouring to make precision attacks on certain factories. The emphasis was on the Midlands and the West, but the enemy's effort was scattered and no real test of the defences occurred; a few planes were shot down and others damaged in widely divergent areas.

5I. Between 25th/26th August, I940, and 6th/7th September, I940, there was noticeable a somewhat greater degree of concentration in the enemy's attacks, though it was still in the Midlands and the West that the main attack fell, over I00 planes attacking Liverpool on four nights in succession.

Forty-eight planes were destroyed by gunfire during this period.

A few aircraft had flown over London by night during this period, but it was on the night of 7th/8th September, I940, following the first heavy raid by day, that London was first singled out as a major objective and one which was thereafter to be continuously attacked.

52. The Fixed Azimuth System broke down completely. The enemy was now operating at greater heights and sound-locators could not always detect the aircraft; at other times more than one plane was operating between two locators and there was no certainty that both equipments were tracking the same aircraft; the assumption that the

main approach to the Capital would be up the Estuary was not always fulfilled (probably owing to the new German navigational aids) and many planes passed outside the flanks of the sound-locator layout; finally, faults developed in the communication system and large sections of the front were put out of action for long periods. In consequence few of the 92 available guns received data on which they could fire.

53. I realised that the mere introduction of more guns would not alone solve the problem, although within 48 hours the number had been increased to 203. I therefore decided, on IIth September, I940, that guns which were unable to fire on the Fixed Azimuth System should be given a free hand to use any method of control they liked.

54. The volume of fire which resulted, and which was publicized as a "barrage" was in fact largely wild and uncontrolled shooting. There were, however, two valuable, results from it: the volume of fire had a deterrent effect upon at least some of the German aircrews, so that, though it cannot be proved by records, I have every reason to believe that one third failed to reach their objective; there was also a marked improvement in civilian morale. Against this there was an expenditure of ammunition which, besides being far greater than was justified by the results achieved, could not be maintained indefinitely without seriously depleting the ammunition reserves.

55. There was a strong suspicion at this time that the German raiders were using two prominent landmarks – the Isle of Dogs and Hyde Park – over which they turned to their various objectives. Two geographical barrages, designed to explode over these two points, were therefore, worked out and were fired for the first time on the night 26th/27th September, I940. There was no marked improvement in the number of raiders destroyed but the plan had the advantage of controlling the ammunition expenditure.

56. It was on Ist October, I940, that radar was first used to control anti-aircraft gunfire. The first sets had actually been received at the end of I939 but a delay in applying them to anti-aircraft work had been caused by their complete inability to give any indication of the height of the aircraft and the intervening months had been spent in trying to overcome this handicap. In this work I must especially mention the untiring and valuable help given by Major-General M.F. Grove-White,

C.B., D.S.O., O.B.E., at that time G.O.C.2 AA Division. The only use to which it had been possible to put the few available sets was direction-finding, but, as the heights still had to be found visibly by a height-finder, there was only a very small improvement on the old system, in that targets could be picked up a little earlier.

57. The first important attempt to provide an improved height-finding apparatus, which would operate against unseen targets, for use with radar arose from the invention of Visual Indicating Equipment. This was an elaborate sound-locator, the findings of which were converted electrically into a visual image on a cathode ray tube.

In practice, the equipment failed to give the results hoped for, since, apart from some difficulty in following the target and suspectibility to bad weather, it suffered from the same limitations as the sound-locators in the Fixed Azimuth System. Its range was limited, it was upset by extraneous noises such as gunfire and the presence of a number of targets at once was confusing.

58. The first real promise of a solution was found in the application of the radar principle to elevation as well as to bearing. Much of this work was achieved by Mr. Bedford, Chief Designer to A.C. Cossor Limited. The existing radar sets were modified as soon as possible by the fitting of this Elevation Finding attachment, and they went into action on Ist October, 1940.The chief limitation of this equipment was that when the angle of sight increased to more than 45 degrees the sets lost all accuracy in bearing.

To test the value of the new equipment orders were given that even against seen targets by day, provided they were over I0,000 feet up, the new unseen methods should be used and the results analysed. The results convinced me that the only real success being obtained was with this radar equipment and that the entire future of anti-aircraft shooting must be associated with it.

59. An entirely new system of unseen barrages was now developed. However great the improvement of the new equipment over the old, it was still far from attaining the required accuracy. In order to increase the chance of destroying the target we considered that it must be used to produce a volume of fire from many guns at once. Guns were, therefore, re-sited in groups, generally of eight and a master site, equipped with the new radar, was selected to control them. The master

site plotted the target and informed the other sites of its position, height and direction. As soon as the enemy entered the barrage belt all guns opened fire independently.

This system was continued until 20th January, 1941, when I came to the reluctant conclusion that it could not be made to produce the success for which I had hoped. Since 1st October, 1940, the anti-aircraft defences had shot down over 70 planes by night and probably destroyed or damaged 53. I shall be referring a little later to our night fighter defences, but it is of interest to mention here that these successes were about four times the number scored by the R.A.F. in the same period.

The chief reason for ordering a change of method in January, 1941, was the limitations of the latest radar methods at angles of sight over 45 degrees. As long as guns, whether individually or in groups, were left to plot targets for themselves, there was in effect a very large blind zone right over the guns themselves and for some distance around them in which they could not operate. If control were vested once more in the Gun Operations Room, the combined information from all sites should eliminate these blind zones.

Consequently sites were ordered to pass their plots to the Gun Operations Room, where predictions were worked out and from which orders to fire would in future emanate. In other words, the plotting on the gunsite was divorced from the shooting and the greater part of the responsibility for the successful conduct of the battle was transferred from the Gun Position Officer to the Commander in the Operations Room.

60. Meanwhile, similar troubles had been experienced with searchlights. Their sound locators had been subject to the same disadvantages as those used with guns and illuminations had consequently been erratic. In the same way as I had found them insufficient for use with the guns and had had to develop methods of unseen fire, so the R.A.F. had found them insufficient for successful co-operation with night fighters.

A further difficulty which arose when searchlights were used with sound-locators was that there was a tendency to over-estimate the speed of sound and to assume that the target was behind its actual position. Consequently, fighters following up an enemy raider frequently found themselves illuminated and an easy target for the enemy rear-gunners.

In order to give the night fighters more opportunity of engaging the enemy, a new technique was introduced known as "Fighter Nights". The theory was that the most likely place for a fighter to intercept the enemy was over the target area and that once contact was made the night fighter would have a very good chance of destroying the bomber.

The disadvantage of the scheme was that in order to safeguard the fighter our guns could not fire or, alternatively, had to be restricted to heights below that at which the fighter had instructions to operate.

Although some results were achieved on moonlight nights, the scheme was not popular. The lack of gunfire incensed the civilian population who thought the gunners were being negligent, and this resulted in a great loss of civilian morale. The enemy bombers, free from all anxiety over anti-aircraft fire, flew straight to their targets and bombed them accurately; nor was this compensated for by a larger number of bombers destroyed by fighters for, in practice, it was extremely difficult for our pilots to see the enemy and even after a "visual" had been made the bomber nearly always shook off the fighter.

The system was tried again during the "Baedeker" raids of 1942 and, after considerable protests on my part, was finally abandoned.

61. Of necessity priority in the provision of radar equipment was given to the guns; but I arranged for the provision at the earliest possible moment of similar equipment for searchlights also and the first sets were deployed towards the end of 1940. These were of the same type as was being employed with the guns; shortly afterwards, a type specially designed for searchlight control, known as S.L.C., which had been delayed in production, became available.

62. Throughout the first three months of 1941 there was an increasing amount of radar equipment coming into service, and a more advanced type for gunlaying, the G.L.II, also began to come from production. These were deployed in and around London in March, 1941.

63. The problems associated with radar were not all confined purely to theoretical matters. Sets deployed in the field produced curious results, and though some of these could be traced, to bad drill or technical faults others appeared to be occurring without any good reason. One of the greatest problems was the appearance on the signal tube of spurious breaks, among which the break caused by the target was apt to disappear. It was not at first clear why these appeared; they

might or might not appear whether the set was placed on high or low ground, close to or clear of buildings.

What was finally established was that the contours of the ground around the set had a pronounced effect upon it and it was suggested that, by pegging out a mat of wire mesh for some 150 feet round the receiver, an artificial level could be obtained which would largely eradicate the trouble. Experiments with a trial mat were a complete success and the principle was adopted universally. What I had not realised was that the project would involve using the whole of the country's stocks of wire net on the first 300 mats.

The project also involved the re-siting of a great number of the sets, as it was not always possible to find sufficient clear space for a mat near to the guns. Some sets were moved over a quarter of a mile from their guns and careful calculations had then to be made to co-ordinate the two positions, as the radar and the guns would see targets from quite a different aspect.

64. It was at this stage, when the equipment position at last began to look easier, that the pressure of manpower problems became severe. I was asked to economise in manpower to the utmost, and the A.O.C.-in-C. Fighter Command and I felt that any cuts which might have to be made must be in the searchlight and not in the gun units.

65. The tactical layout of searchlights had for some time been under discussion with Fighter Command with a view to finding some better means of using them with night fighters. Together we evolved a system by which the lights would be sited in clusters instead of singly. Night fighter pilots had represented that a single beam did not give them enough illumination to see and engage the enemy. Very comprehensive trials of clusters versus single lights were carried out and the majority of the pilots gave their opinion in favour of the cluster of 3 lights. Looking back I think the idea was not sound but it had the advantage that we were able to dispense with some of the administrative troops owing to the greater concentration of detachments. Consequently the actual cut in the searchlight units was kept to a minimum.

66. Technical inventions and improvements came in a flood early in 1941. Among them was the Semi-Automatic Plotter, early versions of which supplied a continuous track of a target and later versions also incorporated a means of deriving future gunnery data. Other devices

are too numerous to mention individually but the sum total was such as to renew the hope that fire control might be restored once again to the Gun Position Officer. The control from the Gun Operations Room, moreover, had proved no better than the old systems.

67. One of the prime movers in the restoration of fire control to gunsites was Major-General R.F.E. Whittaker, C.B., C.B.E., T.D., who had throughout been opposed to my decision to put control in the hands of the Operations Rooms. He carried out experiments with the various new equipments and thereby provided the most valuable contribution to date in the investigation of unseen methods of fire. These new methods of fire control convinced me that we should revert to the plan by which each gun site was responsible for obtaining its own gunnery data.

68. Having now outlined the stages in the development of our methods to combat the raider, I must describe briefly the course of the night battle. Essentially it was one battle throughout but it was possible to detect in it changes in the German policy, each change initiating in some degree a new phase; I must point out, however, that the phases merge one into another to a greater degree even than in the Battle of Britain. No good purpose would be served in a despatch of this nature in detailing all the attacks, since those details did not generally affect the policy of the defences.

69. After the preliminary raids on the West and Midlands, which have already been described, the first phase opened on 7th/8thSeptember, 1940; in this phase the main target was almost exclusively London, which was continuously raided night after night. Supplementary and diversionary raids of smaller size were from time to time scattered across the whole country, so that it was never possible to withdraw into the Capital all the guns I wanted. On I4th/I5th November, I940, a second phase opened in which the main weight of attack was shifted from London to industrial centres and ports, although London continued to receive a succession of smaller raids. The concentration of industry and other objectives in these smaller cities and towns was far greater than in London, and the dropping of a similar weight of bombs could, therefore, cause far greater damage and dislocation than had been achieved in most of the London raids. Coventry was the first town to be singled out and others which in the course of this phase

received particular attention were Liverpool, Bristol, Plymouth, Cardiff and Portsmouth. The guns defending London were at once reduced from 239 to 192, and another 36 were taken from the Thames Estuary. In the later part of January and during the first half of February raiding was hindered by bad weather.

On 19th/20th February, 1941, a third phase began in which, though the objectives remained the same, a more determined attempt was made to put them completely out of action by raids on successive nights, which would take advantage of the dislocation caused the night before. Swansea was the first town so attacked, and other cities, and especially Liverpool, suffered from these methods. In this phase of the battle there was an emphasis on the West although other areas were frequently visited. This emphasis had a very high strategic significance, which caused us to draw 58 guns from the Midlands for the protection of western ports.

The east and much of the south coast had already been largely denied to our shipping; an attack of alarming proportions on our Atlantic sea routes had also developed. A vigorous attack on our western ports might well inflict such damage that the country would, to all intents and purposes, be isolated from the outside world, and every risk had to be taken to prevent this happening.

70. I have already mentioned that a certain amount of the equipment I had at the beginning of the war was on loan from the Royal Navy. Now I was asked for, and agreed to, the return of this equipment. As early as the beginning of 1940 I had agreed to supply Lewis guns and crews for merchant ships. In addition to the return of borrowed equipment, I was asked in turn to lend a large amount of my own equipment in the form of 300 Bofors guns for the protection of shipping, together with the men to man them and 1,000 rounds of ammunition per gun. Thus the Light anti-aircraft defences, which already stood at only 22 per cent, of requirements, were cut to 15 per cent. The Maritime Royal Artillery, thus formed, passed eventually out of my control altogether, but before it left it had given such excellent service as to ensure its continuance.

I was at the same time informed that the R.A.F. would soon be requiring the 20-mm. cannons which I had on loan. My hope that the deficiency might be made good by the employment of Rocket defences was nullified by a decision to give the Admiralty an absolute priority for these weapons.

7I. I thus had to meet the last stages of the Battle impoverished in my Light anti-aircraft resources but with renewed hope that the technical advances of the spring would improve the results of Heavy anti-aircraft shooting.

72. The battle virtually came to an end on I2th May, I94I, after a heavy raid on London. As in every other aspect of the war, so in the air war the Germans changed their tactics as soon as it became evident that we had gained the upper hand. So, while the preparations they had to make for the Russian campaign no doubt influenced the decision, there is no doubt the German General Staff had by May, I94I, come to the conclusion that the war was not to be won by aerial attacks on this country and that the cost of such attacks was heavy. Between Ist April and I2th May, I94I, the successes scored by the guns mounted steadily. During this month and a half 72 planes were destroyed by night by the guns and 82 probably destroyed or damaged. The fighters too were now showing tremendous improvement.

73. At this point I propose to conclude this first part of my despatch. It covers a period in which success in battle was achieved with great difficulty and in which developments in technique were very considerable. At the beginning of the battle our method of defence was still the same as that of three years before; at the end I felt we had begun to make real progress; certainly the foundation of later successes had been laid. What had especially been achieved was the conversion of a large body of troops from ordinary soldiers into skilled technical operators, and this was an essential pre-requisite for successful anti-aircraft gunnery.

I have referred chiefly to the gun and searchlight units, but without the help of the ancillary services, Signals, Medical, Ordnance and Supply, progress could never have been made nor the battle continued. While full credit must be given to the troops of all kinds, and indeed their conduct under very hazardous and trying conditions was beyond all praise, the foundations of success, however, was laid by the scientist, both civilian and in uniform. The Operational Research Group has already been referred to. Its work was brilliant. The technical staff at Command Headquarters, under the leadership of Brigadier Krohn,

C.B.E., M.C., T.D., was and remained throughout the war a vital factor in every scientific advance, and not least must I pay a tribute to those young American scientists who volunteered to help us and who played their part in all our Blitzes. That these gentlemen became available and for many other helpful and friendly acts our thanks are due to Brigadier Claude Thiele, U.S.A., who was one of the first American officer observers to reach this country after the outbreak of war and whose wisdom and help I continually sought throughout the whole course of the war.

PART II
PREAMBLE

I. In the first part of my despatch I described the problems and progress of the anti-aircraft defences during the opening phases of the war and during the first period of sustained attack by the German air forces which lasted from July, I940, to May, I94I.

2. In this second part I propose to carry the report on from that date to the time I relinquished command in April, I945. Though this was a few weeks before the final German capitulation there was no air attack of any kind upon the United Kingdom after that date and therefore this part of my despatch is in effect a report upon the whole of the remaining period of hostilities.

SECTION I.
General

3. I mentioned in the first part of my despatch how the early months of I94I saw an increase in the problems of manpower and how various innovations had to be made and some reduction in the searchlight defences had taken place.

Mixed Batteries.

4. The problem was met by the introduction of mixed units and it must at once be said that, while there were many doubters in the early days,

the mixed units proved a triumphant success. In these units the proportion of women to men was roughly 2 to I. Women carried out every job except those involving heavy manual labour such as loading and manning the gun itself.

The problem, had been considered before the outbreak of war when I asked for the advice of Miss Caroline Haslett, C.B.E., who, after spending days and nights in the field examining the various duties, told me she had no doubt that women were capable of doing all but the heaviest tasks.

It was on 25th April, I94I, that regulations were put into force making women eligible for operational duties. In May, I94I, the first mixed battery began its training and it became operational on 2Ist August, I94I.

5. Two projects were formulated. The first was that all Heavy Batteries coming forward from Training Regiments would in future be Mixed Batteries and the second was that, as the number of trained women increased, some of the existing male batteries should be converted to Mixed Batteries. The Mixed units would only have static and not mobile guns. It was hoped that by the end of I94I there would be provided just under 40 batteries through each project, but this proved an over-optimistic forecast. Nevertheless, it was now clear that we could expect both to remedy existing deficiencies and to continue the expansion of the anti-aircraft defences. I was promised that of the expected total of 220,000 A.T.S. at the end of I942, I could anticipate having I70,000. In actual fact, this estimated figure proved over optimistic as other Army demands on the available women power limited the number of A.T.S. in Anti-Aircraft Command to a maximum, at any time, to just over 74,000.

6. The welfare of these women was one of the considerations which was uppermost in all our minds and this had a considerable effect upon the areas in which they were deployed. I wished to be quite certain that their accommodation would be suitable, and it was also necessary to ensure that they would not find themselves in the probable path of an invading army. A high standard of accommodation was set, but the general labour shortage throughout the country resulted in the programme of building falling behind schedule and it was not always possible to supply the full standard.

7. The possibility of invasion caused additional complications. Plans to counter any invasion, adapted to our increasing resources, were steadily improved. The summer of 1941 found an elaborate and detailed plan prepared, in which the anti-aircraft guns had to be ready for rapid moves in order to fit into the needs of the situation should it arise.

8. Some time previously I had reluctantly accepted a large and expanding programme of static 3.7-inch guns rather than mobile guns because the former were so much more rapidly produced. The task of shifting a static gun was very considerable and a great deal of preparation was necessary before it could be emplaced on a new site. As soon as the Chiefs of Staff advised me which defences must remain and which must be moved in the event of invasion, an interchange of 244 mobile and static guns was ordered so that the number of moves to be made if invasion took place would be cut to a minimum.

9. This interchange had repercussions upon the deployment of Mixed batteries. Some sites where accommodation had been provided for them were now equipped with mobile guns on which women could not be deployed, so that some mixed units had perforce to be put in quarters which were below the desired standard.

10. The original projects had in fact been based upon a degree of immobility in the anti-aircraft defences which could never exist. If the enemy chose to change his objectives, as he later did, units had to be moved in accordance with operational needs rather than with some theoretical accommodation problems of our own. Consequently, as time went on and the deployment of guns changed, the general standard of accommodation for Mixed batteries became further removed from that originally set. So long as reasonable recreational facilities during periods of inaction and satisfactory ablutions at all times were available for them, the morale of women in an operational rôle was always high, and subsequent events proved their great courage. I cannot praise too highly the valuable work these women performed or the splendid spirit which they brought to it.

11. In the emergency deployments of Heavy guns later in the war, women had to be accommodated in emergency conditions if the defences were to remain operative, and they not only accepted those conditions but even chose to remain at their posts when offered an opportunity to leave.

During the temporary concentration of defences on the south coast to protect our invasion forces and later in the emergency deployments to counter the flying bomb, they were accommodated under canvas with all the accompanying inconveniences and finally some units were withdrawn from my command to serve in the anti-aircraft defence of Antwerp and Brussels during a winter campaign, a decision which was the finest possible tribute to the work of the Mixed batteries as a whole.

I2. Although generally women were employed on Heavy guns where units were concentrated, the serious loss of manpower in searchlight units led me to consider whether it might not be possible to employ them in this rôle also. Owing to the impossibility of mixing the sexes in small detachments, any such units had to consist wholly of women and though one searchlight regiment was created in this form and gave a good account of itself, I was dissuaded from extending the experiment for two reasons. First, it was not possible to find a sufficient number of women officers capable of assuming tactical as well as administrative responsibility and secondly, searchlight sites were normally provided with Light Machine-Guns for local air and ground defence, and women, however willing to do so, were not allowed to handle guns of any kind.

Home Guard.

I3. However, further demands for economies in manpower were already upon us. In October, I94I, a cut of 50,000 men for the Field Force was ordered. In order to man the equipment which was now reaching the Command in large quantities, the employment of Home Guards for anti-aircraft defence was once more considered. Home Guard personnel could not, however, do continuous manning and it was not easy to arrange a scheme which could use part time soldiers effectively.

Their terms of service provided that they should not perform more than 48 hours of training and duty in 28 days and in the event of raids taking place they could only volunteer for extra duty with the permission of their civil employers. It was impracticable to permit any of the major defences of the country to be manned on those terms, even if, as later occurred, the terms were somewhat modified.

I4. It was at this time that we had been planning an extension of the anti-aircraft defences by the widespread introduction of Rocket Batteries; the supply of rocket weapons had now increased to the extent that demands for shipping had been met and a surplus was rapidly becoming available for home defence. Unlike other forms of defence the principle involved was simple and required no long and complex training. Rocket weapons appeared to be eminently suitable for operation by the Home Guard and I accordingly proposed the introduction of Home Guard Rocket Batteries. The proposal was approved and units began training immediately.

I5. It was agreed that each man should be called upon one night in eight, so that where I78 men were required to keep a site in action on any one night, a total of I,424 were necessary in order to permit full and continuous manning of the site. These figures will give some idea of the dimensions of the new project, but this was far from being the only difficulty. It was decided that a call for volunteers would be unsatisfactory because many would probably be young men who would shortly be lost under conscription. The responsibility for providing men therefore devolved upon the Ministry of Labour and they selected those who were not otherwise employed on any form of National Service.

I6. Disciplinary control over members of the Home Guard was virtually impossible and it was an easy matter for those who were so inclined to evade all duty. It was due entirely to the service given by the unselfish that the Rocket Batteries became and remained a force which the German aircrews treated with the utmost respect.

I7. Within a year the Ministry of Labour was showing signs of being unable to fulfil demands and men were transferred from Home Guard infantry battalions. The Home Guard infantry battalions, formed when invasion was an ever present threat, contained all the keenest and most enthusiastic elements and whole units might have transferred to an anti-aircraft rôle. But, when called upon to give up men while retaining an infantry rôle, it was natural that they should allow only their least efficient members to transfer to the Rocket Batteries. Arrangements were made whereby one or more Home Guard General Service Batteries were affiliated to the local AA Battery from which the latter could draw recruits. Those unsuitable for AA duty, due either to medical reasons or change of civilian employment, were drafted back to the Home Guard Battalion concerned.

18. In 1942 manpower pressure increased further. In July, 1942, the *ad hoc* sub-committee, charged with relating the requirements and availability of equipments with the availability of manpower for anti-aircraft purposes throughout the world, allotted to Anti-Aircraft Command a ceiling of 264,000; in October, 1942, a reduction to 180,000 was suggested. By introducing what was termed "over-gunning" the ratio of men to guns in Heavy Anti-Aircraft units was further reduced. In places where guns were concentrated, batteries became responsible for more than the normal eight guns and the Home Guard were also introduced to Heavy anti-aircraft gunnery, taking over one or more guns under supervision of the local unit.

Where guns were scattered no over-gunning was possible. The effect in saving therefore became more pronounced as the defences increased and as more guns could be concentrated, rising from about 6 per cent. with 1,500 guns to 15 per cent. with 2,500. By this means the number of Heavy equipments in action was not reduced. Nor was it found necessary to reduce the number of Light guns in action, for the Home Guard took over the defences of certain factories and railways with these weapons and it was agreed that the R.A.F. Regiment should take over the defence of airfields.

19. Anti-Aircraft Command was at the same time largely absolved from the responsibility of holding and draft-finding, which had been such a burden hitherto, so that ultimately this 1942 cut was limited to ten searchlight batteries.

Cuts in Man-Power.

20. The size of this cut was, however, only kept within these limits by reducing the number of male Heavy anti-aircraft batteries from 92 to 64, that is, by replacing men with women in 28 batteries. I regarded 64 as the absolute minimum number of male batteries I should have, since there were certain commitments which I hoped not to have to ask mixed units to undertake. I still envisaged using male batteries only for emergency deployments and I had to retain some male batteries for training and holding purposes. Fortunately the threat of invasion had receded and I was now able to move mixed units into those south and south-eastern areas from which they had been previously excluded.

21. In September, 1943, the question, now a regular annual one,

recurred again. An assessment of German air strength at this time led to the conclusion that certain risks might legitimately be taken in the way of considerably reducing the defences in some of the northern and western areas and cuts were made in all forms of defence, the manpower in Anti-Aircraft Command being reduced by I3,700.

22. In June, I944, further cuts were suggested which had to be postponed because of the attacks by flying bombs; but in August, I944, it was proposed to regard large areas of the country as probably immune from further attack and during September, I944, I lost all Smoke Defences and 28 Searchlight batteries, followed in November, I944, by II male and I0I Mixed Heavy batteries, 34 Light batteries and I4 more Searchlight batteries. Finally in January, I945, I lost 6 male Heavy batteries, 35 Light batteries, 33 Searchlight batteries and at the same time the Home Guard Rocket batteries, which had been allowed to become non-operational in November, I944, were finally disbanded.

23. This bald statement of the progressive reduction in the country's anti-aircraft defences gives no idea of the intensity of the problem which it presented. The men suitable for an infantry or an R.A.S.C. rôle were to be found in every unit under my command and these had to be extracted to meet the urgent requirements of the field force and had to be replaced by less fit men from disbanding units in such a way as to minimise the effect upon the batteries which were at the time heavily engaged in the flying bomb battle.

24. Nor were reductions in the defences the only manpower problems of those difficult years. I have already mentioned that the general labour shortage caused the building of A.T.S. accommodation to fall behind schedule and as the number of mixed batteries increased and redeployments of Heavy guns became more necessary, so the acuteness of the difficulty increased. Finally, we concluded that we must have within Anti-Aircraft Command a labour force which could be applied exclusively to our own needs and early in I943 certain batteries were withdrawn from their operational rôle for this purpose.

These were reconstituted as Construction Batteries and I,800 men were finally employed in this manner. In this unspectacular rôle the Construction Batteries made a most valuable contribution to the defence of the country.

Supplemented by 7,500 unskilled workers from disbanding Light

Batteries, they were largely responsible for the success of a vast building operation during the flying bomb battle to which I shall refer later.

New Equipment.

25. Concurrently the equipment problem became easier. The 3.7-inch gun on a static mounting remained the standard Heavy equipment with a number of similar guns on mobile mountings as a supplement. A special 3.7-inch barrel was designed for the 4.5-inch guns and the conversion of these weapons began at the end of October, 1943; the work was still proceeding at the end of the war but all the 72 4.5-inch guns in the London area were modified by the end of November, 1943; this gun, which was known as the 3.7-inch Mark 6, was remarkable for its high muzzle velocity. A still more effective Heavy gun of 5.25-inch calibre also began to come from production during this period. The first guns of this calibre to go into action were of naval design with twin barrels and these operated from April, 1942. A model with a single barrel, designed especially for anti-aircraft work, began to appear in May, 1943.

The chief Light anti-aircraft weapon continued to be the 40-mm Bofors but it was supplemented by increasing numbers of 20-mm equipment, largely Oerlikon or Polsten guns, and from the beginning of 1944 by an increasing number of twin 0.5 inch Brownings in power-operated turrets.

There was also a steady flow of new radar designs intended to give greater accuracy than the earlier models. These later designs were able to work successfully at high angles of sight. Auto-following was introduced by which the sets were kept on the target, once it had been located, by an automatic electric control; this auto-follow system first operated in action on the American SCR 584 sets during the flying bomb battle.

Though the numbers of the various equipments in action were, until the closing stages of the war, always below the totals regarded as necessary, there was generally a steady and progressive improvement throughout the period covered by this part of my despatch. The only serious setback occurred when war broke out in the Far East. Anti-Aircraft Command gave up 66 Heavy and 216 Light guns for the new theatres of war and for six months afterwards received practically no fresh equipments from production.

26. At the outbreak of war with Japan in December, I94I, the Heavy guns which were available to me totalled I,960, made of up 935 static and 465 mobile 3.7-inch guns, 4I6 4.5-inch guns and I44 of the obsolete 3-inch guns.

At the end of I942 the total was 2, I00, made up of 3 twin 5.25-inch guns, I,200 static and 475 mobile 3.7-inch, 406 4.5-inch guns and I6 3-inch guns.

In June, I944, at the beginning of the flying bomb battle, I had 2,635 guns, made up of 3 twin 5.25-inch and 25 single 5.25-inch guns, I,672 static, 527 mobile and I49 Mark 6 3.7-inch guns and 259 still unconverted 4.5-inch guns.

The position with the Light anti-aircraft weapons when Japan entered the war was that I had a total of I, I97, made up of I,056 40-mm Bofors, 8 obsolete 3-inch guns, 7I miscellaneous types of 2-pounders and 62 20-mm Hispanos.

At the end of I942 the total had increased to I,8I4, of which I,7I7 were 40-mm Bofors, 6 3-inch guns, 5 2-pounders and 86 20-mm Hispano and Oerlikon guns.

In June, I944, the total had risen sharply to 4,589, made up of 2,68I 40-mm Bofors, I,257 20-mm Hispanos and Oerlikons and 65I twin 0.5-inch Brownings.

Rocket projectors in action numbered 4,48I at the end of I942 and 6,372 at the end of I943.

In addition to the increase in the numbers of equipments and to the introduction of new types, certain important inventions were made for use with the older types. The first important one appeared in I943 and was the Automatic Fuze-Setter for the 3.7-inch gun; the earliest designs had the effect of increasing the rate of fire of those guns to which it was fitted by about 50 per cent. while later designs increased it by over 250 per cent. and greatly improved the accuracy of the fuze-setting.

The second invention was the proximity fuze which did away with the need for fuze-setting altogether and was extensively used in the flying bomb battle. With these fuzes the explosion was controlled automatically by their proximity to the flying body; the rapid loading by means of Automatic Fuze-setters was continued with the new fuzes.

Tactical Employment.

27. The tactical plans for the employment of guns in Gun Defended Areas did not change during this period but considerable changes were made in the tactical employment of searchlights.

The scheme for using searchlights in clusters which had been introduced in the autumn of 1940 had not proved as successful as had been hoped; the spacing of lights proved too great for continuous engagement so that night fighters still failed to intercept with searchlight assistance; low-flying raiders were often able to slip through unobserved and the anticipated increase in the range of beams was not noticeable.

In September, 1941, therefore, lights were redeployed on single sites. The basis of the redeployment was a mathematical conception known as the Fighter Box; this was the area within which a night fighter with nothing to aid him except his own eyes and the visual indication of searchlight beams could intercept a bomber which entered that area. After trials had been carried out the size of the box was established as being 44 by 14 miles. The Box system remained the basis of searchlight deployment for the rest of the war.

The country was divided into a complete system of boxes around the various Gun Defended Areas. In the centre of each Box was a stationary vertical searchlight beam around which a night fighter circled until he received an indication that a bomber was entering the Box. At the ends of each Box searchlights were spaced at about 6 miles intervals and in the middle the spacing was about 3½ miles. A series of boxes placed side by side thus created a continuous belt in which lights were thin at the edges, where they constituted an Indicator Zone and dense in the centre which was the Killer Zone.

Later, when enemy penetrations became so shallow that they often failed to reach the Killer Zone altogether the Indicator Zone spacing was thickened and the orbit beam was moved forward if it was thought to be necessary.

28. Just as in March, 1941, the responsibility for fire control had largely passed from Gun Operations Rooms to the gun sites themselves, so now the responsibility for searchlight control tended to shift from Sector Operations Rooms to the searchlight sites. The old form of

control had done much to destroy initiative and it was only by degrees that it was possible to instil into the junior officers the sense of responsibility necessary for the successful operation of the new system. In addition there was at the outset a shortage of S.L.C. Radar equipment. Consequently there developed a distrust of searchlight-assisted interceptions among R.A.F. night fighter crews and Commanders who preferred interceptions ordered on the findings of their own G.C.I. radar. It was towards the successful co-ordination of the two methods of interception that all our energies were now bent, and co-operation became steadily closer and more satisfactory as time went on.

29. Though the main use to which searchlights were put was naturally the illumination of night raiders, they were also employed for a number of other special purposes throughout the war, in an anti-minelaying rôle, to illuminate balloons for our bombers and to make meteorological observations of cloud bases at night. Especially worthy of mention was the system of homing beacons for friendly aircraft which operated from the end of 1939; figures were only kept for a period between September, 1942, and August, 1943, but in that time 525 aircraft were saved from imminent disaster, 600 were homed to alternative airfields and 184 were helped to base.

Re-organisation.

30. The organisation of Anti-Aircraft Command into three Corps and twelve Divisions remained until October, 1942, when a further reorganisation took place. This was prompted by a number of reasons; the desire to economise in manpower, the need for fewer intermediate formations between Command Headquarters and units allowing a quicker dissemination of orders, the need for still closer co-ordination with R.A.F. Groups and the desire to achieve a better balance of responsibility since the shifting of the emphasis in defence southwards had over-loaded Ist Anti-Aircraft Corps.

Corps and Divisions were therefore abolished altogether and were replaced by seven Anti-Aircraft Groups. There were three grades according to the operational commitments in the Group area and establishments appropriate to each grade were worked out. The system was extremely flexible since the grade of any one Group could be changed to meet current needs.

3I. The seven groups were situated as follows:-

Ist. London.
2nd. The Solent, south-east England and southern East Anglia (these two Groups coincided with II Group R.A.F.).
3rd. South-west England and south Wales (coinciding with I0 Group R.A.F.).
4th. North Wales and north-west England (coinciding with 9 Group R.A.F.).
5th. Northern East Anglia and the East Coast as far as Scarborough (coinciding with I2 Group R.A.F.).
6th. North-east England and Scotland (coinciding with I3 Group R.A.F. (except Northern Ireland) and I4 Group R.A.F.).
7th. Northern Ireland.

The defences of the Orkneys and Shetlands remained a separate organisation, responsible in operational anti-aircraft matters direct to Anti-Aircraft Command Headquarters.

In the later stages of the war there were at times concentrations of defences in certain areas quite beyond anything visualised in October, I942, and the local Group Headquarters was not sufficient to deal with the tremendous increase of work. In these circumstances, group boundaries were altered to permit the insertion of an extra Group in the affected area.

Thus, 6th Anti-Aircraft Group took over the Solent area during the preparations for invasion, Scotland becoming the responsibility of a new 8th Group. 6th Anti-Aircraft Group was disbanded when its responsibilities in the South had ended.

The progressive reduction of defences in the North and West in I944 enabled me to disband the 3rd, 4th and 7th Anti-Aircraft Groups and to extend the responsibilities of the 2nd and 5th Groups westwards into their areas.

A 9th Anti-Aircraft Group was especially created in southern East Anglia when, there was a heavy concentration of equipment there in the later stages of the flying bomb battle.

SECTION II.
Attacks by piloted aircraft.

32. In the first part of my despatch I referred to the cessation of heavy night raiding in May, 1941, when the greater part of the German air forces were transferred to the Russian front. After May there were a few major raids (e.g., on Birmingham on 4-5th June, Southampton on 21-22nd June, and Hull on 17- 18th July). The scale of attack, however, gradually decreased, and for the rest of the year, apart from occasional attacks on other targets, the remaining German forces in the West were thrown mainly into the Battle of the Atlantic by attacks on ports and shipping and by heavy minelaying. The position in the Atlantic was still most precarious and the attacks made were designed to increase our shipping difficulties.

33. Attacks on convoys continued, and activity was most intense on the East Coast, Hull being frequently subjected to attacks by aircraft which were either on navigational and operational training or which failed to locate the shipping they had come to attack. The Thames Estuary, St. George's Channel and the Mersey were also continually mined.

34. The fact that much of this activity never came overland and that the defences were not therefore able to do much to hinder it caused us much concern and I therefore proposed that anti-aircraft forts might be situated out in the various estuaries to hamper these attacks.

35. Mr. G.A. Maunsell, a well-known consulting engineer, produced a design for a spider-like tower which, in its fully developed form, would carry 4 3.7-inch guns, 2 40-mm. Bofors, I searchlight and a radar set. Work began on these towers at once but the first was not ready until October, 1942, when much of the minelaying effort had subsided.

Although it had originally been intended to place them in a number of different estuaries, tidal and other difficulties finally caused the project to be limited to the Thames and the Mersey. In the former, in particular, the Maunsell Forts covered an approach which had always been a serious gap in the defence system and they played an important part in the defence of London when heavier raiding began again later.

36. Overland night raiding began again suddenly in April, 1942, and was apparently stimulated largely by a desire for revenge for Bomber

Command's attacks on German cities. The main stream of German raiders kept clear of Gun Defended Areas and in these so-called "Baedeker" raids attacked open towns and cathedral cities; where any of the raiders strayed into range of the gun and rocket defences of a Gun Defended Area, the defences went into action with success. Exeter was particularly a target for the enemy in the first phase of these attacks.

Within 72 hours the defence of 28 towns from Penzance to York which had hitherto been undefended was put in hand. A total of 252 guns were withdrawn chiefly from Gun Defended Areas in the North and West. Success was almost immediate and in the last two raids of the April full moon period the defences destroyed 4 enemy aircraft and probably destroyed or damaged 4 more. With the May full moon raiding began again and Canterbury was subjected to severe attacks, but this form of attack also petered out in the following months.

37. A less spectacular move, of I20 Heavy guns, was made at the same time as the "Baedeker" deployment to augment the defences of ten South Coast anchorages in which was assembling a fleet for the invasion of North Africa in the late Autumn. I was still much concerned, at this time with the shortage of equipment, for almost all new production was being diverted to the Far East and the defences of the west coast ports were dangerously weak. As large American forces were at the time disembarking there, an attack on that area might have had serious consequences. Moreover, there was a distinct possibility that we would have to yield a large number of guns to the field forces under a plan, which did not actually mature, for the invasion of North Europe in I943.

38. Meanwhile on 27th March, I942, a day battle had begun. This was in answer to our own fighter sweeps across the channel and consisted of tip-and-run low level raids on coastal towns by fast fighter-bombers. There appeared to be no military significance in these attacks nor were they on a scale to do much harm.

It would appear that one of the most striking lessons from these raids was the very great value of A.A. guns and balloons in minimising civilian casualties and damage, quite apart from the infliction of casualties on the attacking aircraft. Objectives with no balloons and few guns (e.g., Exeter) suffered badly in these raids, whereas those with adequate static defences came off comparatively lightly.

39. The weapon with which to counter the low-flying raider was the Light gun but the supply of these was seriously limited. Not only had I yielded up some for the Far East but new production was also fully absorbed by that theatre of war. When 189 guns were needed to help defend the anchorages on the south coast I was able only to provide 76, and many of those were withdrawn from the defence of vital industrial plants. Further, no less than 57 different coastal towns between St. Ives and Aldeburgh had been attacked by September, 1942, and the problem of defending all of these and also others which might be subject to attack would have required a number of guns far in excess of those available. As it was, in June, 1942, when guns from production began to come forward once more, we allotted 104 of these to what were termed the Fringe Target towns.

40. Towards the end of September, 1942, it was clear that the attacks, however unimportant from a military point of view, must be stopped and it was at that time that the equipment situation had eased sufficiently to allow steps to be taken. Production had improved and Anti-Aircraft Command was receiving a greater share of it; inland industrial targets had had their defences replaced and these could be denuded once again, and the Admiralty were steadily returning the guns lent them a year previously. My intention was now to join the battle with all the forces I could muster with a view to inflicting such losses on the enemy that he would have to give up this form of attack. No half-measures could be successful. By the end of September, 1942, 267 40-mm. Bofors guns had been deployed on the coast, another 110 could be withdrawn from factories and I was informed that I could expect 142 from production in October, 1942.

41. As was always the case, however, the mere deployment of guns was not in itself sufficient. The raiders approached at heights of less than 100 feet, having found that by this means they could almost always escape radar detection; consequently it was impossible either to warn the anti-aircraft defences in time for the guns to be manned or to scramble fighter aircraft into the air to make an interception. To watchers on the shore the enemy planes could only be seen at the last minute and they used every device which would help them to make an unobserved approach such as sneaking in up undefended valleys and hedge-hopping along the coast.

42. Orders were therefore issued that every Light anti-aircraft gun within five miles of the coast from the North Foreland to Land's End would be constantly manned during daylight hours, but even so it was difficult to secure the necessary degree of alertness when a town might go unattacked for months at a time, while the cold of the approaching winter did not help.

43. To secure freedom of action for the guns we arranged that no R.A.F. plane should cross the coast at less than I,000 feet except with undercarriage lowered, so that all low-flying single-engined aircraft could be assumed to be hostile without the necessity for prior identification.

44. In December, I942, the defences were further reinforced by the addition of large numbers of 20-mm. guns, and other 20-mm. equipments were manned by the R.A.F. Regiment; batteries of 40-mm. Bofors were loaned by Home Forces and the Canadian Forces. By March, I943, the Fringe defences had increased to 9I7 40-mm. guns, I92 20-mm. (with another 232 expected shortly to be available) and 674 light machine-guns of various kinds.

45. The winter successes were limited and the pattern of attack remained similar, though the average number of planes in each attack showed a slight tendency to increase.

46. There were, however, two attacks of an exceptional size and aimed at targets further inland. On 3Ist October, I942, a sweep of 60 raiders made a sharp attack on Canterbury and this was followed by two bomber raids the following night. On 20th January, I943, a similar number, aided by diversionary raids elsewhere, made an attack on London. We thereupon deployed a small number of 40-mm. guns on Heavy gun sites and had a simplified drill worked out for the Heavy anti-aircraft gunners.

47. Meanwhile, the winter had been spent in improving and elaborating the warning system.

Use was made of certain R.A.F. stations on the coast and new marks of radar were deployed. Radio links between these and Light Anti-Aircraft Troop Headquarters were established and the signals organization, besides installing and maintaining these radio sets at the receiving end, also laid a network of land lines for every Troop Headquarters to the guns they controlled. It was now possible to warn guns when an attack was imminent and in April, 1943, an improvement was beginning to be observed in the results when the attacks suddenly ceased.

48. On 7th May, 1943, the German attacks were renewed with much stronger forces and between that date and 6th June, 1943, 15 attacks by about 300 aircraft were made. The guns destroyed 25 and probably destroyed or damaged 13, the R.A.F. destroyed 17 and probably destroyed or damaged 4. Thus the battle was brought finally to a successful conclusion. Altogether 94 different towns had been attacked, of which the heaviest sufferers were probably Eastbourne and Hastings. Though Light anti-aircraft shooting was not as much a science as Heavy anti-aircraft shooting, there is no doubt that it was largely the result of the application of scientific assistance to the Light guns which in the end achieved success.

Smoke Defences.

49. I must now digress in order to refer to the Smoke Defences, the responsibility for which had on 1st April, 1943, been transferred from the Ministry of Home Security to Anti-Aircraft Command. The smoke screens were manned by the Pioneer Corps and once again we were to experience all the disadvantages of a divided control. It was only with the greatest difficulty that sufficient control was obtained to enable us to secure even the most limited efficiency.

50. After the successful attack by Bomber Command upon German dams in May, 1943, it was feared that there might be retaliations in kind and the Chiefs of Staff placed a very high priority upon the defence of our own reservoirs throughout the country. For a short time these were defended by Light anti-aircraft guns and searchlights withdrawn from aerodromes and "Baedeker" towns. Since April, 1943, however, very considerable technical strides had been made in smoke production; chemical, as opposed to oil, smokes were rapidly developed on the basis of earlier work by the Ministry of Home Security and entirely new methods of rapid multiple ignitions were evolved. Training of the Pioneer troops, which had previously been much neglected, was improved and long overdue steps for the improvement of their welfare and health services were taken.

51. Consequently, I was able to suggest that the defence of our dams

might more economically be provided by smoke screens, since what had to be feared was a precision type of attack. For six dams this proposal was accepted and it is worthy of note that this was the only occasion throughout the war when smoke alone was accepted as a sufficient defence.

52. For thirteen other dams, however, the smoke defences were to be supplemented by catenary defences and no guns or searchlights were to be withdrawn until the chains were in place. The task of producing and erecting the necessary masts and chains proved much slower than had been anticipated and as a result, for the greater part of the following winter (1943-44), two conflicting forms of defence were in operation at these dams. Apart from the fact that this was uneconomical, it aggravated the already difficult problem of providing accommodation. The troops were generally placed in remote hills where weather conditions were notoriously bad and it was fortunate that the winter proved to be unusually mild and dry.

53. No attack on the dams actually took place, but the defences remained operational until the disbandment of the Smoke Companies in the autumn of 1944. Other Smoke Companies took part in the defence of southern ports from Great Yarmouth to South Wales during the preparations for the invasion of Northern Europe.

Resumption of Night Attacks.

54. Apart from mine-laying, with the concurrent attacks on coastal towns, the "Baedeker" raids and a few other sporadic attacks, the United Kingdom had been comparatively free of attacks by night ever since May, 1941, but in the autumn of 1943 the German air forces once more began to apply themselves to this form of raiding.

55. The fast fighter-bombers now began to come over at night and they were later accompanied by new fast bombers. At first the raids were comparatively small and of shallow penetration but from October, 1943, they began to increase in size and to aim again at London.

56. I have already mentioned that night fighters might be put on to a bomber either by searchlights controlled from the Sector Operations Rooms or by the R.A.F. Controllers using their G.C.I. radars from G.C.I. stations. The unpredictable behaviour and speed of the present targets sometimes meant that a night fighter failed to secure an

interception because it was limited to one or other of the two forms of control. It was only at this stage that successful co-ordination of the two forms of control began to be achieved, the chief step towards which was the shifting of the control of the searchlights from the Sector Operations Rooms to the G.C.I. station. After this it was possible to change from one method of control to another and back again and so to exploit the advantages of each with perfect flexibility. It was also possible to use without friction both methods in order to maintain the maximum number of night fighters in operation. This series of attacks may be said to mark the peak of searchlight performance, for not only were they used to the best advantage in co-ordination with fighters but their own performance in illumination exceeded everything that had been achieved before.

57. The guns on the other hand were somewhat disappointing and I looked for considerable improvements as soon as experience with new equipment had increased. At this time the Automatic Fuze-setter was just coming in, so were new marks of radar, the 4.5-inch guns were about to be converted into 3.7-inch Mark 6 and 5.25-inch guns were also beginning to be deployed.

58. The new radar sets were very sensitive to interference and on 7th/8th October, 1943, the Germans began to drop strips of metallised paper similar to those which our own bombers had for some time been using over Germany. These had the effect of producing spurious breaks in radar cathode ray tubes which could either be mistaken for aircraft or else appeared in such profusion that an aircraft break could not be identified and followed. It was a move which had been anticipated but to which no satisfactory answer had been found.

59. At first no great trouble was caused because of the limited amount of paper dropped and lack of tactical application in its use. An improved and increased use of it soon followed, however, with very serious effects. Early warning radar equipments were unable to give any accurate estimate of numbers of aircraft approaching nor of the heights at which they were flying nor even where they might be expected to make landfall. Similarly, inland sets found themselves largely unable to track individual aircraft and in places sets were rendered absolutely useless. While, in October, 1943, only the leading aircraft used to drop the paper, by February, 1944, every raider was

doing so and sometimes areas 50 miles long and 25 miles wide were completely infected.

60. Searchlights were the most seriously affected and frequently had to resort to the old and ineffective control by sound-locators. Many gun control radars were affected but a few types were able to continue in service.

6I. There was every reason to anticipate a renewal of heavy attacks on London, for the German air forces had for some time been experimenting with pathfinder technique. The quality of their navigation had greatly deteriorated and it was common for many raiders to lose their way completely during this period and if pathfinder flares had been wrongly placed over open country to have no hesitation in bombing there.

62. The anticipated heavy raids began on 2Ist/22nd January, I944, with 200 aircraft in the first raid; the improvement in gunnery was considerable, eight raiders being destroyed, while searchlights contributed to half of the R.A.F.'s eight successes. Other raids followed and the attacks culminated in a week of intensive raiding beginning on I8th/I9th February, I944. In March, I944, raiding became much more sporadic though still heavy on individual nights.

63. At the same time Heavy and Light guns, searchlights and smoke screens were moving southward for the protection of the invasion ports. Some experience on a more limited scale had been obtained in July and August, I943, when there had been a large increase in coastal defences in the South for a large scale exercise known as "Harlequin". On that occasion the area affected had stretched from Dover to the Solent and the defences there, which already consisted of 266 Heavy guns, 3I9 Bofors and I7I searchlights, were increased by 348 Heavy guns, 432 Bofors and 93 searchlights. After the exercise in September, I943, the additional defences had dispersed.

64. Now, during the spring of I944, we began to build once more the defences all round the coast from Great Yarmouth to South Wales. I was responsible not only for equipment in Anti-Aircraft Command but also for a large number of Heavy and Light guns which were loaned to me by the Field Army, at any rate until the invasion had been launched and they were wanted overseas; I also received assistance both in Heavy and Light guns from the U.S. Army forces on the same terms.

These loaned equipments had to be most carefully woven into the fabric of defence so that their early withdrawal would not disturb the balance of defence remaining.

65. I have already referred to the valuable scientific help given me by the Americans in the early stages of the war; this help was continued right through. There was the closest liaison between us at all times and in the second half of 1943 a specially selected Demonstration Battery from Anti-Aircraft Command had conducted a most successful six months tour in the United States with a consequent valuable exchange of views. In December, 1943, U.S. anti-aircraft units had become operational in the United Kingdom, some batteries being deployed for the defence of London while their main responsibility was the protection of U.S. Army and Air Force installations.

The largest number of U.S. anti-aircraft troops so deployed at any one time had been just over 10,000. During the summer of 1944 English and American Light Anti-Aircraft units exchanged parties of all ranks, each party taking a fully operational rôle with their hosts and this exchange similarly provided a valuable exchange of ideas and did much to foster goodwill. The U.S. forces were naturally anxious to participate in all our major activities.

66. Before any additional defences were introduced for the protection of invasion ports, the equipments between Great Yarmouth and South Wales consisted of 842 Heavy and 332 Light guns and 4 smoke screens. These were supplemented from A.A. Command resources with 252 Heavy and 244 Light guns and 13 smoke screens. In addition we were to receive from our field forces 248 Heavy and 360 Light guns and from the U.S. forces 32 Heavy and 184 Light guns. The total defences of the various ports would therefore amount to 1,374 Heavy and 1,120 Light guns and 17 smoke screens. In addition the Balloon defences were to be increased from 342 to 535. As it turned out these figures had to be reduced by 56 Heavy and 188 Light guns in order to provide a reserve against the possibility of a simultaneous attack by flying bombs which had for some time been feared and to which I shall refer again later.

67. So important in its effect on the whole course of the war was the plan now unfolding and so well known to the German Intelligence that considerable interference from the German air forces was anticipated.

In the event, however, raiding of invasion ports was not serious and in most cases the deterioration in German navigation enabled even those few places which were attacked to escape without serious damage.

68. Apart from some desultory intruder activity in March and April, 1945, these were the last attacks by piloted German aircraft on this country. There were, however, fears towards the end of March, 1945, that a desperate low flying suicide attack on London might be launched and plans were made to increase the Light anti-aircraft defences of the capital from 36 to 412, Anti-Aircraft Command providing 236 of the guns and the R.A.F. Regiment the remaining 140. Whether the attack would ever have taken place or not, had the Germans retained control of the airfields in north-west Germany, it is impossible to say but in the end this deployment never took place.

SECTION III.
Attacks by Robot Weapons.

69. The first official intimation that attacks might be made by pilotless aircraft upon the country were received on 7th December, 1943. The estimated scale of attack at that time was 200 missiles an hour and targets were expected to be London, the Solent and Bristol.

70. Plans were at once made to meet the threat. London was to be protected by a belt of about 1,000 Heavy guns, sited on a line south of Redhill and Maidstone to the southern bank of the Estuary. There was to be a belt of searchlights in front for co-operation with fighters and a belt of balloons behind. A similar plan was made for the defence of Bristol, with a gun belt to the north and a searchlight belt to the south of Shaftesbury and a balloon belt south of Shepton Mallet. Little could be done for the Solent beyond a readjustment of the Isle of Wight defences.

The decision to deploy well inland was taken in order to reduce enemy jamming of radar equipment; to allow fighter aircraft the maximum area for manoeuvre and to leave the coast defences free to engage attacks by piloted aircraft. It was not intended to use either static guns or mixed units in these plans.

The constant attacks by Bomber Command on the launching sites on the French Coast caused the threat to recede, and with the increasing need for a large deployment to protect the invasion ports the plans were at first abandoned and then revived in a very modified form so as to interfere as little as possible with that deployment.

Had the enemy begun his flying bomb attacks before or even at the time the invasion was launched, the strain upon our resources would have been extremely serious, but fortunately at the time the attacks began it was already apparent that no serious scale of attack was to be expected against the ports.

7I. On the night of I2th/I3th June, I944, the first missiles, known by the code name "DIVER", arrived.

72. It was believed that these were only tests and no special deployment was ordered until sustained attacks began on I5th/I6th June, I944. The original plan for the defence of London was then put into operation in the modified form it had had to assume to permit the simultaneous protection of the invasion ports, although certain withdrawals from those defences were made.

Three hundred and seventy-six Heavy and 592 Light guns were deployed and in addition the R.A.F. Regiment on the south coast was operating 560 Light equipments, consisting of I92 40-mm. Bofors and 368 20-mm. guns. To achieve these figures without seriously affecting the defences elsewhere, units of the Royal Navy (including D.E.M.S.I personnel) and the Royal Marines, from the Field Army, from training camps and others were employed. It had been estimated that I8 days, would be necessary to complete this deployment but it was actually completed in a week and was quickly in action since Anti-Aircraft Command Signals had, ever since the first warning in December I943, been laying the necessary lines for intercommunication all over the area. The Signals under command of Brigadier G.C. Wickins, C.B., C.B.E., T.D., were outstandingly efficient throughout the whole war. The personnel was drawn largely from the G.P.O.

For three nights the guns in London fired at those targets which had penetrated the primary defences, but after that they were restricted since it was clear that it was better to allow the flying bombs a chance of passing the more densely populated parts of the Capital rather than to shoot them down into it.

73. Reference has been made in the first part of my despatch to the

peculiar difficulties of Heavy Anti-Aircraft gunnery, the chief of which was that an assumption had to be made as to the behaviour of the target between the initial plotting and the burst of the shell in the sky. Any form of evasive action, however slight, could seriously affect the accuracy of the shooting. Now, for the first time in the war, the guns were presented with a target which did not take evasive action and which obeyed all the assumptions upon which Anti-Aircraft gunnery had been based. It might have been expected that exceptional results would at once be obtained but this was not the case and successes were less than 10 per cent.

74. The whole question had been carefully examined as far back as February, 1944, and it was believed that the targets could satisfactorily be dealt with, especially if certain new American equipments could be acquired in large numbers, provided – and this was especially emphasised – that good results were not expected at heights between 2,000 and 3,000 feet where the target would be too high for light guns and too low for heavy guns and where the effectiveness of Anti-Aircraft fire was likely to be small. I was therefore perturbed to find that it was exactly in this 1,000 feet band that the targets were almost invariably flying. Arrangements were made immediately for a personal representative to fly to America to speed up, if possible, the delivery of the new American equipment, and General Marshall, who interviewed him, promised to send at once 165 of their latest radar sets, the SCR.584, together with all the necessary ancillaries including the No. 10 Predictor. This promise was fulfilled.

75. There were many other difficulties. The spheres of influence of guns and fighters overlapped, and a most awkward system of limiting one or the other according to meteorological conditions was worked out. The radar sets, which had been sited in hollows to avoid enemy jamming, were cluttered up with spurious breaks caused by contours of the ground. The balloon barrage was extended and many guns had to be re-sited, with resulting difficulties over the radar.

76. Above all, the low height at which the targets flew required a higher rate of traverse by the guns than the mobile 3.7-inch was capable of giving. The static 3.7-inch gun, on the other hand, though capable of traversing sufficiently quickly, required an inordinate length of time for its emplacement on concrete. It was at this point that Brigadier

J.A.E. Burls, C.B.E., and the R.E.M.E. Staff produced a platform on which the static 3.7-inch guns could be emplaced quickly, which was portable, and which in the end proved to be one of the keys to success. It consisted of a lattice work of steel rails and sleepers filled with ballast.

I must here pay a sincere tribute to the work of R.E.M.E. from the day the Corps was first formed. Under Brigadier Burls' inspired leadership there was no job they did not tackle.

77. We decided to replace all the mobile 3.7-inch guns with the static version, and the first 32 had been emplaced and were showing improved results when the whole policy of the co-ordination of guns and fighters was changed.

Neither fighters nor guns were being given full scope, for the guns had to ensure that the break on their radar tube was not a friendly plane before opening fire, while the fighters in pursuit of a V.I often had to give up the chase when approaching the gun zone. Lieut.-Colonel H.J.R.J. Radcliffe, M.B.E., at that time my Technical Staff Officer, suggested that we should re-examine the plan of locating the guns on the coast. This plan had always seemed to us to have great advantages from the gun point of view, but there were difficulties from the fighters' point of view in that their scope was thereby limited by having to break off an engagement on approaching the coast and start it again if the target got through the gun zone

It was, however, now very clear that without some very radical re-arrangement, two-thirds of the V.Is would continue to get through to London. The fighters were still having only a limited success, though that success was much better than the guns were experiencing.

Fighter Command were evidently thinking on the same lines, for at a meeting called on the afternoon of I3th July, at their H.Q., after a lengthy discussion the C.-in-C. Fighter Command decided that the guns should be moved to the coast, and orders to that effect were given.

78. The new belt was to extend from Cuckmere Haven to St. Margaret's Bay, and the first guns began to move on I4th July, I944. Apart from the move of all the equipments in the existing belt to the coast, there was a simultaneous move of 3I2 static guns coming in to replace the mobile guns and a further move of 208 Heavy, I46 40-mm Bofors and over 400 20-mm guns in a deployment on the Thames

Estuary to which I shall refer later. The moves involved 23,000 men and women, for with the introduction of the static 3.7-inch gun came the Mixed Batteries and 30,000 tons of ammunition and a similar weight of stores; 3,000 miles of cable were laid for inter-battery lines alone.

In four days the move to the coast had been completed.

79. There were various advantages in this new coastal belt. First, radar sets were freed from the clutter of inland interferences and, since the enemy was not using active jamming methods, they were able to be put to the best possible use; secondly, there was a good chance that many bombs destroyed by the guns might now fall in the sea instead of on land; thirdly, the existing defences on South coast, including those of the R.A.F. Regiment, could now be incorporated in one scheme, and fourthly, the unsatisfactory and alternating limitations on guns and fighters, introduced because of mutual interference arising from the fighters' inability to identify the position of an inland belt, could now be dispensed with, since the line of the coast would clearly reveal the position of the belt to aircraft. The move to the coast was the second of the keys to success.

80. Almost immediately after this the new American equipment, which we were so anxiously awaiting, began to arrive, and as soon as troops could be trained in its operation it was deployed along the belt. Not only was the SCR.584 the most suitable of all the radar equipments available, but its use, in conjunction with the No. I0 Predictor, directed fire with a degree of accuracy hitherto unattained. At the same time the problem of exploding the shells at the correct height was solved by the introduction of the proximity fuze. This equipment provided the third of the keys to success.

8I. As soon as the coastal deployment was in action results began to improve, but although I have emphasised three points which in my opinion did more than anything else to contribute to success, there were also innumerable other smaller matters which each in its own way played its part. No less than 200 modifications, for example, were made to the Heavy guns by my R.E.M.E. Services, while an almost equal number of adjustments had to be made to the American equipments before they could finally be put into action.

82. General Eisenhower himself took the greatest personal interest

in the battle, maintaining that London was as much a base for American troops as for British ones; he insisted on being allowed to increase the defences by the welcome addition of 20 American Anti-Aircraft Batteries equipped with 90-mm Heavy guns. The total of Heavy guns in the belt rose to nearly 600.

83. My ultimate object was to provide an almost robot defence to a robot attack; I visualised the battle as the culmination of the scientific development and training of more than four years and the final proof, if such proof were needed, that the troops of Anti-Aircraft Command, though they must be soldiers first, must become far more than mere soldiers; they must be scientists and technical operators of the highest quality.

84. For the moment training was still a tremendous problem, and there was much more to be done than simply to train Heavy Anti-Aircraft on the new equipment, itself a serious enough problem in the middle of a major battle. Besides lowering the normal base of Heavy Anti-Aircraft fire in order to cover the unprotected height band in which the bombs were flying, we endeavoured to raise the normal ceiling of Light Anti-Aircraft fire. For this purpose arrangements were made to use radar for the first time to control light guns, and light anti-aircraft troops had therefore to be instructed in methods of unseen fire, hitherto a closed book to them.

85. The flying bombs also presented an unparalleled opportunity for trying out equipments still in the experimental stage. It provided all the difficulties of an operational target flying at great speed with the security that no reports of our counter-action would become available to enemy sources. Interspersed with more normal equipment along the belt were anti-aircraft tanks, experimental versions of the Polsten gun, Ministry of Aircraft Production experimental quadruple 20-mm guns, other 20-mm guns with gyro sights, Bofors guns linked to No. 7, No. 9 and No. 10 predictors, Petroleum Warfare Department 9-inch mortars, 2-inch Naval rockets and others. More was learnt about the potentialities of anti-aircraft work in 80 days than had been learned in the previous 30 years.

In addition one Searchlight Regiment was converted to a Rocket rôle and manned 4 twin Rocket Batteries, 512 barrels in all.

86. The original inland searchlight belt did not move to the coast

with the guns and it was only at this stage that it began to give full value. There were now two fighter areas, one out to sea and one behind the gun belt. With the latter the Searchlights co-operated at night. Although the flame from the propulsion unit of the flying bomb made it self-illuminating at night, fighters were not usually able to judge its distance or course without the assistance of a searchlight intersection, especially while making a fast dive and turn towards it. Owing to the low flying height of the bomb a rapid traverse was required and this called for skilful operation, especially since it was essential not to dazzle the fighter, which, at such low heights and high speeds, would then have been in imminent danger of crashing. Of the targets which penetrated the coastal belt at night, searchlights assisted fighters in the destruction of I42, or something over 30 per cent.

87. The continuous nature of the attack, the simultaneous need for training and the constant building of sites (and re-building as they were moved to admit new equipment) caused a very severe strain on the men and women in the battle line. Guns were sometimes manned for I00 per cent. of the 24 hours and often for between 80 per cent. and 90 per cent. Relief forces had to be drawn in from units in other parts of the country.

88. On I9th August, I944, the eastward advance of the armies in France rendered the westward end of the belt largely superfluous, and the portion between Cuckmere Haven and East Hastings was closed down and the units used either to reinforce the remainder or to extend it from St. Margaret's Bay to Sandwich. At the same time units from 2Ist Army Group and from Training Establishments were largely withdrawn so that the burden of the battle devolved more upon the units of Anti-Aircraft Command itself. This had the advantage that a greater degree of uniformity in fire control discipline could be secured, and much rather wild shooting was now eliminated.

89. The re-adjusted belt continued to show improved results until activity ended on 5th September, I944, with the capture by the armies in France and Belgium of the remaining launching sites. The degree of improvement since the period of the inland belt, when the successes were under 10 per cent., is shown in the percentages of flying bombs destroyed in the following successive weeks; these were, in the first phase of the coastal belt, 17 per cent., 24 per cent., 27 per cent., 40 per

cent. and 55 per cent., and, in the second phase of the coastal belt, 60 per cent. and 74 per cent.

90. It had been established early in July, I944, that the Germans were not only launching their flying bombs from ground sites on the French coast, but were also launching a few from specially adapted aircraft. Some of these flew westwards down the Channel, aimed either at Southampton or Bristol, others came in from the North Sea towards London. The latter threat was the more serious, and a deployment was ordered along the coast from the River Blackwater to Whitstable, known as the "Diver Box". The Maunsell Forts in the Thames Estuary proved an invaluable addition to this defence scheme.

9I. On I6th September, I944, attacks were renewed, but many of the bombs came down upon London from the north-east, thereby outflanking the Diver Box to the north. On I8th September, I944, therefore, I6 Heavy Batteries and 9 Light Batteries began to move to the area between the River Blackwater and Harwich. The attackers moved further north and the outflanking continued. On 2Ist September, I944, it was decided to create a new belt as far north as Great Yarmouth; initially intended to consist only of male batteries, it later included mixed batteries as well. Steps were taken to protect Bomber Command aircraft and U.S. Air Force bombers which regularly crossed this strip of coast.

92. On 22nd September I944, orders for the deployment of the "Diver Strip", as it was called, were given.

For a variety of causes, many beyond our control, the deployment was not completed till I3th October, I944. Even this date would not have been achieved but for the excellent work of the R.A.S.C. drivers who drove both themselves and some of their transport to a standstill in their effort to meet the conflicting demands made upon them.

93. Generally, the deployment in the Diver Strip followed the lines which had proved so successful in the Diver Belt. 34 Heavy Batteries were deployed and 36 Light Batteries; the rôle of the latter, however, was changed from that previously used in an attempt to produce an intermediate effect between Heavy and Light anti-aircraft fire. Of the 36 Batteries only I5 were equipped normally, the remaining 2I had 2 static 3.7-inch Heavy guns in place of 4 of their 40-mm. Bofors, these were controlled in I5 instances by No. I0 predictors and in 6 instances

by No. 3 predictors modified for range-finding by radar means. Thus there were in all 5I6 3.7-inch guns and 503 40-mm. guns. Within a month it was clear that the Light Anti-Aircraft units, even when modified for an intermediate rôle, were not providing a satisfactory contribution and they were withdrawn. The total of Heavy guns was increased to 542.

For initial intercommunication 200 wireless receivers were distributed, but these were replaced as soon as land lines could be provided. In the marshy districts of the deployment, where the country was everywhere intersected by considerable streams, this was a considerable task, involving 2,000 miles of cable, much of which had to be carried on poles. Once more our Signals showed their quality.

94. In this new phase of flying bomb activity the average height of the missiles dropped to I,000 feet. Guns firing proximity fuzes could still deal with them though they had to be most carefully sited if they were to do so successfully; the radar sets in particular provided a problem since the need to detect the bombs at long range and the need to eliminate clutter at low angles of sight were mutually antagonistic; searchlights were most affected because the lower the height of the target the more difficult was continuous illumination.

95. The need for constant alertness produced that same degree of strain which had been evident for a time on the South coast, but I had not now available, owing to manpower cuts, the same reserves on which to draw for reliefs.

96. For some time we had been representing to the War Office that the war establishments of Anti-Aircraft Command units were anomalous, based as they were on the assumption that A.A. units were similar to units in a field army which had spells out of the line however continuous the fighting. In a spell of continuous air activity, no unit of Anti-Aircraft Command could anticipate any period of rest, and to base its war establishment on the assumption that air activity would be sporadic was a fallacy. It was agreed therefore that if a spell of continuous air activity threatened or occurred, a special increment could be made to the establishment. This is not altogether a satisfactory solution owing to the consequent lack of team training.

In the present instance it was possible to allow units to rest by day because attacks were almost always made at night, and radar information from sets in both the Low Countries and in England gave detailed advance information of impending attacks.

97. This series of air-launched flying bomb attacks continued until l4th January, 1945, but of a total of l,0l2 plotted only 495 bombs came within range of the guns, for in spite of the extension of the Strip to Great Yarmouth many still outflanked it to the north and many were inaccurately aimed and flew elsewhere than to London. Of the 495 targets only 66 got through and reached London.

98. On l4th October, 1944, that is as soon as the deployment was complete, a decision was taken about providing winter quarters in the area. Events at the approaches to Germany had shown that the war was likely to continue through the winter; and the extreme wetness of the autumn weather made living conditions in the already marshy land extremely uncomfortable. The Mixed batteries were offered the opportunity of leaving the Strip for better quarters inland but unanimously they asked to remain.

The project was a considerable one, involving the building of 60 miles of road, 3,500 huts and the laying of l50,000 tons of rubble and hardcore in the mud as foundation for guns as well as buildings. The cost of the project, which was equivalent to the building of a town the size of Windsor, was £2,000,000 and the building trade estimated the work would take 6 months to complete. It was carried out by the Construction Batteries, reinforced by 7,500 men of Anti-Aircraft Command, the latter being responsible for the collection, loading, unloading and distribution of materials and for providing unskilled labour. The work was completed in 2½ months.

99. On 24th December, 1944, a further deployment was ordered when 40 flying bombs were launched across the Yorkshire and Lincolnshire coasts towards the industrial areas of Lancashire. In spite of heavy snow and fog the deployment was completed in 5 days, for all the necessary preliminary reconnaissance had been carried out some months previously. These defences, known as the "Diver Fringe", extended from Flamborough Head to Skegness and remained in position until the end of hostilities although no further attacks on the North were made. l52 Heavy guns were involved in this area.

l00. During February, l945, information was received that land-launched attacks with bombs of longer range might be resumed from the Dutch coast, and on the 2nd/3rd March, I945 attacks began and lasted until 29th March, I945. Out of I57 bombs plotted, I07 came within range of the guns who destroyed 8I. On eight days I00 per cent. successes were obtained. Only I3 bombs reached London.

Perhaps the most remarkable tribute to the results being obtained by the guns lies in the fact that the A.O.C.-in-C. some weeks before the end of the attack withdrew all his squadrons, except two, for service overseas. The defence in these last weeks rested almost entirely on the guns.

I0I. Although this was in effect the end of the operational activities of Anti-Aircraft Command there was one more development with which I must deal. I refer to the attacks by long-range rockets, the first of which had fallen upon London on 8th September, I944.

I had already been advised of the possibility of such attacks and twelve radar sets had been deployed on the south and south-east coasts to endeavour to track any rockets that were fired.

When the attacks were found to approach London from the east, the sets were re-sited on the east coast and though nine were subsequently withdrawn for use on the Continent, others were brought in to take their place.

It was established that the range was about 200 miles, the maximum height something over 50 miles, the maximum speed more than 3,000 m.p.h. and the landing speed about I,800 m.p.h. In effect it was a high velocity shell of alarming explosive power, the flight of which was long enough to permit calculations to be made as to where it might land. These calculations were not always accurate but at the same time not widely inaccurate. It was, however, not possible to secure satisfactory plots of every rocket that was fired.

I02. I felt convinced that this was the beginning of one of the great problems of the future and I considered whether I could take any steps to deal with it. On I2th December, I944, I proposed that I should be allowed to try shooting at the rockets with a view to destroying them in the air. The idea of shooting at a shell was admittedly revolutionary, but there seemed to me to be no reason why it should not be anything more than a further development of the present unseen firing methods. My proposal was rejected as it was not considered that it had a theoretical background of success sufficient to justify the danger to the civil population beneath the barrage.

I argued that operational shooting was an essential corollary of scientific theory and that only by experience could scientific theory advance; moreover, it was necessary to attempt to make progress before a more powerful rocket came into operation and finally, that war experience was essential for post-war planning. I was asked to prove that there was so much as one chance in a hundred of success and my proposals might go forward.

Experiments both in the matter of plotting, for which special radar sets were now developed by my R.E.M.E. staff, and of gun control instruments were pressed on with.

103. Radar sets situated north and south of the rocket's flight and another set forward in Holland tracked the parabola of flight. During March, 1945, there was an increase in the number of missiles plotted from 44½ per cent. to 48 per cent. The accuracy of the plotting showed a greater improvement. London was divided into areas 2½ miles square; the number which were predicted as falling into the correct square rose from II per cent. to 3I per cent., and there was also an increase in the number which were only one square out from 44 per cent. to 50 per cent., and an overall improvement from 55 per cent. to 8I per cent. of those that were plotted at all.

104. I applied again for permission to fire. If I aimed at one of every two rockets descending and hit, as I estimated, one in 30, the chances were within the limits I had been set, although as 3 in 30 already burst in the air it would be some time before results could be proved. On the 28th March, 1945, I gave orders to the guns to be ready to fire but on the 27th March, 1945, the last rocket had fallen. On 30th March, 1945, the Chiefs of Staff again refused permission for the guns to fire at rockets.

105. The advance in the science of anti-aircraft defence since the beginning of the war has been prodigious, but I believe we are still only touching the fringe of future possibilities. Air Defence is of such paramount importance that we must spare no effort and no expense to maintain our scientific lead.

106. On I5th April, 1945, I handed over my command to my successor.

I07. I would add three names to the few already mentioned as having given outstanding service. There were many others but these can only be dealt with on a separate list. Major-General P.H. Mitchiner, C.B., C.B.E., T.D., M.D., M.S., organized the Medical services in the Command. He was an administrator of a very high order as well as a first class Medical Officer. He rendered great services to the State.

The late Major-General Sir Hugh T. Mac-Mullen, K.C.B., C.B.E., M.C., was Major-General in charge of Administration during the most difficult period of the war. He was outstanding. It was largely due to his administrative skill and tact that the Mixed Batteries settled down so easily and efficiently. Only sickness deprived me of his services.

Major-General R.H. Allen, C.B., M.C., was an outstanding Divisional Commander. He was responsible for the Anti-Aircraft Defences of the West Country. He made up for the limited resources of equipment by his great knowledge of Anti-Aircraft technique and by his skill.

When an attack took place it was always at only a matter of a few seconds warning yet both Gun and Searchlight units were ever on their toes.

Their discipline, judged by percentages of courts-martial and absence without leave cases, was twice as good as that of any other Command or Service.

The Corps of Royal Engineers rendered considerable service in that it trained and supplied the original Regular and Territorial Army Searchlight Units before they became part of the Royal Regiment of Artillery in August, I940.

Other works carried out by the Royal Engineers included the designing of static emplacements and command posts, and making arrangements for a supervision of the construction of gun sites and hutted camps.

The A.T.S., particularly in the Mixed batteries, set a standard of bearing and conduct which in my opinion was not equalled by any other women's service.

The administrative services were not only efficient – they were outstanding. Our sick rate was always small though we never had anything like our quota of doctors.

The R.A.O.C. performed herculean tasks with all the new and

complicated equipments. The R.A.S.C. set a higher standard of driving than in any other Command. The Signals have been mentioned more than once for they were superb and were the one essential requisite in all our schemes.

R.E.M.E. produced an inventiveness, coupled with general engineering skill and enthusiasm, which gave us an answer to every difficulty.

The Chaplains department were the first to introduce the "Padre's Hour" into the Army. Much of the excellent discipline was due to them.

Finally, the Commanders and Staffs serving under me were worthy of the troops they led.

Footnote

I Defensively Equipped Merchant Ships.

3

AIR OPERATIONS BY FIGHTER COMMAND

FROM 25TH NOVEMBER 1940 TO 31ST DECEMBER 1941.

The following report was submitted to the Secretary of State for Air on 29th February, 1948, by Marshal of the Royal Air Force Sir Sholto Douglas, G.C.B., M.C., D.F.C. (now Lord Douglas of Kirtleside), former Air Officer Commanding-in-Chief, Fighter Command, Royal Air Force

PART I: OPERATIONS.

Night Operations.

(a) The Situation on Ist November, 1940

I. At the beginning of November, I940, the most urgent problem confronting the air defences was that presented by the night bomber. For the first ten months of the war the Luftwaffe had undertaken only minor operations against this country; but in June, I940, the enemy began a series of small-scale night attacks on ports and industrial towns. During the next two months, while the daylight battle of Britain was being fought, this night offensive gathered momentum. On September 7th London became its main objective, and the scale of attack increased once more. By the end of October the night offensive had become in many respects a bigger threat to the kingdom than the day offensive, which, for the moment at least, had been successfully beaten off.

2. At that stage London had been raided on every night but one for the last eight weeks. On every night but four during those eight weeks at least a hundred tons of bombs had fallen on or around the Capital; Coventry, Birmingham and Liverpool had all suffered attacks of some weight. So far no intolerable harm had been done to industry or the public temper, although many people had been killed and much material loss and hardship had been caused. But there was every reason to expect that the attacks would continue and perhaps grow heavier; for during the last two months the defences had claimed the destruction of only 79 night bombers – a number equivalent to about a half of one per cent. of the number of night sorties that the Germans were believed to have flown in that time. Obviously, losses of this order were not likely to act as a deterrent.

3. The directive by which I found myself bound when I assumed command on 25th November, 1940, required me to give priority to the defence of the aircraft industry. No formal variation of this directive was needed to make it clear that the defeat of the night bomber must be one of my main tasks.

4. It would be wrong to give the impression that hitherto this problem had been ignored. On the contrary, it had long been foreseen that if the enemy found day attacks too expensive, he would probably turn to night bombing on a substantial scale. But with limited resources it had been necessary to place the emphasis on high-performance, single-seater fighters capable of defeating the enemy by day. Before the war, and in the early stages of the war it was hoped that, with the help of searchlights, these aircraft would also be effective at night.

5. This hope had proved vain. Except at the beginning of the night offensive, when the enemy flew at 12,000 feet or lower, the searchlights were incapable of doing what was required of them. This was partly because they relied on sound locators, which were unsuited to modern conditions, and partly because very often cloud or moonlight prevented pilots from seeing the searchlight beams at the height at which they had to fly.

6. A method of night interception which did not rely on searchlights had been under development (although not continuously) since 1936.

This method rested upon the installation in twin-engined, multi-seater aircraft of the radar equipment known as A.I.

7. On November Ist, 1940, the Command had possessed six squadrons of aircraft fitted with this equipment. All were Blenheim Squadrons, but as the Blenheim was too slow and too lightly armed to take full advantage of its opportunities, Beaufighters were being substituted for the Blenheims as fast as the Air Ministry and the Ministry of Aircraft Production could make them available.

8. But at best the provision of A.I. solved only half the problem. This airborne Radar had a restricted range which could not be greater than the height of the aircraft, subject to a maximum of 3½ miles. Before the A.I. could detect an enemy bomber in the darkness, the fighter had therefore to be brought to within three miles of it at roughly the same height. If searchlights were ruled out, this could only be done by means of directions given to the pilot by a Controller on the ground. It was vital that this controller should have accurate knowledge of the bomber's position. Under my Command, I had No. 60 (Signals) Group, which controlled a chain of some 80 Radar Stations round the coasts, used for giving early warning to the controller of the approach of enemy aircraft across the sea. Over land, information on the raider's position was given by the Observer Corps. Although these sources had proved sufficiently accurate for daylight interceptions, they were not precise enough for successful night fighter operations.

9. Only Radar could provide the answer – special ground search radar stations for the direct control of A.I. equipped night fighter aircraft. Such stations, termed G.C.I. (Ground Control of Interception), were under development when I assumed Command. Nevertheless, the tactics of their employment in conjunction with A.I. night fighters had yet to be evolved from practical experience as and when the G.C.I. stations became available.

10. The Radar Stations used for detecting the approach of enemy aircraft across the sea had only a limited application to this problem, but another kind of ground radar equipment, designed for gun-laying and known as G.L., promised to give good results. Although other varieties of radar equipment were under development, the defects of both ground and airborne search radars were not the most important factors in the establishment of an efficient night fighter defence. Any

success A.I. was likely to achieve depended initially on the skill of the ground controller and then on the operational ability of the aircraft A.I. observer. There was an acute shortage of personnel for both of these highly specialised tasks.

II. It was clear that many problems of method, maintenance and supply would have to be solved before all this delicate equipment could be expected to yield concrete results, and that their solution was likely to take some months. In the meantime, the Air Ministry were anxious that some immediate attempt should be made to improve the situation.

I2. A step in this direction had already been taken in the late Summer, when it was decided that the two Defiant Squadrons in the Command, together with a third Defiant Squadron which was about to be formed, should be turned over from day to night duty. Despite its early successes as a day fighter, the Defiant had proved too slow and too vulnerable to attack from below to be effective against the Me I09, but it was still likely to prove a useful weapon against bombers.

I3. In addition, three Hurricane Squadrons had been turned over to night duty, in the middle of October, I940.

I4. Thus when I assumed Command, the night-fighter force comprised the following squadrons:-

Squadron	*Equipment*	*Station*
No. 23	Blenheim	Ford
No. 25	Blenheim and Beaufighter.	Debden
No. 29	Blenheim	Digby and Wittering.
No. 2I9	Blenheim and Beaufighter.	Redhill
No. 600	Blenheim	Catterick and Drem
No. 604	Blenheim	Middle Wallop
No. I4I	Defiant	Gatwick
No. 264	Defiant	Rochford
No. 73	Hurricane	Castle Camps
No. 85	Hurricane	Kirton-in-Lindsey
No. I5I	Hurricane	Digby

I5. In addition to these first-line units, the Fighter Interception Unit at Tangmere had the task of developing methods of night interception with twin-engined fighters; and sometimes provided aircraft for active operations, No. 422 Flight had been formed recently at Gravesend to study the problem of night interception with single-engined fighters; while a new Defiant Squadron, No 307 (Polish) Squadron, was forming at Kirton-in-Lindsey, No. 420 Flight (later No. 93 Squadron) had just begun to form for the purpose of sowing and trailing mines in front of German bombers. Finally, the formation of No. 54 Operational Training Unit, to specialize in night training, had been ordered.

16. I also had operational control of the guns and searchlights of Anti-Aircraft Command, under Lt.-General Sir Frederick A. Pile, Bart., K.C.B., D.S.O., M.C., and the balloon barrages of Balloon Command under Air Vice-Marshal O.T. Boyd, C.B., O.B.E., M.C., A.F.C. (succeeded on Ist December, 1940, by Air Marshal Sir E.L. Gossage, K.C.B., C.V.O., D.S.O., M.C.).

17. In the early stages of the attack, except in conditions of good visibility, the A.A. guns had to rely on one of three methods of directing their fire. These were: illumination of the bomber by searchlights, which were controlled by sound locators; a combination of rather rudimentary radar and sound locator, or a system of prediction which depended entirely on sound locators. The shortcomings of these sound locators were a great handicap to A.A. gunnery, and the gunners deserve great credit for their achievements at a time when night fighters were almost powerless. By 25th November, 1940, radar equipment for gunlaying was beginning to arrive, and a variant intended for controlling searchlights (S.L.C. or "Elsie") was on the way.

18. Other means of frustrating enemy bombers included measures designed to jam or otherwise interfere with the directional beams that they used to find their targets, and various kinds of dummies and decoys which were intended to attract bombs. With the exception of decoy and dummy airfields, these were not under my control, but liaison was maintained with those responsible for their operation.

(b) *Operations, November and December, 1940.*

19. During the first two weeks in November, London had continued to be the enemy's main target, and was visited by at least I00 German bombers nearly every night. Then, in the middle of the month, came a change. On the night of I4th November, by the light of the full moon, nearly 500 German aircraft delivered an attack on Coventry which lasted from about eight o'clock in the evening until half-past five the

following morning. The attack began with the dropping of large numbers of incendiary bombs by a Unit called K.Gr.I00, which was known to specialize in this form of target marking. More incendiaries, hundreds of high explosive bombs and a number of parachute mines followed. The raid wrought great havoc in the centre of the city, severely damaged 2I important factories, wrecked gas and water-mains and cables, blocked the railways, and put four or five hundred retail shops out of action. Three hundred and eighty people were killed and 800 seriously injured. The Civil Defence Services did excellent work, and, though shaken, the citizens of Coventry remained undaunted.

20. The defences were not unprepared for this move. The A.A. guns put up a tremendous volume of fire, and I23 fighter sorties were flown, day squadrons as well as night squadrons taking part. A few enemy aircraft were seen and some of them were engaged, but none of these combats was conclusive. The A.A. gunners claimed the destruction of two bombers.

2I. Another such raid on Coventry soon afterwards might have created a serious situation. Fortunately the Germans did not consider a second raid necessary, and on the next night London was once again their main objective. But, for the rest of the month and throughout December, provincial towns and cities, including Southampton, Bristol, Plymouth, Birmingham, Sheffield, Liverpool and Manchester, competed with London for their attention. Clearly they had passed to a new stage in their programme and were now seeking to dislocate our means of production and supply.

22. Although this phase of the offensive did not come as a surprise, the ability of the Germans to reach and find their targets in wintry conditions was disturbing. With the help of radio beacons, directional beam systems, and blind-landing devices, the bombers were able to operate effectively in weather which seriously hampered and sometimes precluded fighter operations. As yet the new methods of interception which depended on radar were not perfected, and the less elaborate methods which we had hoped would tide us over this intervening period were largely defeated by this factor of bad weather. Inasmuch, however, as the enemy bomber crews were mainly reliant upon radio beams and beacons for navigation and bomb aiming in conditions of bad visibility, they were correspondingly vulnerable to

radio counter-measures against those aids.There had grown up since the beginning of the war an extensive organisation which had developed a most effective technique for interfering so subtly with radio beams and beacons as to leave the enemy almost unaware of the fact that his own aids were leading him astray. This organisation had been consolidated shortly before I assumed command, in the form of No. 80 Wing, whose invaluable services were almost entirely at my disposal. Operating in association with other forms of decoy, No. 80 Wing was responsible for deflection of a great number of enemy bombers from their targets, while the information it gathered as to the orientation of enemy radio beams from time to time proved a valuable guide to the air defences as to the enemy's intentions. Indeed, until our night fighters were to become a weapon of any significance against the enemy bombers in March of the following year, radio counter-measures were to contribute as much as any other defensive arm towards reduction of the impact of the enemy bomber offensive.

23. On the night of I9th November, a pilot and crew of No. 604 Squadron, using their A.I. in conjunction with searchlight indications and instructions from their Sector Controller, had succeeded in engaging a large aircraft over Oxfordshire. The crew of a Ju88 which crashed later in Norfolk reported that they had been attacked by a fighter on their way from the South Coast to Birmingham; and it seems probable that this was the aircraft engaged over Oxfordshire. If so, this was the first enemy aircraft whose destruction was attributable to a fighter carrying A.I. and belonging to a first-line squadron, although as long ago as July a success in active operations had been claimed by the Fighter Interception Unit.

24. Up to the end of the year fighters claimed the destruction of only three more night bombers, and none of these successes was attributable to A.I.

25. Many novel and unusual means of dealing with the night bomber were suggested about this time and subsequently. The more practicable of these included the release of a free balloon barrage, other forms of aerial mining, and the use of searchlights carried by aircraft.

These are dealt with below under the appropriate headings.

26. On a number of occasions I arranged for fighters carrying equipment which responded to the "beam" transmissions which the

Germans used to find their targets to be sent to "hunt in the beam," but the German crews seem to have anticipated this move and were wary. Fighters sent to patrol the points at which the bombers were expected to cross the French coast on their homeward journey, burning their navigation lights, were no more successful.

27. On the night of IIth December, I tried out for the second time, a measure which had previously been given an inconclusive trial over Bristol. Twenty Hampden bombers were sent to patrol at various specified heights over Birmingham during a concentrated attack on that city. The crews reported seeing a large number of enemy aircraft, but the Hampdens were too unwieldy to bring any of them to action. This experience proved, however, that in suitable circumstances interception by purely visual means was possible.

28. Meanwhile we were taking every possible step to improve the chances of interception by more orthodox means. Up to this time such G.L. sets as were available to assist the fighters had been grouped close together in the Kenley Sector. In consultation with General Pile, I now arranged for them to be more widely spaced to form a "G.L. Carpet," designed to extend over the whole of Southern England from Kent to Bristol and ultimately, we hoped, over a still wider area. I also arranged with General Pile that the searchlights should be grouped in clusters of three, instead of singly, in order to provide a stronger illumination. In addition, I earmarked a number of airfields as night-fighter bases and took steps to equip them with every available aid to night flying.

29. It became clear in December that for the adequate defence of the Kingdom more specialist night squadrons were needed, and I therefore asked the Air Ministry to provide, as soon as possible, a total of 20 such squadrons, to include twelve twin-engined squadrons. Although it was some time before this figure was achieved, substantial additions were made to the night-fighter force during the ensuing months.

30. In the second week of December I was informed that the Air Ministry wished me ultimately to accept responsibility for the "Security Patrols" which had hitherto been flown by aircraft of No. 2 Group, Bomber Command, over airfields in Northern France and the Low Countries.

3I. The use of fighters for this work had already been discussed by my Staff with No. 2 Group, and arrangements were being made for

ir Chief Marshal Sir Hugh C.T. Dowding, Commander-in-Chief of RAF Fighter
'ommand during the Battle of Britain. (HMP)

The General Officer Commanding Anti-Aircraft Command, General Sir Frederick Alfred Pile. The formation of a body of anti-aircraft guns had been announced in 1938 but Anti-Aircraft Command was not formed until 1 April 1939 under General Sir Alan Brooke who then passed control to Sir General Sir Frederick Pile. Pile would remain in command until the end of the war. (Courtesy of Andy Saunders)

Air Chief Marshal Sir William Sholto Douglas pictured in February 1943 during his service as Air Officer Commander-in-Chief, Middle East Command. (Imperial War Museum; ME(RAF)7832)

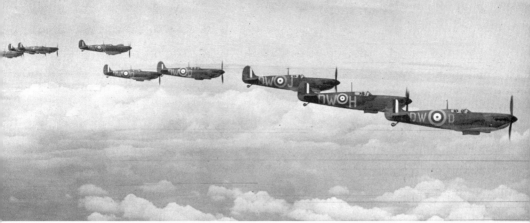

Supermarine Spitfire Mk.IAs of 610 Squadron cruising above the British countryside during the Battle of Britain. The squadron was formed at RAF Hooton Park, Cheshire, on 10 February 1936 as a day bomber unit of the Auxiliary Air Force. On 1 January 1939, the Squadron was re-designated a fighter unit. On the outbreak of war it received Hawker Hurricanes, but by the end of September 1939 had exchanged these for Spitfires, becoming operational on 21 October. When the German offensive opened in May 1940, 610 Squadron moved to Biggin Hill. (ww2images)

Some of "The Few" are seen in this group shot of pilots of 249 Squadron taken at RAF North Weald during September 1940. From left to right are: Pilot Officer Percival R.F. Burton, Flight Lieutenant Robert Barton, Flight Lieutenant Albert Lewis DFC, Pilot Officer James Crossey, Flight Lieutenant Tom Neil, Pilot Officer John Beazley, Squadron Leader John Grandy, Pilot Officer George Barclay and Flight Lieutenant Keith Lofts. This iconic photograph became one of the best known images of the Battle of Britain, especially after it featured in the 1941 Air Ministry publication on the Battle of Britain. (Courtesy of Andy Saunders)

Above: One of the many: the wreckage a Heinkel He 111H-3 on fire at Burmarsh, Kent, on Wednesday, 11 September 1940. The aircraft had been shot down by anti-aircraft fire over London and force-landed at 16.00 hours. The crew of *Unteroffizier* Hofmann, *Feldwebel* Heinz Friedrich (pilot), *Feldwebel* George, *Unteroffizier* Dreyer and *Unteroffizier* Stirnemann were all taken prisoner, though one of the crew (not the pilot) can be seen here being carried away on a stretcher. The aircraft, 1H+CB, was a write-off. (HMP)

Right; Members of the public watch as an anti-aircraft gun crew goes through its paces in London's Hyde Park on the eve of war in the summer of 1939. (US National Archives)

A Bofors 40mm Light Anti-Aircraft gun stands ready to fire on the South Coast.
(Courtesy of Andy Saunders)

The guns of a Heavy Anti-Aircraft battery positioned near the Thames Estuary.
(Courtesy of Andy Saunders)

Barrage balloons being raised. Formed on 1 November 1938, RAF Balloon Command was the organisation responsible for controlling all the United Kingdom-based barrage balloon units just prior to and during the Second World War. By the middle of 1940 there were 1,400 balloons, a third of them over the London area. (HMP)

The wreckage of the last Junkers Ju 87 Stuka to fall on British soil; this was J9+BK flown by *Leutnant* Ernst Schimmelpfennig and *Obergefreiter* Hans Kaden. Both men were killed as the Stuka crashed into the ground at Cheeseman's Farm, Minster, Kent, on 5 February 1941. (HMP)

At 20.02 hours on 14 October 1940, a bomb dropped during a raid on London penetrated thirty-two feet underground and exploded just above the cross passage between the two platforms at Balham Underground Station. Above ground this double decker bus, travelling in blackout conditions, plunged into the crater created by the bomb. The dramatic spectacle of the trapped bus provided one of the iconic images of the Blitz. (HMP)

Firemen playing their hoses on dying embers in buildings along Queen Victoria Street after the last and heaviest major raid mounted by the *Luftwaffe* against the British capital during the Blitz. For six hours on the night of 10-11 May 1941, German aircraft dropped over 1,000 tons of bombs on London, claiming 1,486 lives, destroying 11,000 houses and damaging many important historical buildings. (HMP)

A Bristol Beaufighter night fighter. The Beaufighter came off the production line at almost exactly the same time as the first Airborne Intercept (AI) radar sets. With the four 20mm cannon mounted in the lower fuselage, the nose could accommodate the radar antennas, and the space in the fuselage enabled the AI equipment to be fitted easily. By early 1941, the Beaufighter was proving an effective counter to the *Luftwaffe*'s night raids (HMP)

Released to the press on 3 August 1944, this image shows a V-1 Flying Bomb diving down onto London. The buildings in the foreground are the Royal Courts of Justice (Law Courts) on the north side of the Strand. It is stated that this V-1 fell on Wild Street on 28 June 1944. (HMP)

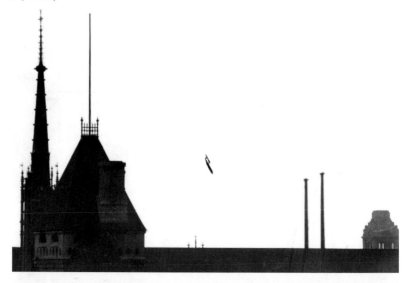

aircraft of No. 23 Squadron to supplement the efforts of No. 2 Group's Blenheims. On receipt of the Air Ministry's letter, I ordered that the whole of No. 23 Squadron should be turned over to this duty, to which the name "Intruder" was now applied. The A.I., whose capture could not be risked, was removed from the squadron's aircraft, navigators were posted to the squadron, and some crews were sent to one of No. 2 Group's Stations to learn all that they could about the operation. The squadron was ready to operate by 18th December and the first patrols were flown on the 21st.

32. A further account of operation "Intruder" is given below, under a separate heading. (Paras. 68 to 72.)

33. On 29th December, the Capital suffered one of its worse raids of the war when a determined attempt was made to destroy the cities of London and Westminster by the dropping of large numbers of incendiary bombs. Nearly 1,500 separate fires were started, some of them of vast dimensions. The weather was poor and the night-fighter force had no success.

(c) *Operations, January to May, 1941.*

34. Early in the New Year the efforts made to apply the principles of Radar to the special problems of night defence began to yield results. Radar equipment began to be available in increasing quantities, although it was sometime before the S.L.C. sets needed by the searchlights arrived in anything like sufficient numbers. The performance of the heavy A.A. guns at night, measured by the number of rounds required to bring down one enemy aircraft, quickly improved and soon surpassed the standard achieved in daylight at the end of the 1914-1918 war.

35. For the fighter force an important step forward was the arrival of G.C.I. sets – hitherto only in the development stage – which enabled a ground controller to follow on a fluorescent screen the track in the horizontal plane both of a selected bomber and of the fighter sent to intercept it.

36. At first these sets could not read height with any accuracy, but their performance in this respect was soon improved.

37. For some time progress was slow, but by March substantial results were being achieved by the night-fighters, and indeed in that

month their claims exceeded those of the A.A. gunners for the first time since June, 1940. Of the 43 night bombers whose destruction was claimed that month, 22 were claimed by the night-fighter forces, and half of these by twin engine fighters using their A.I.

38. From this moment the A.I. fighter became the principal weapon of the night-fighter force. Unlike the single-engined fighter, it was not dependent on moonlight or artificial illumination and could therefore be used in weather which put the single-engined fighter out of court. From March onwards the steadiest results were claimed by A.I. fighters. On the other hand, a number of clear moonlit nights in Spring, on which German aircraft were to be found in large numbers over their target and along the route there to, gave the single engined fighters opportunities which enabled them to surpass, for short periods, the performance of their twin-engined rivals.

39. From that moment, too, the fighter rather than the A.A. gun became the chief means of inflicting casualties on the night bomber. But it would be unwise to draw any hasty conclusion from this fact. Although there was always a friendly rivalry between guns and fighters, it was recognised throughout the war that together – and in conjunction with the balloon defences – they formed a team of which all the members were indispensable. The value of what may conveniently be called the static defences was not to be measured solely, or even mainly, by the casualties which they inflicted on the enemy. Their deterrent effect, not only in causing some bombers to turn away before reaching their target, but in preventing leisurely and methodical bombing from low altitudes by the remainder, was always of inestimable value. The experience of the "Baedeker" raids (which came after the end of the period now under review) proves that if important objectives had been deprived in 1941 of their gun and balloon defences, they could very quickly have been destroyed, regardless of any action by night-fighters. Moreover, it must be remembered that the limitations of Radar at this time made interception at low altitudes extremely difficult. If the guns had not helped to keep the enemy up, successful interceptions at night would have been rare.

40. On the other hand, the guns and balloons were equally incapable of acting as a complete defence in themselves, but required the co-

operation of the more mobile fighter, which was capable of harrying the bomber wherever he flew.

4I. In January and February bad weather frequently defeated all the enemy's attempts to make his bombers independent of extraneous circumstances, by rendering many airfields unserviceable. Chiefly on this account, the German effort declined considerably. March brought a revival, and in April and May the Germans increased their scale of attack still further in an attempt to conceal their intentions with respect to Russia.

42. Early in I94I, the Germans began to show an increasing tendency to concentrate on ports and shipping. There were other signs that an attempt to strangle our sea communications was contemplated, and at the end of February, I was instructed by the Air Ministry to provide additional "watch and ward" for coastwise shipping, and warned, that the German bomber force might be expected to pay special attention in future to ports on the West Coast.

43. Early in March this was followed by a formal directive which required me to give priority to the defence of the Clyde, the Mersey and the Bristol Channel, which were now to rank above the aircraft industry in this respect.

44. I immediately took steps to strengthen the A.A. defences of these areas, partly by moving guns from other parts of the country and partly by pledging a substantial part of the anticipated production in March and April. By the middle of March, the move of 8I additional heavy A.A. guns to the West Coast ports had been ordered, and shortly afterwards further increases amounting to another I04 heavy A.A. guns were arranged. Actual increases exceeded what had been planned: 58 guns were withdrawn from the Midlands in March, and 24 guns came from the factories: by Ist June a further I06 new guns had been deployed.

45. I also modified the deployment of the night-fighter force in order to give increased protection to the Clyde and the Mersey. I considered that the Bristol Channel was already adequately defended by the squadrons deployed to cover the Southern approaches to the Midlands.

46. In spite of the enemy's growing tendency to attack ports and shipping, his attention at this stage was by no means exclusively devoted to such objectives. Many attacks were made on London and

provincial towns, and the operations of German long-range fighters against our bombers and their bases caused some concern.

47. On the night of I0th May the enemy made the most ambitious attack on London that he had attempted up to that time, or indeed was ever to attempt. Although contemporary estimates were lower, it is now known that the German bomber force flew more than 500 sorties on this night. Visibility was good and the results were eminently satisfactory. A total of 60 single-engined fighters were sent to patrol at various heights over London, twenty over Beachy Head, and smaller numbers over the other approaches to the Capital, while twin-engined fighters were used to intercept the bombers as they came and went. These defensive fighters claimed between them the destruction of 23 enemy aircraft, of which the single-engined fighters claimed nineteen. A Defiant on an "Intruder" patrol over Northern France claimed one more, making 24. The A A. gunners, although their fire was restricted by the presence of our fighters, claimed another four, making a grand total of 28 enemy aircraft, or roughly five per cent. of the enemy effort.

48. Perhaps the most remarkable feature of this night's operations was the success of the Hurricane and Spitfire flying in the Bomber Stream. On various other nights in April and May, aircraft on "Fighter Night" patrols, claimed the destruction of twenty enemy aircraft in the aggregate. The impression that "Fighter Nights" was an unprofitable operation is widespread, but these figures show that, given good weather, moonlight, and a substantial concentration of enemy aircraft, these patrols could achieve satisfactory results. It was, however, only at periods when the moon was above the horizon that any success was achieved.

49. Operation "Fighter Night" was, of course, always regarded with disfavour by the A.A. gunners, whose chances of success it diminished. When it was first put into effect, the guns in the target area were forbidden to fire; but it was argued that their silence might cause apprehension amongst the public, and later they were allowed to fire up to heights safely below that of the lowest fighters. Such a restriction of A.A. fire was only justified, of course, when the conditions were particularly favourable to fighters, but the figures just quoted show that in these conditions its justification was beyond dispute. It is interesting to note that, despite the limitation imposed on them, the guns in the

target area were not always barren of success on these occasions. While generally the guns kept the German bombers up to the heights at which the fighters could most conveniently engage them, it would seem that on occasions the fighters must have forced individual bombers down into the A.A. belt.

50. A night of scattered raiding on IIth May brought to an end the intensive phase which had begun eight months before. Thereafter, until the end of the year, the scale of attack was much smaller. Although a few more raids were made on London and the Midlands, the Germans devoted most of their attention for the rest of the year to targets near the coast or at sea, and to minelaying

5I. Undoubtedly the main reason for this change was a new strategic conception by the Germans. Having decided to attack the Russians, they withdrew most of their bombers from the West, leaving behind only a small force to second the German Navy's attempt to blockade the British Isles. To what extent this decision was due to the realisation by the enemy that his night offensive was failing as surely (though not so spectacularly) as his day offensive had failed in the previous Autumn, I do not know. But that the "Blitz" did fail to achieve any strategic purpose is clear enough. In eight months of intensive night raiding, the German bomber force did not succeed in breaking the spirit of the British people or preventing the expansion of our means of production and supply. Moreover, the cumulative effect of the ever-increasing losses which the Germans incurred as the defences got under way cannot have been a negligible factor, even though these losses were not sufficient in themselves to have brought the offensive to a standstill. To the country as a whole, and everyone in it, the end of the night battle was a great relief; nevertheless there was a sense in which it came to those under my command, and indeed to myself, as something of a disappointment. An enemy over whom we felt that we were gaining the mastery had slipped out of our grasp. All arms of the defence were working better than they had ever done before; the first five months of I94I had seen a steady and striking improvement in the results achieved. We were confident – I am confident still – that if the enemy had not chosen that moment to pull out, we should soon have been inflicting such casualties on his night bombers that the continuance of his night offensive on a similar scale would have been impossible.

(d) *Operations, June to December,* 1941.

52. As it was, the minor operations which formed the staple of the German night offensive during the second half of 1941 gave few chances to the defences. Minelaying aircraft, which flew low and could usually avoid gun-defended areas, were particularly hard to shoot down, and although we made many attempts to evolve means of intercepting them, it was not until 1942 that we had much success. But when the enemy did venture overland, the improvement which had been made since the beginning of the year was well maintained. When the Medway towns were attacked in June, for example, the defences claimed the destruction of seven enemy aircraft out of less than 100 operating; on two successive moonlit nights in July, eleven out of about 170 were claimed; and on the first night of November, when some 50 aircraft operated against Merseyside, the defences claimed the destruction of six.

(e) *The Free Balloon Barrage.*

53. Towards the end of 1940, I made arrangements to release Balloons carrying lethal charges in the path of German bombers approaching London. The intention was to use this free barrage on nights when the conditions were unsuitable for fighters; but it did not follow that whenever conditions were unsuitable for fighters they would be favourable for the Balloon Barrage, which had certain positive requirements of its own. These were by no means easy to satisfy. A disadvantage of the scheme was that deployment of the equipment had to be begun many hours in advance, on the strength of a difficult meteorological forecast, and on the chance that when the time came the character of the enemy's operations as well as the weather would favour release.

54. The first release was made on the night of 27th December. Imperfect communications caused a delay of 35 minutes between the issue of the order to release and the ascent of the first balloons. Shortly afterwards the enemy attack died away and the order to stop releasing

the balloons was given. So far as is known the comparatively small number of balloons released had no effect on the enemy.

55. A further release on the night of IIth January, I94I, went much more smoothly. The weather turned out as predicted and I,252 balloons were released over a period of three hours. Some 60 German bombers flew through the area in which the barrage was operating but appeared to be quite unaffected by it, mainly, perhaps, because the balloons were too widely spaced to give a good chance of success.

56. Although arrangements were subsequently made to improve the equipment and system of release, the scheme never achieved any practical success and was eventually abandoned.

(f) *No. 93 Squadron.*

57. No. 93 Squadron was formed in the late Autumn of I940 for the purpose of trailing and sowing aerial mines in the path of German bombers. During its life of rather less than a year the squadron claimed a number of successes, and the destruction of two enemy aircraft – one in December, I940, and one in the following April – was officially credited to it.

58. As time went on, however, the performance of orthodox night-fighter squadrons using A.I. improved so much that I came to the conclusion that the comparatively modest results achieved by No. 93 Squadron did not justify the manpower and effort involved in its continued existence. In November, I94I, therefore, I obtained authority to disband the squadron.

(g) *Airborne Searchlights.*

59. The idea of a searchlight carried in an aircraft is an old one, but the practical difficulties involved are considerable, because of the great weight of the equipment needed to produce a sufficiently powerful light.

60. In I94I this problem seemed to have been solved, thanks to the skill and ingenuity of Air Commodore W. Helmore. Aircraft carrying searchlights were now a practicable weapon and I was ordered to form the equivalentof five squadrons of Havoc aircraft so equipped.

6I. In trials these aircraft succeeded in illuminating and holding their targets while attendant single-engined fighters intercepted them. The crews of the target aircraft reported that the effect when the Havoc suddenly switched on its searchlights and held them in its blinding glare was extremely disconcerting, and hopes ran high.

62. By the time that the Havocs were ready for active operations, however, the enemy effort had dwindled to very small proportions, so that the scheme had no chance to prove its worth in 1941. When, after the end of the period now under review, the Havocs were given their opportunity, they proved too slow to compete on level terms with the orthodox A.I. squadrons against the faster bombers with which the German bomber force was then equipped.

(h) *Deployment of Ground Searchlights.*

63. Reference has been made to the siting of the searchlights in clusters of three during the winter of 1940-41.

64. This arrangement was found to be no solution to the problem, and, in the autumn of 1941, I arranged with General Pile for the searchlights to be re-sited singly.

65. Their primary function was now to help fighters to intercept, since the heavy A.A. guns were no longer dependent on them, and the basis of the new system was what was called the "fighter box."

66. It was found by calculation and experiment that the area within which a fighter pilot could hope to pick up and intercept a bomber with the aid of searchlights alone was a rectangle 44 miles long and 14 miles wide. Accordingly, we divided the whole of the area to be covered by searchlights into rectangles of this size. The searchlights were then so arranged that in the centre of each rectangle there was a stationary vertical beam. Round this beam the fighter circled until an enemy bomber entered the "box." Other searchlights were disposed at intervals of 3½ miles near ithe centre of the box and wider intervals near its borders. As soon as the bomber entered the box the beams of the outlying searchlights (belonging to the "Indicator Zone") began to converge on it, thus indicating its approach to the fighter pilot, who thereupon set a course which would put him in a position to intercept it in the central "Killer Zone."

67. This system was not working with full efficiency by the end of

I94I, but ultimately proved very effective and remained substantially unchanged until the end of the war.

(i) Operation "Intruder".

68. The circumstances in which No 23 Squadron began to fly "Intruder" patrols on 2Ist December, I940, have been described above.

69. It was not until the early spring that the squadron had many opportunities of successful action. With better weather and increased enemy activity it was then very successful, claiming the destruction of three enemy aircraft in March, I94I, two in April, and eleven in May. Thereafter, opportunities were again limited. Nevertheless, it was decided that a second "Intruder" Squadron should be added to the Command, and No. 4I8 (R.C.A.F.) Squadron, equipped with Bostons, began to form in the autumn.

70. No. 23 Squadron, originally equipped with Blenheims, re-armed with Havocs in March and April, I94I, and received a few Bostons later in the year.

7I. Between 2Ist December, I940, and 3Ist December, I94I, operation "Intruder" was carried out on I45 nights and 573 sorties were flown, of which 505 were by Blenheims, Havocs and Bostons of No. 23 Squadron, and 68 by Hurricanes and Defiants of Nos. I, 3, 87, I4I, I5I, 242, 264, 306 and 60I Squadrons, which were employed on this work occasionally on moonlit nights. The destruction of 2I enemy aircraft was claimed, 290 separate bombing attacks on airfields were reported, and ten of our aircraft were lost.

72. Throughout this period the executive control of this operation was something of a problem. To secure the best results, it was essential that the "Intruder" aircraft should arrive at active enemy bases just as returning bombers reached them. This could only be achieved by a close study of information from intelligence and raid-reporting sources on the part of those responsible for ordering the despatch of the "Intruder" aircraft. In accordance with the normal practice in my Command, control of the operation was delegated at the outset to No. II Group, from whose stations No. 23 Squadron was operating. The executive orders were issued by which ever of the Controllers at No.

II Group's Headquarters happened to be on duty at the time, in consultation with the Officer Commanding No. 23 Squadron. It was a matter for consideration whether these Duty Controllers, with their numerous responsibilities, could be expected to give that constant specialized attention to the changing data provided by the Intelligence and Raid-Reporting services which was essential for success. The suggestion that control of the operation should be exercised directly from my Headquarters was made more than once and from more than one quarter in 1941. I did not think it desirable to make any change at this stage, but later, when the necessity of co-ordinating the work of the "Intruder" Squadrons closely with the operations of Bomber Command made a more centralised control almost essential, this solution was adopted.

Day Operations

(a) *Defensive*

(i) Forces Available.

73. At the end of the Battle of Britain, that is to say at the beginning of November, 1940, the strength of the day fighter force amounted to 55½ squadrons, including three and a half squadrons in the process of formation. On paper this was a substantially larger force than the Command had possessed at the beginning of the battle; but really the force available was weaker. Many of our best pilots had been killed, and quantitatively the casualties had proved greater than the training organisation could make good, so that despite such expedients as the transfer of pilots from other Commands, the squadrons were short of their proper establishment of pilots.

74. The long-term measures taken within the Command to ameliorate this situation are described in Part II. In the meantime the position was such as to give some ground for anxiety. Of the 52 operational day squadrons in the Command at the beginning of November, only 26 were, in the most strict sense, first-line squadrons. Another two

squadrons were being kept up to operational strength so that they could act as reliefs in an emergency. The remainder, apart from a half-squadron employed as "spotters," had only a few operational pilots apiece and were suitable only for employment in quiet sectors.

75. The practice of stripping some squadrons of most of their experienced pilots in order to keep others up to strength is clearly indefensible except in a grave emergency, if only because of the invidious distinctions thus created. It had been adopted by my predecessor in the late Summer only because, in the circumstances of that time, it seemed the sole alternative to "telescoping" or disbanding squadrons. As soon as conditions permitted, I abandoned this system, with its categorisation of squadrons as class "A," "B" or "C," and all squadrons in turn were given their chance in the more active Sectors.

76. Although the Battle of Britain is now regarded as having ended on 31st October, 1940, no sharp break was noticeable at the time. Not until some weeks later was it evident that, for the time being, the Germans had abandoned the idea of defeating the Command by a series of mass attacks in daylight. Even then a resumption of these mass attacks in the following Spring or Summer was regarded as inevitable; and in December I asked for a force of 80 day fighter squadrons to meet this situation.

77. The Air Ministry were unable to accept the dislocation of their plan for the expansion of other Commands which the attainment of so large a fighter force by the Spring or early Summer would have entailed, and eventually the strength to which the day fighter force was to expand by April, 1941, was fixed at 64 squadrons.

78. When April came, this figure had been duly reached. However, once again the position was less strong than it appeared on paper. Of the 64 day squadrons shown in the Order of Battle, two and a half were still in process of formation and two, although formed, were temporarily out of the line. The effective strength amounted, therefore, to 59½ squadrons. Many of them had considerably less than their established complement of pilots, and the general level of experience was substantially below that of the previous Autumn.

79. On the other hand, the opposing forces had been weakened numerically by the withdrawal of Units to the Mediterranean and Balkan theatres, and were soon to be reduced still further by

withdrawals to Eastern Germany and Poland in preparation for the campaign against Russia.

80. In the event, of course, the mass attacks made by the Germans in the Summer of 1940 were never to be repeated on a comparable scale, so that after the opening of the Russian campaign, the day fighter force, although still charged with important defensive duties such as the protection of coastwise shipping and the interception of bomber reconnaissance aircraft flying singly, became largely an instrument for containing enemy forces in Northern France and attempting to compel the return of Units from the Eastern Front.

81. But even then the strength of the Russian resistance could not be foreseen; it still seemed likely that the Germans might bring the Eastern campaign to a successful conclusion within a measurable time and then renew their daylight offensive in the West. Accordingly, further additions were made during the second half of 1941 to the day fighter force, which, despite the despatch of seven squadrons overseas in December, reached the end of the year with a strength of 75 squadrons.

(ii) *Operations, November,* 1940, *to February,* 1941.

82. It has been said that, although October 31st, 1940 is now regarded as the last day of the Battle of Britain, the fact that the battle had ended on that day was not apparent at the time.

83. Indeed, the first few days of November, far from constituting a lull, were days of exceptional activity. Nevertheless, 1st November did appear to mark the beginning of a new phase of the offensive. For on that day the Germans turned to a form of attack with which they had opened the battle some months earlier, by sending over bombers and dive-bombers with fighter escort to attack our shipping in the Thames Estuary and the Dover Strait.

84. Before this no mass attacks on shipping had been made for many weeks. The Ju87 dive-bomber, which appeared in substantial numbers on that day, had not been reported in action since 18th August although it now appears that, unknown to the Command and apparently also to the Air Ministry, these aircraft may have been used against shipping at least once in September. When further attacks followed on the next day, it seemed clear that a new stage of the battle had been reached, and on

4th November the Air Officer Commanding No. II Group issued orders which detailed the tactical measures required to defeat this new move.

85. Both before and after the issue of these orders the fighters reported excellent results, especially against the German dive-bombers and the Italian aircraft which took part in a few of the attacks. Doubtless for this reason, the mass attacks on shipping ceased on I4th November and from that date the Ju87 virtually ceased to be employed in daylight operations on the Western Front.

86. Despite its brevity this phase was important, for it brought to a head a conflict between the claims of shipping and the aircraft industry, which had long been a source of anxiety to my predecessor.

87. Since the beginning of the War the primary task of the Command, as laid down in a directive issued by the Air Staff and endorsed by the Chiefs of Staff, had been the defence of the aircraft industry. The Command was, of course, responsible for the air defence of the United Kingdom as a whole, and it also had a somewhat ill-defined responsibility for the fighter protection of shipping close to the coast; but the directive made it quite clear that the aircraft industry had the first claim on the Commander-in-Chief's resources.

88. So far as action by fighters was concerned the defence of the aircraft industry and the general air defence of the country were practically inseparable tasks, for it was an axiom of air defence – though one which the Minister of Aircraft Production was reluctant to accept – that the best way of defending an objective such as a factory was to deploy fighters over the approaches to it rather than concentrate them near the objective itself.

89. This principle did not apply to the protection of shipping. The ships moved mostly on the perimeter of the air defence system and it was seldom possible to be sure of intercepting aircraft which might attack them except by detailing specified fighter units to protect them, either by flying standing patrols near the ships or the adjacent coastline or by assuming an advanced state of readiness at airfields near the coast.

90. The inherent extravagance and relative inefficiency of standing patrols has always been recognised by students of air defence problems; nevertheless there are occasions in which they constitute the only practicable method of defence, and in this case they were the form of

protection which the Naval authorities preferred and for which they constantly pressed.

91. It was not always possible, however, to place our fighters on standing patrol near a convoy without exposing them to the risk of being caught at a tactical disadvantage by the enemy. Another difficulty was that regulations imposed for the benefit of the ships themselves forbade our pilots to come close to the ships, virtually on pain of being fired at.

92. In spite of these difficulties and uncertainties, loyal attempts were made from the beginning of the War to give every practicable assistance to the Royal Navy in their task of safeguarding the convoys whenever they were within range of our fighters. At the same time, attempts were made to place the matter on a more satisfactory basis, and in particular to obtain from the Air Ministry a clear statement of the Command's duties in respect of shipping and the degree of priority to be accorded to them. These attempts culminated at the end of October and beginning of November, 1940, in the receipt of a series of communications from the Secretary of State for Air which gave renewed sanction to the Command's existing practice of protecting convoys whenever possible by holding fighters at readiness rather than flying standing patrols; confirmed that the defence of the aircraft industry was still the primary task of the Command; but added that convoys, and also flotillas and minesweeping craft, must be protected so long as their protection was practicable.

93. This pronouncement did not end my predecessor's perplexities, since – perhaps inevitably – it neither defined the practicable nor assisted him to determine how much of his resources he would be justified in diverting from his primary task to what was clearly a secondary – and yet, apparently, essential – one.

94. The difficulty of the problem will be the more easily grasped if it is borne in mind that, at this stage of the war, practically the whole resources of the Command could have been expended on either of these rival tasks, without glutting the appetite of the Minister of Aircraft Production in the one case or the Naval authorities in the other.

95. The renewal of mass attacks on shipping at the beginning of November brought fresh demands from the Naval authorities. Accordingly, my predecessor again asked the Air Ministry, this time

by means of a formal letter, to clarify their policy in regard to the fighter protection of shipping. In this letter he placed before the Air Ministry a series of proposals based on the practice which had grown up gradually within the Command.

96. No reply to this letter had been received when I took up Command, and I therefore assumed the Air Ministry's tacit consent to the proposals. Henceforward three degrees of fighter protection for shipping were recognized, namely *close escort,* to be given only in special cases and by prior arrangement; *protection,* which meant that specified fighter units were detailed to defend specified shipping units in a given area and over a given period, either by flying patrols or remaining at readiness; and *cover,* which meant that note was taken of the position of the shipping, and arrangements were made to intercept any aircraft which appeared to threaten it.

97. Fortunately the scale of attack against coastwise shipping declined considerably after the middle of November. In the circumstances the Naval authorities remained, to all appearances, reasonably contented with a standard of protection which would probably not have satisfied them had the attacks of early November continued.

98. Only four ships were sunk by air action within fighter range in December 1940, and only two in January 1941, as against eleven in November.

99. Apart from operations against shipping, the enemy continued in November to make the fighter and fighter-bomber sweeps over Kent and Sussex which had been a feature of his operations in October. But in November these sweeps were made at less extreme altitudes than in October, perhaps to avoid causing condensation trails or to reduce the strain on pilots. Consequently they were rather easier to counter. Heavy casualties were inflicted on the enemy's fighters as well as his dive-bombers, and in this month No II Group claimed the highest proportion of enemy aircraft destroyed to their own pilots lost which had yet been recorded.

100. The fighter sweeps virtually ceased in the middle of December and were resumed on a reduced scale in February. In the meantime the Germans made a number of so-called "pirate" raids on aircraft factories and similar objectives. These raids were made by single aircraft, flying

over carefully prepared routes, often in cloudy weather. The German pilots showed great skill in taking advantage of every favourable circumstance of topography and weather to elude the defences. Although the raids were too infrequent to do much harm to our war potential, they caused some anxiety and resulted in great pressure being put on me to provide local fighter protection for the threatened factories.

I0I. The unsoundness of this method of defence, which, if carried to its logical conclusion, would have been impossibly extravagant and would have exposed our fighter force to defeat in detail, needs no elaboration. Nevertheless the Minister of Aircraft Production was so insistent that eventually I devised a scheme whereby a number of aircraft factories were to be allotted fighters for local defence, these to be piloted by the firms' own test pilots. Although put into effect later in the year, the scheme achieved little practical success and was eventually allowed to fall into abeyance. As to its thorough unsoundness from the military viewpoint there can be no doubt; but I think that it may have been worth while at the time simply for its moral effect. Workers who, seeing no fighters in the immediate neighbourhood of their factory, were unaware of the protection that they were receiving from the general air defence system, may have been and probably were heartened by the knowledge that there was a fighter on the factory airfield expressly for the purpose of defending them.

I02. A more important measure taken at this stage concerned the flying of Balloon Barrages. On the outbreak of War the intention had been to fly the balloons at all times. This practice proved so expensive, chiefly because of the large number of balloons carried away or damaged by bad weather, that it soon gave way to a system whereby balloons were close-hauled in doubtful weather and raised only on the approach of hostile aircraft. The disadvantage of this system was that the weather conditions in which balloons were likely to be close-hauled were precisely those in which a "pirate" raider might hope to approach its target undetected, or at least without its purpose being divined in time for the barrage to be raised. Thus, if the barrage commanders interpreted their freedom to close-haul the balloons too liberally, there was a risk that the barrages would be out of action just when they were most needed.

I03. The experience of the "pirate" raids revealed this danger. In consequence I overhauled the machinery which had been set up to inform barrage Commanders of the approach of hostile aircraft, and laid down the principle that some risk of damage to balloons by bad weather must be accepted and that all barrages must be kept flying by day unless there were really strong grounds for close-hauling them.

(iii) *Operations, March to December,* I94I.

I04. At the end of February a decision was reached at the highest level to give absolute priority to the defence of shipping in the North-Western approaches, which was now dangerously threatened by a combination of U-boats and long-range aircraft.

I05. The measures taken in consequence of this decision included the transfer to Northern Ireland of some Units of Coastal Command which had hitherto shared with my Command the task of protecting coastwise trade off the East Coast. Consequently, when announcing this decision on 28th February, the Air Ministry instructed me to provide additional "watch and ward" for this traffic, at the expense, if necessary, of other tasks. At the same time I was warned of the possibility of increased attention by the German bomber force to West Coast Ports.

I06. These instructions were followed on 9th March by a directive which made the defence of the Clyde, the Mersey and the Bristol Channel my primary task.

I07. As has been seen in discussing night operations, I made arrangements in consequence of these instructions to increase the A.A. and night-fighter defences of the West Coast Ports. At the same time, I increased the day-fighter defences of the Bristol Channel and the Mersey by bringing into operation Nos. II8 and 3I6 (Polish) Squadrons, which had been training for some time past at Filton and Pembrey, and by moving the newly formed No. 3I5 (Polish) Squadron to Speke. I did not consider that any addition was necessary to the day-fighter defences of the Clyde, as No. 602 Squadron was already at Prestwick, while Nos. 43, 603 and 607 Squadrons at Turnhouse and Drem could quickly be made available as reinforcements.

I08. On 5th March I gave instructions to all the Fighter Groups to allot a greater proportion of their effort to the protection of shipping and ports. The system of giving "escort", "protection" or "cover" to convoys, according to circumstances, remained in force, but I arranged that "escort"' should be given more generously than hitherto in specially dangerous areas, and that, where attacks were likely to be made without warning, fighters giving "protection" should be kept airborne while the risk continued.

109. The practical effect of these instructions is best shown by a few statistics.

110. In February 1941, my Command devoted to the protection of shipping 443 sorties, or eight per cent. of its total defensive effort by day; in March 2,103 sorties, or eighteen per cent.; and in April 7,876 sorties, or 49 per cent. During April several Squadrons in No. 10 Group each spent more than 1,000 hours of flying time in the discharge of this task. In no ensuing month of 1941 was the proportion of the total defensive effort of my Command by day which was devoted to the protection of shipping less than 52 per cent., the highest proportion being 69 per cent. (in August and again in September). The smallest number of daylight sorties expended on this duty in any month after March was 3,591 (in December) and the largest 8,287 (in May).

111. Besides providing this vastly increased scale of fighter protection, I surrendered from the resources under my operational control, a number of light A.A. weapons for installation in merchant vessels. Other forms of armament now provided for these vessels included rocket projectors and parachute-and-cable projectors.

112. In consequence of these measures the Germans were forced to make an increasing proportion of their attacks under cover of darkness or twilight. After rising to a peak of 21 ships in March, the number of ships sunk by an action in daylight within the radius of fighter action fell to negligible proportions.

113. Various means of protecting ships at night as well as by day were tried, but after dark fighters were at a disadvantage, since their presence tended to confuse the ships' gunners and thus do more harm than good. On the whole the best form of protection for merchant vessels after nightfall proved to be a combination of the A.A. weapons carried by the ships themselves and their escort vessels, and the orthodox use of night-fighters to intercept enemy bombers wherever they could be most conveniently engaged. On the other hand it was important not to

withdraw escorting fighters too early, since the Germans were quick to seize opportunities of attacking ships at dusk. At the end of the last patrol of the day, therefore, fighters had to be landed in the dark. Conversely it was necessary for the earliest patrols to take off long before dawn in order to be in position by "first light."

II4. A word of tribute is due to the pilots who undertook these unspectacular and often tedious duties. Convoy patrols gave pilots comparatively few chances of distinguishing themselves in combat with the enemy, yet they constituted an essential, often exacting, and sometimes hazardous task, since the possibility of a sudden deterioration in the weather, which might render the handling of a high-performance fighter a business requiring all the pilot's skill, was always to be reckoned with.

II5. There remained the problem of protecting shipping outside the radius of action of the short-range fighter. Hitherto my Command had not been concerned with this; but in the Spring of I94I the Air Ministry announced a decision to equip a number of merchant vessels as "Catapult Aircraft Merchant Ships". At least one of these "C.A.M. Ships" would form part of every Atlantic convoy. Each would carry a Hurricane fighter, which could be launched by rocket-catapult on the approach of an enemy aircraft. On completion of his patrol the pilot would either bale out, alight on the sea, or, if, near the coast, make for an airfield on land.

II6. In order to provide the necessary complement of pilots, the formation of the Merchant Ship Fighter Unit began at Speke, in No. 9 Group, early in May I94I. I also made arrangements to train a number of Naval Officers as "Fighter Directing Officers". The latter were to sail in the C.A.M. ships and, making use of radar and radio-telephony equipment, direct the fighters towards approaching German aircraft. The Merchant Ship Fighter Unit absorbed the equivalent of approximately two fighter squadrons.

II7. The Unit despatched its first pilots and maintenance crews on operational service early in June. In August a detachment opened at Dartmouth, Nova Scotia, to administer a pool of replacement aircraft on the Western side of the Atlantic.

II8. German aircraft continued to make occasional "pirate" raids on factories and other objectives in the Spring, but thereafter activity by day, apart from operations against shipping, consisted almost entirely of reconnaissance flights and occasional "tip-and-run" attacks on coast towns in England and Scotland. Offensive operations by German fighters virtually ceased in the early Summer. On a few occasions in the Autumn Me I09 fighters were seen over Kent and Sussex, but the only offensive action worthy of the name which was taken by German fighters in the second half of I94I was on Christmas Day, when two aircraft appeared off the South Coast and opened fire on buildings near Hastings. This was the prelude to a new low-level fighter and fighter-bomber offensive which was to take place in I942.

II9. The interception of "pirate" raiders and other aircraft flying singly was a difficult task, especially in cloudy weather, when problems arose similar to those which surrounded night interception. As early as December I940, the principle of using Beaufighters fitted with A.I. by day in bad weather was established, and as experience grew it became evident that in such conditions the only reasonable chance of success was offered by the same combination of A.I. in the aircraft, and G.C.I. on the ground, as was used at night.

I20. The next step was the use of G.C.I. by day for controlling fighters without as well as with A.I. In August I94I, I made provision for this to be done throughout Nos. I0 and II Groups, although at this stage G.C.I. Stations in No. II Group were not required to keep watch by day in good weather.

I2I. Another step taken about this time was the development of a plan for intercepting aircraft capable of flying at very great heights, which it was thought that the Germans might be planning to use against us. After fighters of No. I0 Group had practised making very high-altitude G.C.I. interceptions of Fortresses of Bomber Command, my staff devised a system of control whereby the country was divided into a number of regions each-containing an "area control" connected with a "central control" designed to co-ordinate their activities. This scheme was to prove useful in I942 when the Germans sent a number of high-flying Ju86 P reconnaissance aircraft over this country.

I22. With the decline in the volume of overland activity by the Luftwaffe towards the end of I94I, I considered it reasonable to contemplate a relaxation of the principles of balloon-barrage control which had been re-affirmed in the Spring. Technical improvements which made it possible to raise balloons to their operational height more quickly than hitherto favoured a change which seemed called for by an increased volume of flying by our own aircraft, to which the barrages were in some circumstances an impediment. In November trials were made with a system whereby a large number of provincial barrages were grounded throughout the 24 hours except when German aircraft were known to be about. It was not until 1942, however, that this system was finally adopted.

(b) *Offensive.*

(i) Operations up to 13th June, 1941.

123. During the Battle of Britain the initiative in daylight operations lay with the Germans. Nevertheless, even before the battle was over a time was foreseen when our fighter squadrons would seize the initiative and engage the German fighters over the far side of the Channel. The necessary operational instructions were drawn up as early as the third week in October, 1940, and revised in the first week of December.

124. By the latter date it was possible to contemplate something more ambitious than a mere pushing forward of fighter patrols, and on 29th November, I instructed the Air Officer Commanding No. II Group to look into the possibility of combining offensive sweeps with operations by Bomber Command.

125. In the middle of December the German fighter force, which had suffered heavy losses since the Summer, virtually abandoned the offensive for the time being. Clearly, the moment had come to put our plans into effect and wrest the initiative from the enemy.

126. Broadly speaking, the plan which we now adopted visualized two kinds of offensive operations. In cloudy weather, small numbers of fighters would cross the channel under cover of the clouds, dart out of them to attack any German aircraft they could find, and return similarly protected. In good weather fighter forces amounting to several squadrons at a time, and sometimes accompanied by bombers, would sweep over Northern France. The code-names chosen for these operations were respectively "Mosquito" (later changed to "Rhubarb," to avoid confusion with the aircraft of that name) and "Circus"; but in

practice it was necessary to restrict the name "Circus" to operations with bombers, and fulfilling certain other conditions which will become apparent as this account proceeds.

127. "Rhubarb" patrols were begun on 20th December, 1940, and provided valuable experience alike for pilots, operational commanders, and the staffs of the formations concerned. I encouraged the delegation of responsibility for the planning of these patrols to lower formations, and many patrols were planned by the pilots themselves with the help of their Squadron Intelligence Officers.

128. It was obvious from the start that in many cases pilots engaged on these patrols would not succeed in meeting any German Aircraft, and they were authorised in this event to attack suitable objectives on the ground. Nevertheless, I considered it important that the primary object of the operation – namely, the destruction of enemy aircraft – should not be forgotten, and discouraged any tendency to give undue emphasis to the attacks on ground objectives.

129. Between 20th December, 1940, and 13th June, 1941, 149 "Rhubarb" patrols, involving 336 sorties, were flown, of which 45 were rendered abortive by unsuitable weather or other extraneous circumstances. German aircraft were seen in the air on 26 occasions, to a total of 77 aircraft, and on 18 occasions were engaged. The destruction of seven enemy aircraft was claimed for the loss of eight of our pilots, and 116 separate attacks were made on a variety of surface objectives, including ships, road vehicles, airfield buildings, grounded aircraft, artillery and searchlight posts, German troops and military camps.

130. Operations on a larger scale began with a sweep off and over the coast of France by a total of five squadrons of fighters on 9th January, 1941. The first operation with bombers followed on the next day, when dispersal pens serving landing grounds on the edge of the Foret de Guines, South of Calais, were attacked. Altogether eleven of these "Circus" operations were executed up to 13th June, the objectives for the bombers including the docks at Dunkirk, Calais and Boulogne, a number of airfields and one industrial plant known to be working for the Germans. In addition more than forty sweeps were made during this period by fighters without bombers.

131. After the first three "Circus" operations an inevitable difference

of view between Bomber and Fighter Commands as to the primary object of these attacks became apparent. The principal aim of my Command was to shoot down enemy aircraft, while Bomber Command, naturally enough, attached more importance to the bombing. It was, however, the view of the Chief of the Air Staff that the bombing of objectives in France with the resources available for operation "Circus" could have no decisive military effect at this stage of the War, and that it would be a pity to spoil the chances of the fighters by making them conform to the requirements of a bomber force bent exclusively on inflicting material damage by bombing, and prepared to linger over the target area for that purpose. On his instructions, the Air Officer Commanding-in-Chief, Bomber Command, and myself, held a conference at my Headquarters on 15th February, 1941, when we agreed that the object of operation "Circus" was to force the enemy to give battle in conditions tactically favourable to our fighters. To compel the Germans to do so, the bombers must do enough damage to make it impossible for them to refuse to fight.

132. The early "Circus" attacks were not always successful in producing these tactically favourable conditions, even after agreement on this point had been reached. This was largely because, in practice, there was still a tendency for our forces to operate too low down. There is no doubt that ideally our lowest fighter squadron should never have flown at less than about 18,000 feet, the highest being somewhere about 30,000 feet. To achieve this it would have been necessary for the bombers invariably to fly at 17,000 feet or more. This was not always practicable, if only because of the time required by the Blenheim bombers then used for these operations to reach that height. Nevertheless, it was thought advisable to lay down this principle as a *desideratum,* and this was done when I issued fresh instructions for operation "Circus" during the third week in February. In the next three operations the bombers flew at heights between 15,000 and 17,000 feet and in the following two at 10,000 and 12,000 feet respectively.

133. Towards the end of May the weather declined, and between 22nd May and 13th June no "Circus" operations were attempted. Up to this point no major fighter battle had occurred, the enemy having been content, on the whole, to pounce on stragglers or otherwise attempt to exploit any favourable tactical situation which might develop. In the

absence of such favourable circumstances he had usually avoided combat. In this sense the operations had proved slightly disappointing. On the other hand, statistically the results were fairly satisfactory so far as they went, the destruction of 16 aircraft and probable destruction of a substantial number of others being claimed for the loss of 25 of our pilots; and much valuable experience had been gained. Moreover, by a combination of "Circus" and "Rhubarb" operations our ultimate object, which was to seize the initiative, harass the enemy, and force him on to the defensive, had undoubtedly been achieved.

134. Besides these "Circus" operations, fighter sweeps, and "Rhubarb" patrols, a series of bombing attacks on shipping and what were called "fringe targets" by aircraft of Bomber and Coastal Commands, with fighter escort, were made between 5th February and 12th June, 1941. These operations differed from "Circus" operations inasmuch as the primary object was not to force enemy fighters to give battle, but to damage or destroy the target. The fighter force therefore conformed to the requirements of the bomber force and did not seek battle unless attacked.

135. Sixteen such operations were undertaken during the period stated, the size of the bombing force ranging from three to eighteen aircraft, and that of the fighter escort from one flight to eight squadrons. A number of combats with German fighters developed, in which we claimed the destruction of one German aircraft for approximately every one of our pilots lost. A considerable volume of fighter-reconnaissance was carried out in connection with these operations.

(ii) Operations, 14th June to 31st December, 1941.

136. On 14th June an improvement in the weather permitted the resumption of the "Circus" offensive, and an operation which had been planned towards the end of May was put into effect. A similar operation on 16th June was followed on 17th June by the most ambitious "Circus" yet attempted. This involved an attack on a Chemical Plant and Power Station near Bethune by eighteen Blenheim bombers, escorted by no less than 22 squadrons of fighters. The enemy fighter force reacted vigorously, and although we lost nine pilots, those who returned

reported a very favourable outcome of their combats. It seemed that the long expected "fighter battle on terms tactically favourable to ourselves" had come at last.

137. On the same day the Chief of the Air Staff instructed me to devise, in consultation with my colleagues at Bomber and Coastal Commands, the most effective means possible of checking the withdrawal of Luftwaffe Units to the East – where the German attack on Russia was imminent – and, if possible, forcing the enemy to return some of the Units already withdrawn.

138. A meeting to discuss this question took place at my Headquarters, on 19th June, and was attended by the three Commanders-in-Chief and members of our staffs and by the Air Officer Commanding No. II Group and two of his staff.

139. We came to the conclusion that the best plan would be to attack objectives within range of escorting fighters – in other words, to intensify the "Circus" offensive. Since the enemy had reacted most energetically so far to the "Circus" against a target near Bethune on 17th June and another against a target in that area on 21st May, we concluded that the industrial area which included Bethune, Lens and Lille was probably his most sensitive spot. By attacking this area it was hoped to induce him to concentrate in North-East France such fighter units as he still had in the West. Bombers without escort might then hope to reach West and North-West Germany in daylight round the flank of the defences, and this in turn might force the enemy to bring back fighters from the Eastern Front in order to defend the Fatherland.

140. As a corollary to this offensive, night attacks would be made on communications in the Ruhr, and shipping attempting to pass through the Straits of Dover would also be attacked. This two-pronged offensive would, we thought, constitute a threat to communications between France and Germany which the enemy could not afford to ignore.

141. These proposals met with the approval of the Air Ministry, and an agreed list of "Circus" objectives was drawn up. It was arranged that aircraft of No. 2 Group, Bomber Command, should attack them in co-operation with fighters of my Command, and, as a secondary task, should also attack shipping and "fringe targets."

142. On 3rd July, the Air Ministry informed me that the formula defining the object of operation "Circus," which had been agreed upon

in February, must be abandoned and that the object must now be "the destruction of certain important targets by day bombing, and incidentally, the destruction of enemy fighter aircraft."

143. Two days later Stirling bombers of No. 3 Group were used in these operations for the first time instead of Blenheims of No. 2 Group. This change, together with the tactical adjustment which the new policy laid down by the Air Ministry made necessary, imposed a slight and temporary handicap on the fighter force. As soon as experience had been gained under the new conditions, a small formation of Stirlings was found to suit the fighters better than a larger formation of Blenheims. Towards the end of the month the Stirlings ceased, however, to be available for "Circus" operations, as Bomber Command required them exclusively for other purposes.

144. During the first few weeks of the intensive period, which may be regarded as beginning on 14th June, our pilots reported outstandingly good results in combat, and early in July it seemed that something like complete ascendancy had been gained over the opposing fighter force. For a short time in the middle of June the German fighter-pilots had offered determined opposition, but they now seemed, as in the Spring, reluctant to engage unless specially favoured by circumstances.

145. The results reported by our pilots during the next few weeks were not quite so good, although still much in our favour, and at the end of July the Air Ministry decided to review the results achieved up to this time.

146. To assess these results with any approach to accuracy was a matter of great difficulty. Our pilots had reported the destruction of enemy fighters in large numbers; but in operations on this scale there is room for much honest error, and even if the claims were accepted at their face value, it was impossible to know how many German pilots had baled out of their damaged aircraft, descended safely by parachute, and lived to fight another day. We believed that our information about the enemy's Order of Battle was good – as, indeed, it subsequently proved to be – but our knowledgeof his capacity to replace losses was scanty. We had good reason to think that so far our attempt to force the Germans to bring back units from the Eastern Front had failed, but suspected that towards the end of July some experienced individual pilots had returned in order to stiffen up the mass. We also had

information which suggested that reserve training units in France had been called upon to replace losses. The effect of the bombing attacks was virtually unknown.

147. As for our own losses, so far as Fighter Command was concerned these had been heavy, but not so heavy as to cause serious embarrassment. Our losses in pilots during the first two weeks of the intensive period had been far lighter than at the height of the Battle of Britain; and our losses in aircraft over the same period not beyond our capacity to replace. Bomber Command had lost fifteen aircraft in "Circus" operations since 14th June, and in the course of a daylight attack on German capital ships at Brest and La Pallice had suffered the rather more serious loss of sixteen bombers out of 115 despatched.

148. Losses like this, incurred when attacking an objective on the left flank of the German defensive system, suggested that attacks round the right flank into Germany might not prove such a practicable undertaking as had been hoped.

149. It was in these circumstances that a conference was held at the Air Ministry on 29th July to decide whether "Circus" operations should continue. It was agreed that some of the conceptions formulated at the conference of the Commanders-in-Chief on 19th June had been too sanguine; the daylight bombing of Germany, in particular, no longer looked like being practicable on any appreciable scale for some time to come, and it was agreed that for the medium and heavy bombers of Bomber Command night operations should normally take precedence over day operations. On the other hand it was equally clear that, if anything was to be done to contain the enemy fighter force in the West, offensive operations by Fighters must not cease; and it seemed to me that the co-operation of a bomber force was necessary to make these operations effective. The Chief of the Air Staff upheld this view; and it was decided that the "Circus" offensive should continue.

150. Up to this time 46 "Circus" operations had been carried out since 14th June. In those six weeks escort and support had been given to 374 bomber sorties and over 8,000 fighter sorties flown. We had lost 123 fighter pilots but it was hoped that many more German fighters than this had been destroyed. In addition, over 1,000 fighter sorties had been flown in support of 32 bomber operations against shipping, including the operations against the German capital ships on 24th July and an

attack on the docks at Le Havre on I9th June. Fighter sweeps without bombers accounted for approximately another 800 sorties, and operation "Rhubarb" – resumed on I6th July after a month's pause – for a further 6I. Altogether the six weeks' intensive effort had meant the expenditure of nearly I0,000 offensive sorties by my Command. This was an impressive total, but to preserve perspective it must be remembered that the effort devoted to defensive purposes was still greater, approximately this number of sorties being expended during the same period on the protection of shipping alone.

I5I. The "Circus" offensive was resumed on 5th August and 26 operations were carried out during the month. Blenheims of No. 2 Group provided the striking force for 24 of them and Hampdens of No. 5 Group for the other two. As the enemy gained experience in repelling these attacks his opposition grew more effective, and the balance of advantage showed a tendency to turn against us. This being so, it was for consideration whether the scale of the offensive should be reduced, if not at once, at any rate as soon as there was any sign of a more stable situation on the Eastern Front.

I52. Apparently the same considerations occurred simultaneously to the Chiefs of Staff. Consequently, the problem was studied at the end of August and beginning of September in the Air Ministry as well as at my Headquarters and at Headquarters No. II Group. The outcome was that, although it was now clear that the offensive had not succeeded in forcing the return of German Units, at any rate in substantial numbers, from the Eastern Front, and could not now be expected to do so, it was generally agreed that it ought to be continued, although on the reduced scale which the declining season was likely to impose in any case. A suggestion made by the Air Officer Commanding No. II Group, which I endorsed, was that, instead of being largely concentrated against the French departments of the Nord and Pas-de-Calais, the attacks should now be delivered over a wider area so as to induce the Germans to spread their fighters more thinly along the coasts of France and the Low Countries.

I53. Accordingly, twelve "Circus" operations were carried out in September and two during the first week of October. The objectives attacked by the bombers included two targets at Rouen, one at Amiens, one at Le Havre and one at Ostend.

154. By this time it was clear that demands from other theatres of war were likely to cause a shortage of fighter aircraft at home for some time to come. For this reason, and also because the weather was growing less favourable and the situation on the Eastern Front had reached a stage at which it was unlikely to be materially affected by the "Circus" offensive, on 12th October I instructed the three Group Commanders concerned with offensive operations that in future "Circus" operations must only be undertaken in specially favourable circumstances, but that a rigorous offensive should be continued against shipping and "fringe targets".

155. Early in October the Hurricane bomber, which had been under development for some time, became available for active operations, and armed with this weapon the Command assumed responsibility for what was called the "Channel Stop". The object of this operation, which hitherto had been performed mainly by Blenheims of No. 2 Group with fighter escort, was to close the area between the North Foreland, Ostend, Dieppe and Beachy Head to all hostile shipping by day.

156. When the Air Ministry decided to reduce the scale of the "Circus" offensive in September, I made arrangements at their instance to increase the scale of scope of operation "Rhubarb". Hitherto pilots had seldom been lucky enough to meet German aircraft, so that their only alternative to inaction had been to make rather aimless attacks on surface objectives. I might have taken advantage of this situation by imposing a rigid "target policy," but up to the present I had judged it inadvisable to lay down any rule which might give the impression that attacks on surface objectives were as important as the destruction of enemy aircraft. Pilots were therefore given a free hand in this matter so long as they observed the general bombardment instructions which reflected the attitude of H M. Government to questions of humanity and international law.

157. Although the relative importance of enemy aircraft and surface objectives as objects of attack had not changed, my staff and I felt that the time had come to subordinate the ideal to the real by recognizing that on nine occasions out of ten our pilots were not likely to see any German aircraft and must either attack surface objectives or do nothing.

158. Accordingly, new instructions for operation "Rhubarb" were

issued in October. Pilots were now to proceed to a selected surface objective, and if they met no German aircraft on the way, that would be their target. If they did meet German aircraft, then the destruction of those aircraft would take priority.

159. Categories from which the surface objectives were to be selected were drawn up by my staff in consultation with the Air Ministry; they included canal barges, railway tank wagons, electrical transformer stations and, for a season, factories engaged in distilling alcohol from beet. On 20th October, H.M. Government withdrew a long-standing ban on the attack of moving goods trains, so that we could now attack tank wagons on the move as well as in sidings.

160. Factories distilling alcohol and a number of other targets on land were also attacked in November by fighter-bombers with fighter escort. The fighter-bombers, which attacked from heights below 5,000 feet, suffered rather heavy losses from A.A. fire in these operations and also in some of their attacks on shipping. In the past the Blenheim bombers used by No 2 Group for these "shipping strikes" had come up against the same difficulty, despite attempts by accompanying fighters to silence the German gunners by attacks with cannon and machine-guns.

161. Meanwhile, on 21st October, I carried the reduction in the scale of the "Circus" offensive a stage further by imposing on No. II Group, as the Group principally concerned, a limit of six such operations a month.

162. In practice there was only one "Circus" after this date. This was carried out on 8th November in conjunction with a high-level fighter sweep and a low-level attack by fighters and fighter-bombers on an alcohol distillation plant. An unexpectedly high wind added to the difficulties of the undertaking, which resulted in the loss of sixteen fighter aircraft and thirteen pilots. Later in the day another aircraft and its pilot were lost in the course of a fighter sweep.

163. Although not by any means disastrous, losses on this scale were unwelcome in view of the shortage of aircraft that was expected to make itself felt during the next few months. I therefore decided to restrict No II Group to three "Circus" operations a month in future instead of six.

164. A few days later the Air Ministry informed me that the War Cabinet had called attention to the desirability of conserving resources

in order to build up strong forces by the Spring of 1942. Since the wording of the letter in which the Air Ministry conveyed this information made it clear that no risks must be taken by pressing attacks in unfavourable weather, I now imposed a still more stringent limitation on the Air Officer Commanding No. II Group, who was asked to undertake no more "Circus" operations without reference to me.

165. The outbreak of War between the United States of America and Japan in December provided still further grounds for conservation, since it was clear that the supply of aircraft from America was likely to cease or at least be greatly reduced for some time to come. Consequently the constant drain imposed by even minor operations could no longer be afforded.

166. In point of fact, wintry weather was already upon us, and after 8th November no more "Circus" operations were carried out. The intensity of our other offensive operations was also substantially reduced as the year drew to its close.

167. A word must be said here about some of the special offensive operations, outside the normal "Circus", anti-shipping, fighter-sweep and "Rhubarb" categories, in which the Command participated between 14th June and the end of 1941.

168. Reference has already been made to Bomber Command's attack on the German warships at Brest and La Pallice on 24th July. In connection with this operation six squadrons of fighters from No. II Group provided escort for two diversionary attacks on Cherbourg and another fourteen took part in a "Circus" against Hazebrouck, while the equivalent of nine squadrons from No. 10 Group gave support over Brest and the Western end of the English Channel. Since only five squadrons of single-seater fighters with long-range tanks were available, the degree of support that could be given over Brest was necessarily disproportionate to the size of the bomber force, which suffered accordingly.

169. On 12th August a force of 54 Blenheims of Bomber Command attacked two Power Stations at Cologne in daylight. A squadron of Whirlwinds accompanied them on the first 135 miles of their outward journey, and on their return journey a wing of long-range Spitfires met them near the Dutch Coast, while another Spitfire wing made a sweep

over Flushing in support. Two "Circus" operations over France by a total of nineteen fighter squadrons and twelve Hampdens of Bomber Command were carried out as diversions. Eleven aircraft of the bomber force despatched against the Power Stations were lost, but Bomber Command expressed themselves as well satisfied with the results achieved. In the light of our subsequent knowledge of the enemy's system of deploying and controlling fighters at that time, it now appears unlikely that diversions so far from the scene of the main attacks could have had any effect on the opposition in that area.

I70. On I8th December and again on 30th December, Bomber Command made further attacks on the German warships at Brest. Fighter support was provided by ten and nine squadrons of the Command respectively. As before, the results were satisfactory from the fighter aspect, but once again the bombers suffered substantial losses.

(iii) Results Achieved by the Offensive.

I7I. It would be unwise to attach too much importance to statistics showing the claims made and losses suffered by our fighters month-by-month throughout the offensive.

I72. The experience of two wars shows that in large-scale offensive operations the claims to the destruction of enemy aircraft made by pilots, however honestly made and carefully scrutinized, are a most inaccurate guide to the true situation. Moreover, the results achieved by an offensive can rarely be judged by a mere statistical comparison of casualties suffered and inflicted. Except when an operation has been launched purely for the purpose of procuring the attrition of the opposing force, a broader view than this must be taken of the strategic purpose and the extent to which it has been achieved.

I73. In the present case the original object was to wrest the initiative from the enemy for the sake of the great moral and tactical advantages bestowed by its possession. Later the Command was entrusted with the task of co-operating with Bomber and Coastal Commands in order, first to prevent the enemy from withdrawing any more flying units from the Western Front after the middle of June, and secondly to induce him to return some of the units already withdrawn by that time. These may be designated respectively objects numbers one, two and three.

I74. Object number one was achieved within a few months of the opening of the offensive. By the Spring of I94I the initiative in major daylight operations had passed from the Germans, who did not subsequently regain it.

I75. Objective number two was also achieved, inasmuch as the Germans did in fact retain on the Western Front throughout the second half of I94I approximately the same first-line fighter force as was present in the late Spring. In particular, two Geschwader of particularly high quality, which might have been usefully employed elsewhere, remained in Northern France to oppose the "Circus" offensive and our other offensive operations. It is, of course, most unlikely that, even without the offensive, the Germans would altogether have denuded the Western Front of fighters: so long as even the threat of an offensive was present, a substantial defensive force would doubtless have been retained in the West in any case. Still, the fact remains that throughout the Summer and Autumn of I94I roughly one third of the total establishment of German first-line single-engined fighters was contained on the Western Front.

I76. Object number three was not achieved. Such moves between East and West as occurred were by way of exchange rather than reinforcement.

I77. To turn to subsidiary achievements, the offensive against shipping went far to deny the Dover Strait to the enemy in daylight, so that the Germans were induced to pass more and more of their shipping at night. This produced favourable conditions for the emploment of naval forces. Furthermore the offensive as a whole, and particularly the "Circus" offensive, brought about a substantial attrition of the German fighter force in Northern France during the Summer, at a substantial cost to ourselves. Such an effect could not, by its very nature, be other than transitory so long as the enemy's means of replacement remained intact; for any slackening of the offensive, whether caused by bad weather or our own losses, would enable him to restore the situation more or less quickly. One of the clearest lessons which was later seen to emerge from this experience was that fighters operating from this country over Northern France could, at a sufficient cost, inflict such losses on the opposing fighter force as would bring about a local and temporary air superiority. But this achievement could, of itself, have no decisive military value: the ability to create this situation was valuable only if means were to hand of exploiting it by some further move capable of producing a decision.

178. This condition was not fulfilled in 1941. Consequently the operations just described, although they achieved two of the three objects for which they were undertaken, and also provided valuable experience, were necessarily indecisive. This was, indeed, recognized as inevitable when the intensified offensive was begun, for its underlying strategy rested upon the assumption that the decisive theatre lay, for the moment, in the East. Nevertheless these operations pointed the way to the events of 1943 and 1944, when the temporary reduction of the opposing fighter force was to be deliberately and successfully undertaken as a necessary prelude to the decisive military gesture which was to lead to the defeat of Germany.

PART II:
STRENGTH, FIGHTING VALUE AND
ORGANISATION.

(a) *Expansion of the Operational Training System.*

179. At the beginning of November 1940, the first-line strength of Fighter Command stood nominally at 67½ squadrons. Outwardly, therefore, the Command was stronger than at the beginning of the Battle of Britain, when only 58 squadrons were available. In reality it was weaker. After several months of intensive fighting some of the squadrons had only a few pilots fully up to operational standards, and the first-line strength was backed by insufficient depth. At the height of the battle the supply of new pilots had failed to keep pace with losses and it had been necessary to improvise measures to avert a crisis.

180. Superficially this weakness was due to the inability of the operational training organisation within the Command to keep pace with our losses. In reality the trouble went deeper. It is true that if there had been a larger reserve of pilots in the Operational Training Units

the decline in the effective strength of the first-line squadrons could have been avoided or postponed. But such a reserve could only have been accumulated in the first place either by withholding pilots from the first line or by increasing the supply from the Flying Training Schools. Neither course was practicable in the circumstances of the time. The real "bottleneck" was the restricted Capacity of the Flying Training Schools, and it was not within my competence to remedy this shortcoming, which was perhaps an inevitable consequence of the change from peace to war.

181. Nevertheless, this experience pointed to the desirability of expanding the operational training organisation so that full advantage might be taken of the increased supply of pilots from the Flying Training Schools which would eventually become available. On Ist November 1940, three Operational Training Units were in existence and the formation of another had been ordered. On 5th November my predecessor proposed to the Air Ministry that two more should be added and that all six should be incorporated in a Fighter Operational Training Group within the Command.

182. The sequel was the formation in December 1940 of No. 81 Group under the Command of Air Commodore F.J. Vincent, D.F.C. On 31st December, No. 81 Group assumed control of the six O.T.U.s then in existence or being formed. During the succeeding twelve months the number of O.T.U.s was increased to eleven. In the course of the year No. 81 Group did 263,604 hours flying and turned out 4,242 pilots – an average of more than 350 a month.

(b) *Pilot Strength of Squadrons.*

183. Nevertheless, the supply of pilots continued to be a source of anxiety during the greater part of the period covered by this account. The nominal establishment of a fighter squadron stood on Ist November 1940 at 26 pilots. In practice the average strength was a little over 22. Heavy calls were already being made on the Command to send pilots to the Middle East, and it was also necessary to find instructors for the expanding operational training organisation and for Flying Training Command. In these circumstances there was little prospect of raising the strength substantially within a measurable time. For this and other

reasons I agreed soon after assuming Command that the establishment of a fighter squadron should be reduced to 23 pilots.

184. In practice even this lower figure was not achieved for many months. By the beginning of January 1941, the average strength had fallen to 21 pilots a squadron, and it remained at this level until well into the Spring. Since it was thought that the Germans were likely to resume mass attacks on the United Kingdom in the Spring or Summer, this situation caused me some anxiety. The view taken by the Air Ministry was, however, that the general strategic situation and the requirements of other theatres of war justified a reduction in the strength of Fighter Command below the level postulated in the previous Winter.

185. I believe that if the Germans had delivered a second daylight offensive in 1941 with such forces as they could then have mustered, Fighter Command would have given as good an account of itself as in the previous Summer. But no second Battle of Britain was fought. Instead, the Germans turned their attention mainly to other theatres, and the initiative in the daylight battle passed to ourselves.

186. As the year went on, the benefit of the expanded operational training organisation and an increased flow of pilots from the Flying Training Schools began to be felt, so that in spite of substantial losses in offensive operations and the posting of many pilots to other Commands, Fighter Command reached the end of 1941 with a surplus of pilots in the squadrons. The proportion of seasoned veterans was, however, inevitably somewhat low, for of those who had survived, many had been claimed by other theatres and others had been assigned for the time being to other duties.

(c) *Number of Squadrons and Fighting Value.*

187. Of the 67½ squadrons in the Command on 1st November 1940, twelve were specialist night squadrons and the rest were primarily day squadrons. Shortly after this, one of the night squadrons – No. 73 Squadron – was transferred to the Middle East.

188. In December 1940, I estimated that for the adequate defence of the country in the coming Spring, 20 night and 80 day squadrons would be required.

189. The Air Ministry were unable to contemplate the provision of

so large a force by the Spring. Instead, an immediate target of 81 squadrons was set and was reached by the beginning of April. This force comprised sixteen orthodox night squadrons (including one "Intruder" Squadron), one aerial mining squadron, and 64 day squadrons. Some of the squadrons had considerably fewer pilots than their establishment, but even so the force was numerically a good deal stronger in first-line and depth than that which had resisted the German onslaught in the previous Summer. On the other hand the general level of training and experience was somewhat lower. A high proportion of the pilots who fought in the Battle of Britain were seasoned men who had fought successfully at Dunkirk or elsewhere over France and Belgium. The majority of these had now been killed or posted away and had been replaced largely by pilots who had been hurried through the O.T.U.s in the Autumn or whose operational training had been hampered by Winter weather.

I90. In respect of equipment the Germans seemed at the time to be drawing ahead. Of the 64 day squadrons in Fighter Command at the beginning of April, I94I, one was equipped with the Spitfire VB and 29 had Spitfires II or Hurricanes II. The rest were equipped with types that were not altogether a match for the Me I09F which the Germans were now using. However, it seems that only about half the opposing fighter force was equipped with this aircraft by the early Spring; the other half still had the Me I09E. In reality, then, there was probably little to choose between the two forces in this respect.

I9I. On the other hand we had made a good deal of progress in the practical application of Radar to the problems of night defence, and although we were not yet capable of inflicting prohibitive casualties on the night bomber, we were in a much better position to deal with this menace than in I940.

I92. At this stage the Command was called upon to provide six squadrons as reinforcements for the Middle East, while one squadron – No. 232 – was temporarily withdrawn for training in Combined Operations. Before Midsummer, however, the formation of seven new squadrons was begun, so that when, in the middle of June, I was required to intensify my offensive campaign over Northern France, the strength was back at the old figure of 8I squadrons.

I93. A further expansion during the second half of the year had always been contemplated by the Air Ministry, although from my point of view it would, of course, have been preferable to have the extra squadrons in the Spring or early Summer. It was now decided that the aim should be to build up the Command, if possible, to a strength of 89 day and 25 orthodox night squadrons by the end of 1941. There was also a new requirement for units to carry airborne searchlights to assist in night interception; for this an additional ten flights, or the equivalent of another five squadrons, were required.

194. In practice the needs of other theatres made it impossible to carry out this programme in its entirety. A decision by the Air Ministry to send Beaufighters overseas, although doubtless justified in the circumstances, reduced the supply of these aircraft at home and so hampered the expansion of the night-fighter force. Again, the desirability of guarding against a German break-through at the Eastern end of the Mediterranean made it necessary for Fighter Command to surrender to the Middle East Command six more day squadrons as a contribution to a force which was to be built up for this purpose. These squadrons left England in December and after they had sailed were diverted, because of events in Malaya, to the Far East. With them went No. 232 Squadron, which had returned to the Command in July after being absent for training in Combined Operations earlier in the year.

195. The outcome was that the Command reached the end of 1941 with a strength of 100 squadrons – comprising 23 night defensive squadrons, two "Intruder" Squadrons, and 75 day squadrons – in addition to ten "Turbinlite" Flights (as they were called), whose function was to carry airborne searchlights. In the event these "Turbinlite" Flights, despite the skill and enthusiasm of those concerned with them, were to accomplish little, for by the time they were used in substantial numbers the enemy had virtually ceased to send over the slower bombers with which they might have coped successfully.

196. Thus by the end of the year, the Command had achieved approximately the strength which I should have wished to have at my disposal in the Spring and Summer. The squadrons had, however, been drained of most of their more seasoned members, and the general level of experience was not so high as I could have wished. But since the size of the opposing force left in the West after the opening of the

German campaign against Russia in June was only about a third of that which had opposed us in I940, there is no doubt that at this stage the country was adequately defended.

I97. On the other hand, the enemy was working on internal lines of communication and could have moved back units from Poland or the Mediterranean more quickly than we could have brought squadrons from overseas. It would be a mistake, therefore, to conclude that we were needlessly strong.

I98. From August to December two Hurricane Squadrons were detached for service on the North Russian Front in No. I5I Wing under the command of Wing Commander H.N.G.Ramsbottom-Isherwood, A.F.C.

(d) *Expansion of Group and Sector System.*

I99. During the period covered by this account a considerable expansion of the Group and Sector system took place, mainly in accordance with plans laid before the period began.

200. The need for new Fighter Groups on the flanks of Nos. II and I3 Groups had become apparent at an early stage of the War. Indeed, a Group in the West of England was visualised in the Command's tentative plans even before war broke out. Accordingly, Nos. I0 and I4 Groups had been formed during the Battle of Britain. Thus by the beginning of November, I940, there were five Groups and 23 Sectors in existence, as against the three Groups and eighteen Sectors required by the approved prewar programme.

20I. Furthermore, on the fall of France it had become necessary to plan a further extension of the air defence system up the West Coast. Clearly another Group would be needed to take charge of the Sectors which were to be formed in Wales and the West Midlands. Accordingly, No. 9 Group began to form at Preston early in August, I940, and on I6th September its first Air Officer Commanding, Air Vice-Marshal W.A. McClaughry, D.S.O., M.C., D.F.C., took up his appointment.

202. At the beginning of November, I940, the development of this Group had not yet reached the operational stage, mainly because the necessary airfields and communications were not yet ready. Consequently, such specific fighter defence as it was possible to allot

to the area for which the Group would ultimately become responsible was still being provided by No. I2 Group.

203. In the middle of October special measures had been set in train to bring No. 9 Group to the operational stage as rapidly as possible. These efforts continued, with the result that on Ist December the Group was able to assume operational control of two of the four Sectors (later increased to five) which were allotted to it. By the middle of March, I94I, No. 9 Group had assumed responsibility for all its Sectors in daylight, although No. I2 Group, with its better night-flying facilities, continued to defend one Sector at night.

204. Before this a Sector, planned before the War, had been established in Ulster, where one fighter squadron was established in the Summer of I940. At the same time improved facilities for operating fighters under the control of No. I3 Group were set up in South-Western Scotland.

205. These measures, of which some had been executed and all had been planned when the period under discussion opened, now bore fruit, and the twin problem of providing adequate defences in the West and protecting shipping between the Rhinns of Islay and the Bristol Channel was much eased in consequence.

206. In the Spring of I94I, there were six operational fighter Groups and 29 Sectors in existence. On the outbreak of war the flanks of the air defence system had stood on the Firth of Forth and Spithead, although there was an outlying detachment at Filton for the defence of Bristol. In a little over eighteen months the system had been so expanded that the Command was now able to operate short-range fighters, under close control, over almost every part of Great Britain and Northern Ireland and adjacent waters, with the exception of North-West Scotland.

207. Towards the end of I940 the Command was asked to form two new Sectors in this last area in order that shipping in the Minches and objectives in the Western Highlands and the Hebrides might be brought under the shelter of the Fighter Command "umbrella". Although this desire was natural, its accomplishment was far from easy. There were no airfields suitable for short-range fighters on the mainland, and the nature of the country made it impossible to construct them. From a practical viewpoint there was much to be said for placing the

responsibility for this distant area on Coastal Command, whose long-range fighters could operate in safety from airfields in the Hebrides. However, the Air Ministry rejected this solution, and eventually a compromise was adopted, whereby short-range fighters to be provided by Fighter Command would be supplemented by long-range fighters, which would be provided by Coastal Command. The latter would operate under Fighter Command when used for controlled interception.

208. The arrangements necessary to put this scheme into effect were not completed until 1942, and it may be noted that in the sequel, although two fighter Sectors were duly set up with Headquarters at Stornoway and Tiree, and remained in being until 1944 and 1943 respectively, it never became necessary to base there any flying units of Fighter Command.

209. In the Summer of 1941 I was instructed to provide an increased scale of defence for certain Naval anchorages in Northern Ireland and it was decided that the number of Sectors in Ulster should be increased to three. This necessitated the formation of a new Fighter Group and accordingly on 25th September, No. 82 Group under the command of Air Commodore G.M. Lawson, M.C., and with its Headquarters at Belfast, assumed operational control of these three Sectors.

210. As a result of these and other developments, the Command comprised, at the end of 1941, seven operational Groups and 33 Sectors – ten more than had existed at the beginning of the period covered by this account.

(e) *Adoption of Section of Two Aircraft and Three-Squadron Wing as Standard Tactical Units.*

211. During the Battle of Britain it became clear that from the tactical viewpoint there was much to be said for sections consisting of two or four aircraft rather than three, which was then the standard number. When a formation broke up in a dog-fight it was desirable that it should break into pairs, so that individual pilots could give and receive mutual protection. A section of three aircraft could not do this.

212. Since administrative arrangements were based on the sub-division of a squadron into two flights each comprising two sections of three aircraft, there was a conflict here between operational and administrative interests. But the tactical superiority of the section of

two or four was so clear that some sacrifice of administrative convenience was obviously justified. Accordingly, it was decided that the section of two aircraft should be adopted, and in the Spring of 1941 a new sub-division of the squadron into two flights each comprising three sections of two aircraft was standardized throughout the Command.

213. Another change which arose out of experience gained in the Battle of Britain concerned the use of Wings consisting of three or more squadrons. Such wings had sometimes claimed exceptionally good results in combat with large enemy formations, and there was a body of opinion which favoured a more frequent use of them. Against this it was argued that in many cases, if time were consumed in assembling large wings, it would be impossible to attack the enemy formations before they reached their targets.

214. A conference to discuss this point was held at the Air Ministry in October, 1940. At this meeting it was confirmed that Wings of three or more Squadrons were the proper weapon to oppose large enemy formations when conditions were suitable; but as to what constituted suitable conditions for their employment no definite decision was reached. A more concrete suggestion was that some of the squadrons in the Command should be disposed and organized in such a way as to facilitate their employment as wings when occasion called for it.

215. It was my view that the best way of defending an objective was not so much to interpose a screen of fighter squadrons between that objective and the enemy, as to shoot down a high proportion of the enemy force sent to attack it, irrespective of whether the objective was bombed on a particular occasion or not.

216. On assuming Command, therefore, I adopted the suggestion made at the conference. Provision was made to operate three-Squadron Wings from a number of Sectors in South and South-East England, and in February, 1941, the sanction of the Air Ministry was obtained for the appointment of Wing Commanders second-in-command at fifteen of the principal Stations in the Command. I arranged that these Officers should concern themselves with the operation and training of the day squadrons in their Sectors and, where there were three-Squadron Wings, Sector Commanders were encouraged to rely on them to lead the wings in battle on important occasions.

2I7. By that time we had turned to the offensive, and it was as an offensive weapon that I had begun to visualise the wings. If there had always been some controversy as to their practical usefulness in defensive warfare, their advantages for offensive use were clear enough. It so happened that no opportunity was to arise in I94I to test them on the defensive, since the Germans did not resume their mass attacks of I940. The wings became, however, an essential weapon of our own daylight offensive, which began to gather weight early in the year and was greatly intensified after the middle of June.

(f) *Growth and Development of Artillery and Balloon Defences.*

2I8. The development of the Group and Sector organisation in Fighter Command was accompanied by a considerable expansion of the artillery and balloon defences.

2I9. I exercised general operational control over these defences and was responsible for their disposition and co-ordination with other means of defence. I was not responsible for their administration nor, in the case of the artillery defences, for training or technical development, apart from the provision (during part of the period) of aircraft for anti-aircraft co-operation and exercises.

220. It is therefore necessary to mention here only a few of the more important organisational and technical changes, such as had a close bearing on the operation or disposition of the defences.

22I. One of the chief of these was the reorganisation of A.A. Command which occurred at the end of I940. Three A.A. Corps were created, the number of A.A. Divisions was increased from seven to twelve and these formations were re-grouped so as to facilitate co-operation with the formations of Fighter Command. Co-operation at the Command level had always been and remained excellent, but to secure effective co-ordination at lower levels was more difficult. Inevitably the requirements and interests of guns and fighters must sometimes conflict, and to achieve a satisfactory adjustment between them through two different chains of command was not an easy problem. This change did not prove to be the final answer to it, but it was a step in the right direction.

222. Other important changes belonging to this period concerned the deployment of search-lights.

223. At this stage of the War searchlights were used to illuminate enemy aircraft for the benefit of both guns and fighters. In 1940 they gave disappointing results in both capacities, partly because they relied on sound locators which could seldom cope satisfactorily with the speed of the modern bomber and partly because clouds and haze often made them ineffective. As a means of overcoming the second difficulty, recourse was had to the expedient of siting them in clusters of three so as to provide a stronger illumination. This arrangement was found in practice to confer no advantage sufficient to compensate for the drawback of wider spacing, and in September, 1941, General Pile and I decided that the lights should be resited singly. In the meantime calculations had been made to determine the size of the area in which a single night-fighter aided by searchlights could hope to effect an interception, and the pattern in which the searchlights were deployed was based on this conception. The method of operating this "fighter box" system of searchlight-aided interception has been described above. (See Part I, paragraphs 63-67).

224. The following table shows the numbers of heavy and light A.A. guns and searchlights deployed on various dates, together with the approved scale on the outbreak of War:

	Heavy A.A.	Light A.A.	Searchlights
Scale approved before the War.	2,232	1,200	4, 128
Outbreak of War.	695	253	2,700
End of 1939.	850	510	3,361
July, 1940.	1,200	549	3,932
May, 1941.	1,691	940 }	See below
December, 1941.	1,960	1,197 }	

225. Although the approved scale of searchlight defence on the outbreak of War stood at 4,128, a total of 4,700 lights was recommended. Early in 1941 the figure of 4,532 lights actually deployed was reached, but subsequently the need for economy in manpower led to a reduction.

226. It was hoped that the introduction of the "U.P." A.A. rocket projector would do much to remedy the shortage of heavy A.A. guns, but the effective use of this weapon by A.A. Command was delayed by a number of factors, including shortages of ammunition. It was not

until the crisis had passed, therefore, that they could be used for home defence in substantial numbers.

227. The total number of balloons authorized to fly and actually flying in the various barrages at the beginning of the period covered by this account was 1,958 and 1,741 respectively. In the Spring of 1941 it was 2, 191 and 2,115. Subsequently a further expansion brought the number of balloons, actually flying at the end of 1941 up to 2,340 – some 900 more than the total initial equipment of the barrages on the outbreak of War.

(g) *Expansion of the Raid Reporting Radar Organisation.*

228. In common with other forms of Home Defence, the Radar Chain of coastal stations of No. 60 (Signals) Group in my Command entered into a phase of intensive expansion to complete early warning radar cover to our Western sea approaches and also to face the problem of the enemy low-flying raiders. During 1941 the constructional programme involved nearly 100 radar stations – equivalent to setting up all the stations of several B.B.C.s within a period of a few months only. The War Cabinet had instructed that the highest priority should be accorded to this effort. The burden of this work fell heavily on the No. 60 Group organisation. Short of technicians for installation, calibration, and maintenance duties, an acute shortage of the crews of radar operators to man the new stations also had to be faced. No. 60 Group nevertheless proved equal to the task, despite the fact that officers, airmen and airwomen in the Group were almost exclusively non-regular personnel of the R.A.F.V.R. without any previous service experience. 1941 was certainly the most hectic year of its existence.

229. The expansion of the Group and Sector organisation in my Command permitted a decentralisation of the radar reporting system. Originally all radar information had been reported to a Filter Room at Command Headquarters at Stanmore, the tracks of aircraft being passed on to the Operations Room. At the end of 1940 it was possible to decentralise the Stanmore Filter Room and split it between Fighter Groups throughout the country. This was also in accord with a decision to delegate the Air Raid Warning control from my Command Headquarters to the Headquarters of each Fighter Group. Owing to the heavy telecommunications re-arrangements involved, the complete

decentralisation of radar reporting was not achieved until September, I94I.

230. Together with the great expansion of the radar chain and the decentralisation of the reporting system, there was an equivalent technical progress, not only with regard to equipment, but also in the handling and filtering of the radar information. The Operational Research Section of scientists at my Headquarters, working in conjunction with No. 60 Group, made many improvements to extract the maximum benefit from the available radar information. This application of the scientific method to the use of weapons through the medium of Operational Research Sections began first on problems within Fighter Command and subsequently spread throughout all Royal Air Force Commands.

(h) *Organisation to resist Invasion.*

23I. Any account of the activities of the Command during this period would be incomplete without some mention of the preparations made to resist an invasion of the United Kingdom.

232. The roles to be played by the Home Commands in this eventuality had been laid down in broad terms by the Air Ministry in the Summer of I940. It was then assumed that an invasion would fall into three distinct phases, beginning with a large-scale offensive against Fighter Command, continuing with an airborne invasion, and culminating in the seaborne invasion by which alone the Germans could hope to bring about our final defeat. It was thought that the third phase might in turn fall into three sub-phases, namely the preliminary concentration of shipping, the voyage across, and the attempt to establish a bridgehead. The Air Staff plan laid down the functions to be performed by the Command in each of these phases and sub-phases.

233. On consideration it seemed doubtful whether all these phases and subphases would be distinguishable in practice, and in devising arrangements to carry out the spirit of the plan, it was thought inadvisable to allot different roles to the squadrons during the voyage across on the one hand and the attempt to establish a bridgehead on the other. Instead, the various tasks which might devolve upon the fighter force in consequence of these activities by the enemy were grouped together in order of importance. Priority at this stage was given to the

protection of our Naval forces against enemy bombers.

234. As experience grew, other modifications were made, and throughout the period it was necessary to keep constantly under review an elaborate complex of operational and administrative arrangements. It would be tedious to describe these arrangements in detail, more especially since, after the success of the Command during the preliminary phase of the German invasion plan in 1940, it never became necessary to repeat the experience or deal with subsequent phases.

235. One aspect of these preparations called, however, for something more concrete than planning. This was the defence of airfields against various forms of attack.

236. Before the War the necessity for providing for the local defence of our airfields against anything more than sabotage or low-level air attack had not been grasped. Consequently, when it was realised that airfields in this country might be seized by airborne troops or landing parties, measures had to be improvised.

237. The general defence of the country against enemy troops, whether airborne or seaborne, was, of course, the responsibility of the Army. On the other hand it had always been recognised as a principle in the Royal Air Force that Station Commanders were responsible for the local defence of their Stations. At the same time it was obviously essential that local defence schemes should fit into the general defence plan and be approved by the appropriate military Commander.

238. On the outbreak of War the resources of the Royal Air Force were insufficient to give adequate protection even against the dangers that were then foreseen, and help had to be obtained from the Army. Detachments of troops were supplied to undertake Station defence duties jointly with Royal Air Force personnel.

239. The consequence was a bewildering division of responsibility for defence against the various forms of attack that might be made; and it was quite clear that in many cases Station Commanders, who were answerable to their Group Commanders for the local defence of their Stations, would in practice be unable to exercise effective control over the miscellaneous units nominally at their disposal.

240. This problem was common to all Home Commands, but it was particularly urgent in Fighter Command, since fighter stations were a

vital element in the defence system and some were peculiarly vulnerable by reason of their geographical position.

24I. In the Spring of I94I the experience of Crete focussed attention on this problem, which was already causing me grave anxiety, and various means of improving the situation were suggested. Few of these were of practical value, for although the necessity of securing the fighter bases was now generally recognised, the resources at my disposal were not adequate or suitably organised to effect the desired object.

242. It has already been pointed out that the local defences of Stations were manned partly by Army and partly by Royal Air Force personnel. This in itself was a source of weakness, particularly since there was a tendency for the Army detachments allotted to these duties to be changed at frequent intervals. The creation of a Royal Air Force defence force had begun in I940, but towards the end of that year a halt was called to the scheme, pending a decision as to whether theWar Office or the Air Ministry should ultimately bear the responsibility for defending the Stations.

243. To enable Station Commanders to dispose their resources to the best advantage, each was given the services of a Station Defence Officer. Many of the Officers appointed by the Air Ministry to fill these posts were past their first youth and lacked the resilience of mind and body required for service in the field.

244 There was a great need, in addition, for officers to be attached to the Staffs of the Fighter Groups for the purpose of inspecting Station defences and supervising training. After repeated requests, the services of one Army Officer at each Group were obtained; but the instructions given to these officers by the military authorities limited them, in effect, to the performance of liaison duties for which they were not needed.

245. Finally, there was in many cases a fundamental difference of view, which written orders seemed powerless to adjust, between Station Commanders and the Army Officers responsible for the general defence of their area, as to their respective duties and responsibilities in relation to their superiors and to each other.

246. There is no doubt that the problem was a difficult one, involving many issues which it lay outside the competence of a Commander-in-Chief to decide and on which even now no opinion can be properly

expressed. The solution eventually adopted, which led to the formation of the R.A.F. Regiment, did not become effective until after the close of the period with which this account is concerned. In the meantime the system of divided responsibility continued with all its evils. Consequently, despite much hard work at all levels, many Stations in my Command were far from impregnable throughout those months of 1941 when enemy landings by sea or air were at least a possibility.

4

AIR CHIEF MARSHAL SIR RODERIC HILL'S DESPATCH ON AIR OPERATIONS

BY AIR DEFENCE OF GREAT BRITAIN AND FIGHTER COMMAND 1944-45

AIR OPERATIONS BY AIR DEFENCE OF GREAT BRITAIN AND FIGHTER COMMAND IN CONNECTION WITH THE GERMAN FLYING BOMB AND ROCKET OFFENSIVES, 1944–45

The following report was submitted to the Secretary of State for Air on 17th April, 1948, by Air Chief Marshal SIR RODERIC HILL, *K.C.B., M.C., A.F.C., Air Marshal Commanding, Air Defence of Great Britain, Royal Air Force, from* 15th *November,* 1943, *to* 15th *October,* 1944, *and Air Officer Commanding-in-Chief, Fighter Command, Royal Air Force, from* 15th *October,* 1944, *until the end of the war in Europe.*

PART I:
PRELIMINARY

(a) *Command and Higher Organisation of A.D.G.B. and Fighter Command.*

I. Towards the close of 1943 the Allied fighter, tactical reconnaissance, and tactical bomber forces in the United Kingdom began to assemble under the command of Air Chief Marshal Sir Trafford Leigh-Mallory, K.C.B., D.S.O., in readiness for the landing in northwest Europe which was to take place in the spring. The name of the Allied Expeditionary Air Force was given to this combination, part of which was set aside, under my command, for the defence of the British Isles.

2. The Force that I commanded was functionally a successor to Fighter Command. For the time being, however, that name was abandoned, and the old name of Air Defence of Great Britain was revived.

3. I commanded Air Defence of Great Britain from its inception on I5th November, I943, until I5th October, I944, when the Allied Expeditionary Air Force was disbanded. My Command then became an independent one and the name Fighter Command was restored. Thereafter, I held the post of Air Officer Commanding-in-Chief, Fighter Command, until the end of the war with Germany.

4. Throughout the life of Air Defence of Great Britain, and especially after the landings in Europe had begun, the control over my handling of operations which was exercised by Air Chief Marshal Leigh-Mallory in his capacity as Air Commander-in-Chief was little more than nominal. His energies were engrossed by offensive tasks. As the Armies in France pushed on, these tasks made it necessary for him to spend more and more of his time on the Continent. I was obliged, therefore, with the Air Commander-in-Chief's knowledge and consent, to deal directly with the Air Ministry, the British Chiefs of Staff, and governmental bodies on many points of operational policy. On the other hand, Air Chief Marshal Leigh-Mallory continued to exercise, through his staff, a close supervision over certain aspects of administration, especially those affecting personnel.

5. On I7th November, I943, I received from Air Chief Marshal

Leigh-Mallory a directive which defined the functions of my headquarters "under the general direction of the Air Commander-in-Chief" as follows:-

(*a*) To be responsible for the air defence of Great Britain and Northern Ireland.

(*b*) To command Nos. 9, I0, II, I2, I3, 60 and 70 Groups and exercise operational control of fighters in Northern Ireland.

(*c*) To control operationally the activities of A.A. Command, the Royal Observer Corps, Balloon Command, "and other static elements of air defence formerly controlled operationally by Fighter Command".

(*d*) To conduct "defensive and offensive operations which involve the use of squadrons of both A.D.G.B. and T.A.F. as heretofore under instructions issued to both headquarters, until fresh instructions are issued".

(*e*) To develop air interception methods and apparatus for eventual use in A.D.G.B. and other theatres.

6. The reference in article (*d*) to offensive operations by squadrons of the Tactical Air Force was hardly more than a convenient fiction. Its purpose was not so much to place these operations under my control, as to prevent them from prematurely absorbing the energies of the Air Officer Commanding and staff of the Tactical Air Force, to the detriment of their more important task of preparing for the coming events in Europe. Although the operations were planned and their execution ordered from the headquarters of No. II Group, which was part of my command, they were supervised until the I5th March, I944, by the Air Commander-in-Chief himself. Thereafter they were directed by the Air Marshal Commanding, Second Tactical Air Force (Air Marshal Sir Arthur Coningham, K.C.B., D.S.O., M.C., D.F.C., A.F.C.). This arrangement was typical of a series of complex relationships brought about by the special circumstances of the time. In effect it meant that the Air Officer Commanding, No. II Group (Air Vice-Marshal H.W.L. Saunders, C.B., C.B.E., M.C., D.F.C., M.M.), while he never ceased to be constitutionally my subordinate, acted for certain

purposes as the agent first of Air Chief Marshal Leigh-Mallory and later of Air Marshal Coningham.

7. My real task, then, was that set out in articles (*a*), (*b*), (*c*) and (*e*) of the directive, and as much of article (*d*) as related to operations by formations under my own command. In short, it was primarily a defensive one. Although squadrons of A.D.G.B. were to play their part in operations over France during the assault phase of the European operations, the Overall Air Plan issued by the Air Commander-in-Chief showed that my most significant responsibility even in that phase would be to stand guard over the base. Obviously, we were approaching a stage at which the needs of the offensive must have priority. The directive of the l7th November emphasized the need for economy in defence "in order to make greater provision for offence", and called upon me to suggest changes in organisation with this need in mind. My problem, in fact, was to ensure, with limited resources, that the United Kingdom was securely defended from air attack as a base for the great operations by land, sea, and air which were being planned.

(b) *Resources Available.*

8. In the circumstances some "rolling up" of the Group and sector organisation seemed clearly justified. No. I4 Group, in the north of Scotland, had already been amalgamated with No. I3 Group before the time of my appointment. During the next few months I secured approval for further reductions. By 6th June, I944 (D Day) the number of operational fighter Groups had been reduced to four and the number of active sectors from I9 to I4 – less than half the number in existence at the end of I94I. Still further reductions were made later.

9. Plans for translating the Air Commander-in-Chief's directive into practice were worked out by my staff and his in consultation. The basic strength of A.D.G.B. was fixed at ten day-fighter and eleven night-fighter squadrons. In addition six night-fighter squadrons earmarked for allotment to No. 85 Group – a Group formed for the purpose of defending the overseas base after the land forces should have advanced beyond the lodgment area – were to be put under my command for the time being. So long as I retained them I should be responsible for the night-fighter defence of the lodgment area as well as the United Kingdom and the waters between. Similarly, six day fighter squadrons

intended ultimately for No. 85 Group were to be put at my disposal to enable me to keep German reconnaissance aircraft at bay, and perform a number of other tasks arising directly out of the situation created by the coming assault. Finally, another fifteen day-fighter squadrons were to remain nominally in A.D.G.B., but be lent to the Second Tactical Air Force for the duration of the assault phase. Only in an emergency would these squadrons revert to my operational control before the end of that phase. It was agreed, however, that if a serious situation should arise, the Air Officer Commanding, No. II Group, would be justified in using any part of his uncommitted resources (other than American units) for the daylight defence of his Group area. A few aircraft of the Royal Navy would also operate under my control.

I0. Thus, the maximum number of Royal Air Force, Dominion and Allied squadrons on which I was expected to call – including the fifteen squadrons lent to the Second Tactical Air Force – would be 48: rather less than half the number that had been considered necessary for the defence of the United Kingdom at the end of I94I, when the main theatre was in Russia.

II. However, since I94I much progress had been made in the technique of fighter interception, especially at night. The German Air Force, on the contrary, was known to have lost a great deal of its hitting power since those days, and its offensive spirit had declined. Furthermore, great advances had been made in the technical methods and equipment on which the "static" elements of the air defence system relied. Against this I had to reckon with the psychological difficulty of maintaining the fighting spirit of men placed on the defensive while their opposite numbers were fighting an offensive battle. But despite this handicap, and despite the numerical limitations of the forces under my operational control, it was my opinion that the air defences would give a good account of themselves against any attack by orthodox weapons that the German Air Force might deliver.

(c) *Appreciation of the General Situation before the start of the German Flying Bomb Offensive.*

I2. From the time of my appointment until the beginning of the flying-bomb offensive a week after D Day, coming German air operations against the United Kingdom were expected to consist of attacks by both orthodox bombers and "secret weapons". The two kinds of attack might be delivered either at different times or, more probably, together.

I3. Numerically the capabilities of the German bomber force could be judged with a fair degree of accuracy from our knowledge of its strength and disposition. To foresee how this potential hitting power would be used in practice was more difficult. For planning purposes we assumed that orthodox opposition to the landings in France might take the form of minor daylight attacks along the south coast before D Day, and attacks on the beaches and anchorages thereafter. Night attacks on a scale of 50 long-range-bomber sorties a night for two or three nights a week, increasing to I50 sorties a night for very short periods, seemed likely to occur during the weeks preceding D Day. Ports, concentration areas, and concentrations of shipping would be the most probable targets. Slightly heavier attacks would be possible if the enemy should decide to punctuate nights of maximum activity by comparatively long intervals of quiet.

I4. Whether the German bomber force would operate on a major scale in daylight on D Day or the succeeding days was problematical. If it did, the enemy would doubtless choose the most favourable tactical conditions by attacking targets on his own side of the Channel.

I5. All this was theoretical. But our estimates were based on practical experience. While our plans were going forward, the enemy came to our assistance by disclosing part of his hand. Early in I944 the German bomber force delivered the series of night attacks on London and other towns which has been called the "baby Blitz". Thanks to the watch which we were able to keep on its movements, these attacks did not take us by surprise. The defences were ready. Although the Germans used their fastest bombers, which stayed over England only for brief periods, we were able to inflict a higher rate of casualties than the German night defences could inflict on our bomber forces during their long flights over Europe. Moreover, the navigation, target-marking, and bombing of the Germans when faced by our defences proved to be very poor. Thus the attacks were extraordinarily ineffective. After this experience, I felt confident that we should be able to deal with any attempt by the German bomber force to interfere with the concentration of the Anglo-American land, sea, and air forces in preparation for the assault.

I6. The threat from "secret weapons" was harder to assess and more disturbing. By the autumn of I943 a mass of information collected over a long period was beginning to convince even the most sceptical that the Germans were preparing novel means of air attack. When I took up my appointment in the early winter, few men in responsible positions doubted that those means included both a long-range rocket of some kind and also some form of flying missile, or pilotless aircraft. Evidence received a few weeks later made us virtually sure that certain new constructions in northern France, which we called "ski sites" [1] were meant for the launching of missiles of the latter kind against this country.

PART II:
THE FLYING BOMB CAMPAIGN.

(a) *Appreciation of the Threat up to "D" Day and Plans to meet it.*

I7. Against a flying missile launched from the ground two methods of defence were possible. We might conduct a "defensive offensive" against the places where the missiles were made or stored, the constructions required for their launching, or the means of communication between those places. Some or all of these objectives might be attacked either separately or in combination, provided that we were able to locate them. Alternatively, or in addition, we might try to render the missiles harmless once they had been launched.

I8. Early in December, I943, the Chiefs of Staff decided to pursue the first method while exploring the possibilities of the second. Accordingly, on the 5th December the Second Tactical Air Force and the American Ninth Bomber Command began a series of bombing attacks on the "ski sites". The Strategic Air Forces, in the shape of our own Bomber Command and the American Eighth Bomber Command, also contributed their quota. By the end of the year, 3,2I6 tons of bombs had been dropped on the sites – about the weight that fell on London in an average fortnight during the night "Blitz" of I940-4I. So far as the Air Ministry could judge, the effect of these attacks was to "neutralize" twelve sites and seriously damage another nine. But since

88 "ski sites" had been located by this time, and the existence of another 50 was suspected, the neutralization of all the sites with the bombing resources that could be spared from other tasks seemed likely to prove a long-drawn business.

I9. Meanwhile, early in December the Air Commander-in-Chief, at the instance of the Air Ministry, had instructed me to study the problem of defending the country against attack by pilotless aircraft and draw up plans accordingly. By way of assistance I was given an "appreciation" which embodied what was known at the time about the missiles that the Germans were getting ready to use against us. According to this document, these missiles flew at something between 250 and 420 m.p.h. and a height which might be anything from 500 to 7,000 feet. I was to assume that an attack by two missiles an hour from each of I00 sites might begin in February, I944.

20. These estimates of speed and height were so broad as to make detailed planning difficult; but on 20th December, in reply to a questionnaire from my staff, the Air Ministry committed themselves, with reservations, to the opinion that the missiles would probably fly at an average speed of 400 m.p.h. and a height of 7,500 feet. Later these estimates were reduced to 350 m.p.h. and 7,000 feet, and still later to 330 m.p.h. and 6,000 feet. The views of the Chiefs of Staff as to when the attacks were likely to begin were also modified from time to time, as our bombing offensive against the "ski sites" got under way.

2I. In devising measures to deal with pilotless aircraft, my staff and I worked in close touch with General Sir Frederick A. Pile, Bart., G.C.B., D.S.O., M.C., General Officer Commanding, Anti-Aircraft Command, and his staff, who helped in the preparation of all detailed plans which involved guns and searchlights as well as fighters.

22. It was clear at the outset that to prepare a detailed plan of defence would take several weeks. I therefore decided to submit a preliminary outline plan. I took as my point of departure the fundamental proposition that a pilotless aircraft was still an aircraft, and therefore vulnerable to the same basic methods of attack. Of course, as there was no crew, such an aircraft could not be made to crash by killing the pilot; on the other hand, it would be incapable of retreat or evasion, except, perhaps, to a very limited extent.[2] Nevertheless, if the missile should prove in practice as fast as was believed at first, the performance of the

fighters on which we normally relied would be inadequate.

23. However, on balance, and considering the uncertainty of our knowledge, it would clearly have been unjustifiable to exclude any of the normal methods of defence which we were accustomed to use against piloted aircraft. Accordingly, I recommended in my outline plan, which I submitted to the Air Commander-in-Chief on the 16th December, that aircraft, guns, searchlights, and balloons all be deployed against pilotless aircraft in such a manner as to avoid causing mutual interference. I pointed out, however, that the missiles might well prove too fast for our fighters, and in any case would make difficult targets for A.A. gunners. I recommended, therefore, that the bombing offensive against the installations in France be continued with the utmost vigour. I also asked to be kept informed of the progress made by two committees which had been set up at the Air Ministry to investigate the possibility of radio and electro-magnetic counter-measures.[3]

24. During the second half of December General Pile and I completed our detailed plan on these lines. On the 2nd January I submitted the plan to the Air Commander-in-Chief, who approved it and submitted it in turn to higher authority. Meanwhile, the Allied bomber offensive against the "ski sites" was achieving good results and the likelihood of imminent attack seemed to be receding. On 22nd January the Chiefs of Staff came to the conclusion that the date by which we must be ready for attacks by pilotless aircraft to begin could safely be put back until the 1st March; later they postponed it still further, until the middle of the month. Since intensive preparations for the European operations were due to begin on the 1st April, we were thus faced with the possibility that the first use of pilotless aircraft by the Germans might coincide with these preparations, or even with the assault itself.

25. Hence, by the time the Chiefs of Staff came to examine the detailed plan it had been overtaken by events. Circumstances now called for a modified plan which would provide simultaneously for defence against pilotless aircraft and the needs of the offensive. Early in February the Chiefs of Staff asked that such a plan should be prepared. In the meantime, General Pile and I received authority to proceed with the administrative arrangements which would have to be

made before any deployment on the lines laid down in the existing plan could be ordered.

26. During the next few weeks, therefore, we overhauled our plan and devised a modified version of it which aimed at meeting the threat from pilotless aircraft mainly with resources not directly required for the European operations. We called this modified version the "Concurrent Air Defence Plan for 'Overlord' and 'Diver'", or, more briefly, the "'Overlord'/'Diver' Plan"[4]. I submitted it to the Air Commander-in-Chief towards the end of February. After receiving his approval, it was approved in turn by the Supreme Commander and the Chiefs of Staff. On 4th March I gave instructions for copies of the plan to be sent to the Commands and Groups which would be directly concerned if it were ever put into effect.

27. With minor amendments, this was the plan on which we acted three months later, when the attacks began. Some account of it, and of its relationship to the earlier detailed plan out of which it grew, must therefore be given at this stage. Such an account may provide, perhaps, an insight into the conditions in which a major defensive operation of this kind has to be contrived. For in such cases a Commander must not only take into account a number of factors, political as well as military and logistic, which are governed by the capabilities of his own side; he must also reckon, first and last and all the time, with what the enemy may have up his sleeve.

28. Both the "Overlord/Diver" Plan and the earlier plan were based on the fundamental principles postulated for the first outline plan of the 16th December. But some of the assumptions which had been made when the original outline and detailed plans were made were modified by altered circumstances or fresh intelligence by the time the second plan was made. For example, as I have already pointed out, estimates of the performance of the weapon which we had to counter differed from time to time. Again, as the bombing offensive against the "ski sites" began to achieve its purpose, the Air Ministry revised their estimates of the probable scale of attack. But the broad concepts which determined the general nature of our defensive measures remained substantially unchanged.

29. Much, therefore, remained common to both plans. Both plans, for example, relied on the ability of our existing radar chain stations to

detect pilotless aircraft in the same way as they detected ordinary aircraft. After taking expert advice I had come to the conclusion that the stations would be able to do this, and that we should be able to tell pilotless from piloted aircraft by "track behaviour" – that is to say, the characteristics of their flight as interpreted by the radar responses. Similarly, members of the Royal Observer Corps would, presumably, be able to recognise pilotless aircraft by their appearance and the noise they made.[5] All that was required under this head, then, was to lay down a procedure for reporting pilotless aircraft by the means already in existence, and instruct all concerned in its use. For this both plans provided.

30. Again, at every stage the principal object that General Pile and I had in mind was the defence of London, which was the target threatened by the vast majority of the "ski sites". Secondly, we had to provide for the defence of Bristol, which was threatened by a smaller number of "ski sites" near Cherbourg. Thirdly, we had to bear in mind the possibility that, as a counter-measure to our preparations for the European operations, pilotless aircraft might be used against assembly areas on the south coast, and particularly round the Solent.

3I. In each case, fighter aircraft were to be the first line of defence. For the defence of London the arrangement envisaged in both plans was that whenever an attack in daylight seemed imminent, fighters of No. II Group would patrol at I2,000 feet on three patrol lines, 20 miles off the coast between Beachy Head and Dover, over the coastline between Newhaven and Dover, and between Haywards Heath and Ashford respectively. Once an attack had begun, additional aircraft would patrol these lines at 6,000 feet. At night, fighters would patrol under the control of G.C.I., Type I6, and C.H.L. radar stations, and would be reinforced, if necessary, by further aircraft under Sector control.

32. At Bristol and the Solent the facts of geography promised a longer warning and more room to manoeuvre as well as a lighter scale of attack. Consequently I did not propose to fly standing patrols for the defence of those places. Should attacks appear imminent, however, fighters would be held ready to intercept by normal methods.

33. Under both plans, guns and searchlights would provide the next line of defence, and would, of course, become the first line of defence

if at any time the state of the weather or any other factor prevented the fighters from operating. For the defence of London, General Pile and I proposed under the first plan to deploy 400 heavy A.A. guns in folds and hollows on the southern slopes of the North Downs, where their radar equipment would be liable to the minimum of interference from "jamming" by the enemy. We also proposed to use 346 light A.A. guns, to be deployed largely on searchlight sites, and 216 searchlights. In front of Bristol we proposed to put 96 heavy A.A. guns and 216 light A.A. guns, with 132 searchlights. Thirty-two heavy A.A. guns, 242 light A.A. guns and a smaller number of searchlights would defend the Solent.

34. It was here that the most important differences between the two plans lay. The original plan called for the deployment of a grand total of 528 heavy and 804 light A.A. guns and more than 350 searchlights. Clearly, to muster as many guns and searchlights as this would not be easy. General Pile and I proposed to find half the required number of heavy A.A. guns from within Anti-Aircraft Command by depleting the defences of places not directly threatened by pilotless aircraft; the other half would have to come from the resources of 21 Army Group and Home Forces, and thus would consist very largely of guns already earmarked for the European operations. In the case of light A.A. guns and also of searchlights, 21 Army Group would have to provide an even higher proportion of the total.

35. Some risk would, of course, be involved in removing guns from places like Oxford, Birmingham, and the Clyde to defend London, Bristol, and the Solent against flying bombs. But the risk was one that I felt we should be justified in taking, since otherwise there was no possibility of finding the resources required for adequate defence against the threat from pilotless aircraft as we conceived it in December, when the plan was made.

36. By February, when we came to draw up the revised plan, the position had changed. Virtually every gun and searchlight that could be spared would shortly be needed for the European operations; and it was essential that the "Diver" defences should make the smallest inroad on the "Overlord" resources that was compatible with an adequate scale of defence. Fortunately, the success of the bombing attacks on the "ski

sites" held out the hope of achieving an adequate scale of defence on cheaper terms than had seemed possible two months earlier.

37. Accordingly, General Pile and I carefully reviewed this part of our original plan. We came to the conclusion that substantial savings in both guns and searchlights could and must be made. We therefore proposed to reduce the number of heavy A.A. guns to be deployed on each of the sites in the belt defending London from eight to four. This would save 208 guns. We hoped that by the time the attacks began 128 American 90 mm. guns, using electrical predictors and a new type of radar called S.C.R.584, might be available to replace a corresponding number of our 3.7-inch guns with their mechanical predictors and G.L. Mark III radar; for there was every indication that the S.C.R.584 and electrical predictors would be particularly effective against pilotless aircraft. But as this equipment had yet to arrive from the United States and crews be trained in its use, we dared not count on it: we therefore prepared alternative plans to cover either contingency. We also proposed to reduce the number of light A.A. guns in front of London from 346 to 246.

38. No reduction in the number of heavy A.A. guns defending Bristol seemed possible, and we decided to leave this figure at 96. In view of the great need of light A.A. guns for "Overlord" we proposed, however, to reduce the strength of these from 216 to 36. We also proposed to do without searchlights in this area, other than those provided by the normal layout. Under the revised plan, all the Bristol guns, both heavy and light, would have to be withdrawn by "D" Day; but we hoped that by that date the threat to that city, never very serious, would have been neutralized by bombing.

39. As for the Solent, fortunately that area would, in any case, be heavily defended against orthodox air attack during the final stages of preparation for "Overlord". In these circumstances no special "Diver" deployment would be needed there, apart from a few searchlights. We visualized, however, a possible re-disposition of the "Overlord" guns to fit them for a dual role. Here, again, there would be a substantial saving.

40. Under the original plan, balloons would provide a third line of defence for London. For this purpose I had originally proposed to put a permanent[6] barrage of 480 balloons immediately behind the guns on

the high ground between Cobham (Kent) in the east and Limpsfield in the west. It so happened that I was already seeking authority from the Chiefs of Staff to reduce the balloon defences of the country by 500 balloons: by appropriating this saving to defence against pilotless aircraft the problem of providing the "Diver" barrage could be solved. As these balloons were not needed for "Overlord" there was no need to alter these proposals in the revised plan.

4I. It was, then, with the revised plan ready for action that we awaited the beginning of the German attacks. To say that this plan represented a compromise between the requirements of "Overlord" and those of "Diver" would not be strictly true; for the defence of the base against "Diver" was itself an essential "Overlord" requirement. But it provided at once the largest appropriation that could be spared for the job, and the smallest that was likely to be effective against the threat which was then foreseen. The number of guns to be deployed, in particular, was no more than a bare minimum. In the circumstances it was impossible for us to budget for more guns; but we took care to frame the plan in such a way that the numbers could easily be increased if further guns should happen to become available. I also took the precaution of pointing out that if the pilotless aircraft should fly between 2,000 and 3,000 feet instead of at the greater altitude expected by the Air Ministry, the guns would have a very awkward task, for between those heights the targets would be too high for the light anti-aircraft guns and too low for the mobile heavy guns which at that time could not be traversed smoothly enough to engage such speedy missiles.

42. In the event, the threat which materialised in the summer was to prove a very different one from that foreseen in February when the plan was made. This was not only because the height at which the pilotless aircraft flew had been over-estimated, but also because the forecasts of the enemy's capabilities with which the Air Ministry provided us were based on knowledge which was incomplete in one important respect. Consequently, when the attack developed we soon found that we needed not only more than the 288 heavy and 282 light A.A. guns postulated in the revised plan, but more than the 528 and 804 respectively for which we had budgetted in our original, superseded plan.[7]

(b) *The Eve of the Attacks*

43. Ironically enough, the emergence of this undiscovered factor which upset our calculations was due to the very success with which we had bombed and neutralized the "ski sites". By the end of April most of the sites had been rendered unfit for use. Although the Germans repaired some of them, from that time onwards there were never at any time more than ten "ski sites" in a state to fire.

44. Fortunately for them, the Germans soon realised how vulnerable the "ski sites" were, and began to build other launching sites which were more carefully hidden and harder to destroy. By simplifying the plan of construction and using pre-fabricated parts, they were able to complete these new sites very quickly.

45. Since the armistice the Germans have told us that they began this new programme of construction in March 1944. However, it was not until the 27th April that the first of the "modified sites", as we called them, was seen on a reconnaissance photograph. By the middle of May twenty such sites had been located, and by the 12th June the number had risen to 66. Forty-two were aligned on London and the rest on Bristol or south-coast ports.

46. The "modified sites" made difficult bombing targets. When Typhoon bombers carried out an experimental attack on one of them on the 27th May the site proved hard to find and the results were poor. Besides being small and well concealed, the sites comprised few buildings at which bombs could be aimed. Unlike the "ski sites", they seemed to be intended as launching points and nothing more. The conclusion was that any stocks of pilotless aircraft held locally would not be kept on the sites themselves, but stored elsewhere or dispersed in the wooded country amongst which all the sites were placed.

47. At least partly for these reasons, we made no further attacks on the "modified sites" until after the Germans had begun to launch missiles from them. Meanwhile, the officers at the Air Ministry and elsewhere who were responsible for offensive counter-measures were debating whether to attack certain other constructions, usually referred to as "supply sites". They believed that these constructions had something to do with the storage or maintenance of pilotless aircraft; but they were not sure. Nevertheless, two attacks on one of the sites

were made about the end of May. From that time onwards, little was done to hinder the enemy's final preparations for the offensive.

48. This state of affairs was a natural consequence of the awkwardness of the "modified sites" as bombing targets, and our uncertain knowledge of the enemy's plans. I believe, however, that aligned with these causes was a psychological factor. It must be remembered that for many months past the chief threat had seemed to come from the "ski sites". The use of our bomber forces against the "ski sites" had therefore been felt as a necessary, but still an unwelcome diversion of effort at a time when interest was focussed on the coming European operations. To the officers responsible for directing offensive operations the success of the attacks on the "ski sites" must have come as a great relief. In the circumstances, they would have been hardly human if they had not been more reluctant than perhaps they realised to recognise that the neutralization of the "ski sites" had not averted the menace after all.

49. I think, therefore, that at the end of May and in the first half of June the threat from the "modified sites" was under-estimated, not in the sense of a failure to apprehend it intellectually, but in the sense that it was not felt as keenly as the original threat from the "ski sites" six months earlier. If it had been, I do not doubt that the "modified sites" would have been attacked as vigorously then – despite their shortcomings as targets – as they were a few weeks later, when "Diver" had begun.

50. Whether this would have had much effect on the subsequent course of events is another matter. The question is one to which no final answer is possible. My own opinion is that a well co-ordinated series of attacks on the "modified sites" during the weeks immediately preceding the "Diver" campaign would have been worth making, but that nothing short of the destruction of all the sites would have prevented the Germans from using their new weapon sooner or later. Nor does my belief that the menace of the "modified sites" was under-estimated necessarily imply that I think the omission to attack the sites was wrong in the light of the knowledge available at the time. Even if their dangerousness had been fully realised, there would still have been strong arguments against attacking them. And while it is easy to be wise after the event, at the time there was no means of knowing how

imminent the danger was. On the contrary, until some 36 hours before the first pilotless aircraft was launched, such intelligence as was available suggested that the "modified sites" were not likely to be used for several weeks.[8]

5I. The fact remains that during the first half of June the Germans were able to press on with their preparations to bombard us with pilotless aircraft, virtually unmolested by our bomber forces.

52. At that stage, one of the tasks of my Command was to prevent German reconnaissance aircraft from approaching the areas where our forces were concentrating. In this we succeeded even beyond our expectations. Partly on this account, the landings in Normandy early on the 6th June achieved complete tactical surprise. Even on subsequent days, when the Germans had had time to appreciate what we were doing, air opposition was far from energetic. Naturally enough, the Air Commander-in-Chief and his staff were jubilant, and had little time or inclination to think of pilotless aircraft.

53. It was equally natural that my staff and I, with our defensive preoccupations, should not entirely share this optimism. It seemed to us that things were going almost too well. So much was at stake for the enemy that we dared not believe he would let us have everything our own way. We could not help suspecting that he still had something up his sleeve.

(c) *The Attacks: First Phase* (I3th *June to* I5th *July*).

54. Events were soon to substantiate our doubts. Shortly after midnight on the night of the I2th-I3th June the German long-range guns opened fire across the Channel. In this there was nothing novel; what was unusual was that for the first and last time during the war, a town some miles from the coast was shelled. Eight rounds fell at Maidstone, one at Otham, two-and-a-half miles to the southeast, and twenty-four at Folkestone. The bombardment doubtless achieved its purpose, inasmuch as it gave some people the impression that a novel weapon was being used and tended to create an atmosphere of uncertainty and rumour. At least one Me.4I0 flew over the London area during this phase and was shot down by anti-aircraft fire near Barking.

55. At 0400 hours the shelling stopped. A few minutes later an observer on duty at a Royal Observer Corps post in Kent was passed

by an aircraft which made "a swishing sound" and emitted a bright glow from the rear. In common with all his colleagues, he had been briefed to recognise pilotless aircraft; and in accordance with his instructions he shouted "Diver". The missile continued over the North Downs "making a noise like a model-T Ford going up a hill" and fell to earth with a loud explosion at Swanscombe, near Gravesend, at 0418 hours. During the next hour three more of the missiles came down at Cuckfield, Bethnal Green, and Platt (near Sevenoaks) respectively. No casualties were suffered except at Bethnal Green, where six people were killed and nine injured; in addition a railway bridge was demolished.

56. The attack then ceased for the time being. I came to the conclusion that so small an effort did not justify the major re-disposition of the anti-aircraft defences required by the "Overlord-Diver" Plan. The Chiefs of Staff agreed. I therefore gave orders that the plan was not to be put into effect until we could see more clearly what was going to happen. In the meantime the existing defences were authorised to engage pilotless aircraft on the same terms as ordinary aircraft. I had already arranged that a visual reconnaissance of the most likely launching areas should be flown; and at the instance of the Air Ministry several attacks were made on three of the so called "supply sites" on the 13th, 14th and 15th June. These absorbed the whole of the bombing effort that could be spared from other tasks. Accordingly the "modified sites" still went unmolested, although it is now known, and was strongly suspected at the time, that the missiles had been launched from sites of this class.

57. At 2230 hours on the 15th June the attacks were resumed on a much heavier scale. During the next twenty-four hours the Germans launched over 200 pilotless aircraft – or, as we soon began to call them, flying bombs or "doodle bugs" – of which 144 crossed the coasts of Kent and Sussex and 73 reached Greater London. Thirty-three bombs were brought down by the defences, but eleven of these came down in the built-up area of Greater London.[9]

58. Clearly we were confronted on the morning of the 16th June by a situation very different from that of the 13th. I was of the opinion that the time to execute the "Overlord-Diver" Plan had now come; and in the course of the day the Chiefs of Staff agreed that this should be done.

That afternoon I attended a "Staff Conference" over which the Prime Minister and Minister of Defence presided. One of the decisions then reached was that, in consultation with General Pile, I should redistribute the gun, searchlight, and balloon defences "as necessary to counter the attacks". Another was that for the time being the guns inside the London area (as well as those outside) should continue to engage flying bombs. We abandoned this arrangement two days later, after experience had cast doubt on the assumption that most of the bombs that were hit exploded in the air.

59. Before going to the conference I had given orders for deployment of the "Diver" defences to begin. By the early hours of the 17th June the first A.A. regiment to move had taken up its new positions and the deployment of the balloon barrage had also begun. When drawing up the plan we had calculated that deployment would take eighteen days to complete and that it would be wiser to allow twenty-five days; the Air Ministry had expected to be able to give us a month's warning. In the event we had received no warning at all, apart from that provided by the Germans themselves on the 13th June. In the circumstances it was imperative that we should get the job done quickly. The original time-table went by the board. Thanks to the administrative arrangements which had already been made and to remarkable feats by both Anti-Aircraft Command and Balloon Command, the whole of the planned deployment was virtually complete by the 21st June, only five days after the issue of the order to deploy.

60. All this time the attacks were continuing at the rate of about 100 flying bombs a day. Our fighters were bringing down about thirty per cent. of the bombs and the static defences some eight to ten per cent.; but more than half the bombs which crossed the coast were getting through to Greater London. I soon realised that a scale of static defence which might have been adequate against such attacks as eight or ten "ski sites" could have delivered was not going to suffice against the effort of which the "modified sites" were showing themselves capable. In consultation with General Pile, therefore, I arranged for the gun defences to be substantially reinforced. By mid-day on the 28th June 363 heavy and 522 light A.A. guns were in action. Further weapons, including light guns manned by the Royal Air Force Regiment, anti-aircraft tanks of the Royal Armoured Corps, and rocket projectors, were

either in position or on the way. I also arranged for the strength of the balloon barrage to be doubled.

6I. Meanwhile Tempest V, Spitfire XIV, Spitfire XII, Spitfire IX, Typhoon, and at night Mosquito aircraft of No. II Group had been in action against flying bombs since the beginning of the main attack. As we have seen, their rate of success at this stage amounted to about thirty per cent. of all the bombs which crossed or approached the coast. On the I6th June I had issued orders defining their area of patrol as the Channel and the land between the coast and the southern limit of the gun-belt, and prohibiting them from passing over the gun-belt except when actually pursuing a flying bomb. I soon found that in good weather the fighters were much more successful than the guns, which were badly hampered by the fact that the flying bombs did not fly at the height of 6,000 or 7,000 feet previously estimated by the Air Ministry, but at that very height of 2,000 to 3,000 feet which we had always realised would make the gunner's task most difficult.[10] On the other hand, when the weather was bad, poor visibility hampered the fighters, and in these conditions the guns were likely to prove the more effective weapon. Accordingly, I arranged on the I9th June that in very good weather the guns should abstain from firing in order to give the fighters complete freedom of action. Conversely, when the weather was bad, the guns would have freedom of action and no fighters would be used. In middling weather fighters would operate in front of the gun belt and enter it only when pursuing a flying bomb. When a fighter entered the gun belt for this purpose the guns would, of course, withhold their fire; otherwise the guns inside the belt would be free to fire up to 8,000 feet. Outside the gun belt gunfire was prohibited in these circumstances, except that light A.A. gunners linked to the communications network might open fire on targets they could see, provided no fighters were about.

62. These rules for engagement, which I ordered to be codified and issued to those concerned on the 26th June, were intended to prevent mutual interference between guns and fighters. For reasons which I shall explain later, they did not altogether achieve this aim. But before coming to this question it will be appropriate to review the progress of the German attacks and of our counter-measures up to the date in the

middle of July when the question of an important change in our defence plan came to a head.

63. The scale of attack for the first two weeks was, as I have said, of the order of 100 bombs a day. After a period of deliberation at the outset, the authorities responsible for offensive counter-measures embarked on a series of bombing attacks on the "modified sites". A number of sites were neutralized, but the number remaining was always sufficient to have launched a scale of attack several times greater than that which we actually experienced. In other words, the factor limiting the German effort was not the number of sites available, but something else – most probably the rate at which the flying bombs could be supplied to the sites. It was therefore arguable that the attacks on the "modified sites" amounted to locking the stable door after the horse had been stolen, and were a waste of effort. The authorities decided to continue the attacks, however, in order to harass the launching crews and thereby reduce their efficiency. I cannot say how far that object was achieved, since my staff were never able to establish any statistical relationship between the bombing attacks on the "modified sites" and the rate or quality of the enemy's fire. The Germans have told us since the armistice, however, that the bombing of the "modified sites" made little difference to them.

64. At the same time the authorities responsible for offensive counter-measures appreciated that the factor limiting the scale of attack was probably supply. Information from intelligence sources cast increasing doubt on the relevance of the so-called "supply sites" and showed that the key-positions were probably certain underground storage depots situated in limestone quarries in the valley of the Oise and an abandoned railway tunnel in Champagne. Successful bombing attacks were made on several of these depots, and in two instances were followed by a noticeable decline in the scale of attack. In both cases, however, the effect was only temporary. Apparently the Germans were able to improvise other channels of supply. Hence, while I was much relieved by the offensive counter-measures undertaken by the Tactical and Strategic Air Forces, I realised that they were not likely to put a stop to the German attacks. The loss or preservation of thousands of lives, much valuable property, and a substantial productive capacity, would turn on our ability to provide an effective system of defence for

London with the resources under my operational control. At that time our land forces in France had not advanced beyond the lodgment area: the capture of the launching sites in the imminent future seemed very doubtful. The flying-bomb attacks might well go on for many months.

65. And in fact the attacks continued at the same rate of roughly I00 flying bombs a day until the end of the first week in July, when the effort fell for about ten days to an average of less than 70 a day. This decline may have been partly due to good weather, for the Germans usually saved their biggest efforts for days when the weather was likely to hamper the defences. But I incline to the view that it was largely the result of a specially successful attack on one of the main storage depots which was made by Bomber Command on the night of the 7th July. Except during this same second week in July, when both good weather and a reduced scale of attack helped our fighters to shoot down a higher proportion of the bombs than usual, about half the bombs that crossed the English coast went on reaching Greater London. In sum, during the five weeks which ended at sunrise on the I5th July, just under 3,000 flying bombs came within the compass of the defensive system.[II] Our fighters shot down rather more than a tenth of them into the sea, and a few were brought down into the sea by A.A. fire or fell into it of their own accord. Of the remaining 2,500 odd which crossed the coast, fighters, guns, and balloons respectively destroyed or brought down about half over the land, fighters claiming ten and guns four casualties to every one claimed by the balloon defences.

66. Outwardly these results were not too bad. Nevertheless, I was far from satisfied that the defences were working properly. In the first place, an average of 25 bombs a day was still reaching Greater London. The overall average since the beginning of the attacks amounted to nearly 40 bombs a day. London had endured heavier bombing than this in I940; but for various reasons an intermittent drizzle of malignant robots seemed harder to bear than the storm and thunder of the "Blitz". Nor were the material results of the bombardment inconsiderable. Between the I3th June and the I5th July it killed about 3,000 people, seriously injured I0,000, and irreparably damaged I3,000 houses. Although no objectives of vital importance to the war effort were hit, many public buildings such as churches, hospitals, and schools appeared in the casualty list.

67. Secondly, although the performance of the defences as a whole had improved continuously since the beginning of the attack, and although the fighters had done particularly well during the last two weeks, I saw many signs that the limit of improvement with our existing methods had been reached. I was reluctantly convinced that unless some radical change was made, the future was more likely to bring a slow decline than further progress.

68. The circumstances which led me to this view can only be understood by reference to the special problems of the various arms of the defence. In order to gain an intimate knowledge of those problems I had decided early in the attack to share in the fighter operations as a pilot, using various aircraft in turn. Personal experience convinced me that the first problem confronting the fighters was the speed of the bombs, which was rather greater than we had expected before the attacks began.[12] The fastest aircraft I had were a wing of Tempest Vs and a wing of Spitfire XIVs. These could not be everywhere at once. One of my first moves, therefore, was to obtain the Air Commander-in-Chief's consent to my borrowing at first a flight and later a wing of Mustang IIIs from the Second Tactical Air Force. These aircraft were very fast at the height at which the bombs flew and made a valuable contribution to the improved results achieved by the fighters after the first week in July. By the 15th July I was using a total of thirteen single-engined and nine twin-engined (Mosquito) squadrons against flying bombs. Six of the Mosquito squadrons alternated between this work and operations over the lodgment area, two of them doing bomber-support work as well. I found that, while some pilots took readily to the work of shooting down flying bombs, the majority preferred shooting down enemy aircraft over France. To instil enthusiasm for the novel and impersonal business of shooting at pilotless missiles, and ensure that pilots were not kept long enough at the task to make them stale, was not the least of my anxieties.

69. In order to get as much speed as possible, I arranged that aircraft which were to be used exclusively against flying bombs should be stripped of their armour and all unnecessary external fittings, and that their paint should be removed and their outer surfaces polished. The engines were modified to use I50-octane fuel and accept a higher boost

than usual. In this way we managed to increase the speed of some of the single-engined fighters by as much as 30 m.p.h.

70. Even with these modifications the fighters had only a small margin of speed over the flying bombs. Nevertheless they did have a margin. It was reported that a demonstration by a German pilot with a captured Spitfire had convinced Hitler that our fighters could not catch the flying bomb. This was true of the Spitfire V, and almost true of the Spitfire IX; but it was not true of the Spitfire XIV or the Tempest. Even so, these aircraft had no more than a fractional superiority. Hence the problem was essentially one of time and space. For interception over the sea we used a method of close control from radar stations on the coast, or alternatively a method of running commentary. At best the radar chain could give about six minutes' warning before the flying bombs reached the coast; but in practice the time available to the fighters over the sea was always less than this, not only because of inevitable time-lags but because we dared not risk our modified aircraft on the far side of the Channel, where they might be surprised by German fighters. Later the Royal Navy were to come to our assistance by providing a chain of small craft which operated at three mile intervals seven miles off the French coast, carrying observers who warned our pilots by means of signal rockets and star-shells that flying bombs were on their way. This improvised system was in the final stages of development about the time when the main attack came to a close.

7I. Over the land we used the method of running commentary from radar stations and Royal Observer Corps Centres, supplemented by various devices such as signal rockets, shell-bursts, and searchlight beams, for indicating the approach of flying bombs to patrolling pilots. The weakness of this method was that sometimes several pilots would go after the same flying bomb, leaving other bombs to slip through unmolested. However, there was nothing else we could do, for the absence of low-looking radar made close control over the land impracticable.

72. The majority of the flying bombs crossed the coast between Cuckmere Haven and St. Margaret's Bay. The distance thence to the southern edge of the gun belt was in most places about 30 miles. The flying bombs covered this distance in five minutes. Five minutes, then,

was the time available to the pilot of an overland fighter to select his target, get within range of it, and shoot it down, unless gunfire had been restricted or he took advantage of the rule which allowed him to enter the belt in pursuit of his quarry. In this case he would have an extra minute or so before he reached the balloon barrage. Thus there was rarely time for a stern chase unless the pursuer started with a substantial advantage in height. On the whole the most effective procedure was to fly on roughly the same course as an approaching bomb, allow it to draw level, and fire deflection shots as it passed, being careful not to fire when it was closer than 200 yards lest it should explode in the air and blow up the attacker.[13] The hot gases emitted by a bomb immediately in front of the fighter made a steady aim difficult, so that short bursts and frequent aiming corrections were required. Usually several bursts were needed to inflict enough damage to explode the bomb or bring it down. Another method useful on occasions but hardly suitable for general adoption, was to get close beside the target and tip it over by inserting the wing of the fighter underneath that of the bomb and then raising it sharply.

73. Thus, in many respects the fighters had a stiff task. That which faced the guns was, if anything, more awkward still. Theoretically, pilotless aircraft ought to have made ideal targets for anti-aircraft artillery, since they flew on courses which could be accurately predicted from the data on which the technical devices normally employed had been designed to work. For the first time in the war, the gunners were presented with targets that could not dodge. In practice this advantage was outweighed by the speed of the missiles and the critical height at which they flew. They were too high and went too fast to make good targets for light A.A. guns, but were too low and crossed the field of vision of the heavy A.A. gunners too swiftly to give adequate time for the radar and predictors to be used and the guns be laid by hand. These difficulties could be minimised so far as the heavy guns were concerned by replacing the mobile guns used in the original "Diver" deployment by static guns which could be electrically elevated and traversed and were fitted with improved fuse setters and other devices which made them quicker to operate and more accurate. Unfortunately the static guns required concrete emplacements which took some time to instal. A steel mattress, known as the "Pile Mattress," which was devised by

the R.E.M.E. detachment at Anti-Aircraft Command provided a way out of the difficulty; and the task of replacing the mobile guns by static guns was started towards the end of June.

74. Another change which General Pile found necessary at an early stage was the removal to higher ground of the radar sets belonging to the heavy guns. At the start these were placed in hollows because the "Overlord/Diver" Plan had been made in anticipation of attempts at "jamming" by the enemy. Successful bombing attacks during the "Overlord" preparations had, however, virtually deprived the Germans of this resource, and so it was possible to move the sets to more exposed positions in which the contours of the ground caused less interference.

75. Another variation from the plan concerned the light guns. Originally these were to have been deployed on searchlight sites, but after the attacks had begun, General Pile came to the conclusion that better results would be achieved by concentrating them in front of the heavy gun belt. He also found that by linking troops of four guns each to a heavy-gun predictor and G.L. radar set he could use the light A.A. guns against "unseen" as well as "visual" targets.

76. Towards the end of June we began to receive the S.C.R.584 radar sets and improved predictors which we had been eagerly expecting since February. These two items of equipment were destined to contribute very largely to the ultimate success of the guns. An intensive training programme which had to be organised with such resources as could be spared from operations was, however, indispensable before they could be used on any considerable scale.

77. With the balloon barrage the problem was largely the arithmetical one of achieving a sufficient density to give a reasonable chance of success. We found, however, that in practice the theoretically computed rate of success was not always attained: somehow more bombs slipped through the barrage than should have done so according to the laws of probability, if our assumptions were correct. One difficulty was that the "double parachute links"[14] used to arm the balloon cables in normal barrages had not been designed to cope with aircraft travelling much faster than 300 m.p.h. For this reason we did not arm the cables of the balloons deployed during the first few days of the attack. But we soon came to the conclusion that an imperfect arming device was better than none; and by the 21st June all cables were armed. I received a large

number of suggestions for increasing the effectiveness of the barrage in other ways, such as by adding "whiskers", nets, kites, and other forms of drapery. Many devices of this kind were tried, and some were of value, but as most of them increased the physical difficulty of handling the balloons in one way or another, I had to adopt a somewhat cautious attitude lest the best should prove the enemy of the good.

78. A slight re-disposition of the barrage proved necessary in order to prevent bombs which penetrated to its northern edge from being brought down in built-up areas. The notion of keeping the balloons up in all weathers – which was contained in the original "Overlord/Diver" Plan but afterwards abandoned – was considered a second time after the attack had begun, but once more found impracticable. We therefore used a system of control which was less flexible than that used for normal barrages, but served its purpose adequately. In order that our pilots should not lose their lives by colliding with the barrage we perpetrated a pious fraud on them by allowing them to believe that the balloons would fly continuously.

79. So much for the problems that confronted the individual arms of the defence and the chief measures taken to solve them. There were, of course, many smaller problems with which I have not space to deal. But the biggest problem of all was not confined to one arm: it was of wider consequence and consisted in securing the right kind and degree of co-operation between guns and fighters. Since in a sense these were rival weapons, the task had always been a troublesome one from the early days of the war; nevertheless, so far as operations against orthodox aircraft were concerned, with experience a satisfactory working solution had been found. During the "Baby Blitz," for example, the co-operation between guns and fighters had been most satisfactory. I found, on the other hand, that as the Germans must have intended, the novel problem presented by the flying bomb created a host of new difficulties. For example, it was sometimes hard for a pilot to realise that he was approaching the gun belt in time to avoid infringing the rule against entering it. Conversely, gunners in the belt who were engaging a flying bomb did not always realise in time that a pilot was legitimately entering the belt in pursuit of this or another missile, and would go on firing to the peril of the pilot's life. The crews of the guns on the coast and elsewhere outside the gun-belt were in a

still more difficult position, for except in bad weather they always bore the onus of ensuring that no fighters were about before they could open fire. In the excitement of the moment, when the attention of the gunners was concentrated on their targets, it was only too easy for a fighter travelling at six miles a minute to slip unnoticed into the field of fire. Consequently numerous infringements of the gun-belt by fighters, and many unintentional engagements of our fighters by the guns, were reported, especially in middling weather when guns and fighters were simultaneously in operation. Charges and counter-charges mounted; and with deep misgiving I began to sense a rising feeling of mutual distrust between pilots and gunners.

80. I felt very strongly that this state of affairs could not be allowed to continue. If the causes of friction were not removed, the situation would inevitably grow worse. As the first four weeks of the attack went by, the overall achievement of the defences improved. To all appearances, the machine was growing more efficient. But this improvement brought me scanty satisfaction. I knew that the point would soon be reached at which this friction would become the limiting factor, and no further improvement would be possible. Looking further ahead, I realised that, whatever temporary advantages our existing practice might bring, we could not afford to sacrifice the spirit of co-operation between gunners and pilots which had been steadily built up in the past.

81. I came to the conclusion that the only solution was to give guns and fighters freedom each in their own sphere. On the I0th July, therefore, I decided to prohibit fighters from entering the gun-belt, whatever the circumstances, after the I7th July. At a conference held to discuss this change, General Pile pointed out that an obvious corollary to it was to move all the guns inside the belt, so as to have them all in one place and provide both guns and fighters with clearly-defined spheres of operation. The logic of this argument was irrefutable; and I agreed to examine detailed proposals for moving all the guns into the belt except a few which would remain on the coast to act as "markers".

82. The great advantage of the principle of separate spheres of operation for guns and fighters was that it would lessen the chances of misunderstanding by creating a clear-cut situation. It would also ease

the task of the gunners by giving them a free hand in their own territory. Not the least important point was that when not in action they would always be free to train, whereas under the existing arrangements when gunfire was restricted and fighters were operating they were condemned by the presence of our aircraft to an enervating inaction. At the same time the change would reduce the field of action open to the fighters. In order that the necessity for making this sacrifice might be clear to pilots, I instructed my Deputy Senior Air Staff Officer, Air Commodore G.H. Ambler, C.B.E., A.F.C., to prepare an explanation which could be circulated to lower formations. At this stage no question of changing the geographical position of the gun-belt had been raised.

(d) *The Re-deployment of the Guns (mid-July).*

83. Nevertheless, there were strong arguments in favour of such a move. Originally we had deployed the guns on the North Downs largely because the "Overlord/Diver" Plan had been drawn up at a time when jamming of our radar by the Germans was a threat which could not be neglected. The desire to reduce this threat or minimise its effects if carried out had done much to dictate this choice of situation. Now, as we have seen, by D-Day successful bombing of German wireless and radar stations had virtually removed the possibility of jamming. This fact and its significance had not become fully apparent until after deployment had begun.[15] Consequently we had carried out the deployment as planned, though shortly afterwards, as already related, General Pile had taken advantage of the absence of jamming to move some of the heavy-gun radar sets to better and more exposed positions within the original deployment area.

84. By the middle of July what had been a reasonable hope a month before had become a practical certainty. Clearly, little danger from jamming need be feared. Consequently there was no need to hide the guns and their radar sets away in folds of the Downs if a better position could be found for them. Was there such a better position, and where was it?

85. These questions were far from simple. The guns could not really be considered in isolation; they were part of a defensive system, which also included fighters, searchlights, and balloons. If, nevertheless, the subject was approached from the sole viewpoint of the operational

effectiveness of the guns, there was much to be said for moving the gun-belt away from the Downs and putting it on the coast. In this position the gunners would get a better view of their targets; the hampering effect of ground echoes on their radar sets would be reduced to a minimum; and they would be able to use shells fitted with "proximity fuses", which were potentially more effective than normally-fused shells, but could not be used inland because they were dangerous to life and property. Added to this was the important point that if the guns were on the coast the majority of the bombs that they brought down would fall harmlessly into the sea.

86. From a more general aspect there was one weighty argument against moving the guns to the coast. To do so would split the operational area of the fighters into two, and thus, to all appearances, infringe the principle of separate and clear-cut spheres of operation for guns and fighters which I was anxious to establish. Up till then the fighters had been by far the most successful weapon against flying-bombs; out of 1,192 bombs which had been destroyed or brought down up to sunrise on the 13th July, they had accounted for 883. No move which threatened to impair their effectiveness was to be undertaken lightly. Still, to a great extent interception over the sea and interception over the land were already separate problems. Hence in practice the disadvantage of having three spheres of operation for guns and fighters instead of two would not be so great as it looked at first sight.

87. These considerations struck Air Commodore Ambler with great force when he sat down to write the explanation of the new rules for engagement which I had instructed him to prepare. The correctness of the decision to banish fighters from the gun-belt was not in question; nor did he dissent from the proposal to put all the guns in one place. But he felt that to bring this about by moving the guns already on the coast to the North Downs was only going half-way. What was wanted was to put all the guns together in the place where they could function best. In his considered view this meant adopting the opposite course, and sending forward the guns already on the Downs to join those on the coast. The disadvantage of splitting the operational area of the fighters would, he thought, be more than outweighed by the increase in effectiveness of the guns in the latter position.

88. To clarify his mind, Air Commodore Ambler incorporated his

arguments in a formal appreciation. Armed with this document, he came to see me on the morning of the l3th July and put his views before me.

89. His arguments convinced me that unless discounted by some faulty technical assumption, the tactical theory behind the case for moving all the guns to the coast was sound. At the same time I learned that Sir Robert Watson-Watt, the Scientific Adviser on Tele-communications to the Air Ministry, had made an independent study of the problem and reached substantially the same conclusions as Air Commodore Ambler. Sir Robert's opinion, coming from such a distinguished pioneer of radar, carried all the more weight since better conditions for the radar equipment of the guns was one of the main advantages claimed for the proposed change.

90. On the other hand the matter had necessarily to be considered from many aspects besides that to which Air Commodore Ambler, as an Air Staff Officer, had properly confined himself. Even if I accepted the argument that the material and moral effect on pilots of splitting their sphere of operation into two would be no worse than that of excluding them from the existing gun-belt, many practical and administrative factors had still to be taken into account. Hundreds of guns, with all their equipment, were now in position on the Downs. Great reserves of ammunition had been collected there. Thousands of miles of telephone cables had been laid over a period of six months. Accommodation had been found or improvised for the gunners. The best positions available for the guns themselves and their equipment had been selected. In short, a small city was spread out between Redhill and the Thames. The proposal was that we should pick up this city bodily and transport it thirty or forty miles further south. On top of this, for the last two weeks men had been busy building permanent emplacements for the guns among the apple orchards and on the slopes of the chalk hills in Kent and Surrey. The organism was taking root. To transplant it might still be possible, but would not long remain so. Air Commodore Ambler's proposal, with all its consequences, must be endorsed or rejected without delay.

9I. I decided to think the matter over during the day and hold a conference late that afternoon, primarily for the purpose of discussing it with General Pile. In the meantime I took steps to acquaint him with the proposal so that he might be in a position to give a considered opinion when the time came. My reflections were punctuated by the intermittent clatter of the bombs, which continually reminded me of the hourly toll of lives and property. The attack that day was the lightest we had had yet; nevertheless sixteen flying bombs crashed into Greater London.

92. General Pile came to the conference with three of his staff. At my request, Sir Robert Watson-Watt also attended, as did the Air Officer Commanding, No. II Group, with two of his staff, a representative of the Air Commander-in-Chief, and several of my own staff officers.

93. I opened the conference by outlining the situation. I then asked General Pile whether he supported the proposal to move all the guns to the coast, leaving the balloons where they were, and creating two areas for fighters, one between the balloons and the new gun-belt, and the other in front of the gun-belt, over the sea. He replied that he was in full agreement with it: and in fact, the merits of siting the guns along the coast had been under consideration in A.A. Command for some time. From the gunners' point of view, such a deployment would present notable advantages. General Pile now proposed that the guns be deployed between St. Margaret's Bay and Beachy Head, and asked that they be given freedom of action inside a strip extending 10,000 yards out to sea and 5,000 yards inland.

94. Air Vice-Marshal Saunders, the Air Officer Commanding, No. II Group, might have been expected to demur, since the plan would throw a barrier across the area in which his fighters operated. On the contrary, he welcomed the proposal, which he said was "certainly the most satisfactory plan that had yet been produced". Sir Robert Watson-Watt also spoke in favour of the plan, and undertook to produce improved radar equipment for controlling fighters over the sea.

95. On hearing these opinions, which confirmed the conviction that had been growing in my mind throughout the day, I decided to adopt the plan. This left two courses open to me. On the one hand, since the forces which I intended to re-dispose had already been allotted to me for the defence of London against flying bombs, and no move of guns from one defended area to another was involved, I might regard the change as a tactical one and act at once on my own responsibility. On

the other hand, bearing in mind that no move involving so many guns had ever been made on purely tactical grounds before, I might adopt a more proscriptive attitude and refer the matter to higher authority first, as I should have done, for example, if I had proposed to move guns from, say, Manchester to the "Diver" belt, or from Birmingham to Bristol.

96. I decided in favour of the former course. I felt that the situation had reached such a point that no delay could be accepted. If the work on the gun-emplacements on the Downs were allowed to proceed even for another week, the opportunity to shift the guns would be lost. They must be shifted now, or anchored where they were. It seemed to me, rightly or wrongly, that if I were to pause and consult higher authority at this juncture, controversial questions of such magnitude might arise and the further authorities who might claim to be consulted would be so numerous, that I should not reasonably be able to count on a decision before it was too late. Time was running out. It was now or never.

97. I therefore gave instructions before the meeting closed for the new arrangements to be set in train forthwith. General Pile returned to his headquarters, and within a few hours advance parties were on their way to the coast.

98. During the following week vehicles of Anti-Aircraft Command travelled an aggregate distance of two-and-three-quarter million miles in consequence of this decision. Stores and ammunition weighing as much as two battleships, as well as the guns themselves and 23,000 men and women, were moved to the coast, and telephone cables long enough in the aggregate to have stretched from London to New York were laid. By dawn on the 17th July all the heavy guns were in action in their new positions, where they were joined by the light guns two days later.

99. After the conference I acquainted the Air Commander-in-Chief with its outcome. He asked me whether we could not make a trial deployment on a small stretch of the coast. I replied that half-measures would be worse than useless, and that, taking the view that no more than a tactical re-orientation of resources already at my disposal was involved, I had decided to order the complete move on my own responsibility, and in fact had done so. In accordance with his custom

where purely defensive measures were concerned, he did not question my judgment and made no further comment.

100. I was greatly relieved to hear that evening that the move had begun without a hitch, for I was convinced that, whatever the risks involved, we were now on the right track. I had made my decision in full knowledge of the issues at stake and the responsibilities which I was incurring. I was aware that the immediate effect on the performance of the fighters was bound to be adverse, and that if improved results from the guns did not counterbalance this loss within a few weeks, and things went wrong, I alone should be held to blame.

10I. In the event, I did not have to wait so long. Within a few days the Air Ministry informed me officially that the Air Staff considered that I ought not to have ordered a major re-deployment of the guns without prior reference to themselves. The move itself was not explicitly disapproved, but I was left in no doubt that thenceforward I should be held personally responsible for the outcome and that any blame or credit that might accrue would be laid upon my head.

102. Despite this intimation the Air Staff continued to give me full support; and I found that at the price of incurring a formal stricture I had purchased an appreciably greater degree of operational freedom than I had hitherto enjoyed. This was to be invaluable in subsequent operations. Happily the performance of the guns in their new positions vindicated the change of plan before many weeks were out, thus proving incontestably the soundness of the deployment which had grown out of Air Commodore Ambler's proposal. The Air Staff were as good as their word in the matter of responsibility for the decision to move the guns; and the effect of the move on the operational results eventually obtained received notice in a letter of approbation sent by the Air Council to my Command at the close of the main attack.

(e) *The Attacks: Second Phase (I7th July to Ist September).*

103. Nevertheless the next few weeks were an anxious time. The new system went into effect at dawn on the I7th July. During the following six days 204 bombs reached Greater London out of 473 that came within the compass of the defences. These figures reflected a substantially lower rate of destruction than that achieved during the last week under the old system, although a somewhat better one than we

had obtained during the first four weeks of the attacks, before the defences had got into their stride. Analysis of the week's figures showed that – as critics of the new plan had predicted – improved results from the guns and from an expanded and denser balloon barrage had not sufficed to outweigh a sharp decline in the achievement of the fighters.

I04. Still, it was encouraging that the performance of the guns had improved at all during a week which had begun with a major upheaval and afforded little time for the gunners to get used to their new positions. As for the decline in the performance of the fighters, this was no more than I had expected. I was not disheartened. Thanks to the energy and skill of the operational and administrative staffs of all Services concerned, the change from the old system to the new had been made without any serious setback. The machine had been brought safely to its new position. It was in running order, as witness, for example, the bringing down of sixty bombs between sunset on the 20th and sunset on the 2Ist July.[16] Already the gunners were showing that they knew how to make good use of their opportunities. I felt that one of my main tasks must now be to ensure that the forces directly under my command were made thoroughly familiar with their part in the new plan.

I05. I realised that this was a task I must undertake myself. My own staff had their hands full: to devise and apply measures which would ensure that the safety of our own aircraft was not endangered by the "Diver" defences was only one of many duties that called for much careful staff work and painstaking liaison. The Air Officer Commanding, No. II Group, and his staff were preoccupied with matters arising out of the operations in Normandy. Realising that this would be so, I had arranged that the Sector Headquarters at Biggin Hill should become a co-ordinating centre for "Diver". I found, however, that the practical, hour-to-hour supervision of operations left the Sector Commander and his staff with little time for other work; and it seemed to me that, in any case, the study and dissemination of tactical doctrine and the promotion of disciplined enthusiasm amongst pilots faced with a novel weapon ought to proceed from a rather higher level than that of a Sector Headquarters.

I06. I daresay that, if the circumstances had been slightly different, the best answer to this problem might have been the creation of a Task Force commanded by an officer of air rank answerable to myself for all fighter operations against flying bombs. It would have been necessary to make such an officer responsible for studying tactical methods and the technique of improvised training under operational conditions, as well as for the actual conduct of operations. This would have meant giving him a small staff. I had not the resources to do this, nor the smallest chance of persuading the Air Ministry to provide them. Indeed, in the circumstances this hope would have been quite unreasonable, and I did not entertain it. I felt that this was a case where I must give a direct lead to the Station and Squadron Commanders concerned with flying bombs.

107. Here my practice of sharing actively, and frequently in the fighter operations stood me in good stead. Trying to shoot down a missile travelling at six miles a minute while flying at the same speed and a height of perhaps a thousand feet across a narrow belt of undulating country bounded by balloons and guns was a business whose subtleties were not readily appreciable from an office chair. I found that a practical acquaintance with this business had its uses. Not only did it help me to acquire a fund of tactical knowledge that I could hardly have gained in any other way; above all it enabled me to talk on a basis of common understanding and endeavour with the pilots whose devotion it was my task to foster.

108. An incidental advantage of the abolition of the inland gun-belt was that it gave the searchlights, which remained when the guns had gone, more scope to assist night fighters. Another unlooked-for benefit of the move was that it brought the headquarters of the A.A. Batteries close to the bases from which our fighters were operating. Immediate and personal contact between Battery Commanders and Station Commanders suddenly became possible and even easy. I found during my first visits to stations after the move that advantage was not always being taken of this proximity. I was shown – as I had been shown for the last five weeks – aircraft whose pilots alleged that the guns had fired at them; I was shown marks of damage said to have been thus inflicted, and fragments of shell-casing which appeared to have entered aircraft or fallen on airfields. In each case I suggested that the Station Commander concerned should pocket the more portable of these

exhibits and, armed with this evidence, go and discuss his grievances, real or imaginary, with the local Battery Commander.

I09. The hint was taken. The consequences were profound and striking. As a result of these meetings between Station and Battery Commanders, the first requisite of understanding between two parties whose interests must occasionally conflict – the realisation that the other side also has a viewpoint – was attained. The mists of suspicion whose gathering had troubled me so much were dispersed almost overnight. On subsequent visits to the same stations I was again shown aircraft that had suffered minor damage from anti-aircraft fire. But this time, instead of having to listen to grievances against the gunners, I was told of pilots who had flouted discipline and good sense by venturing too near the guns. In short, pilots and gunners were beginning to understand one another's problems and work together. Unity was restored. The process reached its climax towards the close of the main attack. Flying towards the south coast on the 28th August, I could see over Romney Marsh a wall of black smoke marking the position of the "Diver" barrage. From time to time a fresh salvo would be added to repair the slow erosion of the wind. On the far side of the barrage fighters were shooting down flying bombs into the Channel; on the nearer side more fighters waited on its fringe to pounce on the occasional bomb that got so far. The whole was as fine a spectacle of co-operation as any commander could wish to see.

I10. That day 97 bombs approached these shores. The defences brought down 90[17] and only four reached London.

III. Some weeks before this the fact that we were gaining mastery over the flying bomb had become clear to ourselves and also to the Germans. During the second week after the re-deployment of the guns, the defences brought down a higher proportion of the bombs that came within their compass than in any previous week; and only a little more than a quarter of the total got to London.

II2. In the following week there was a spell of bad weather, and the fighters did not do so well; but the gunners, whom this factor affected much less, again did better than before. For the first time since the beginning of the attack they maintained a higher rate of destruction than the fighters over a full week. About this time the Meteor, our first jet-propelled fighter, came into service, and I decided to match jet against jet by trying it out against the flying bomb. At first only a few of these aircraft were available, and various problems, including that of limited endurance, had to be overcome before we could get the full benefit out of the Meteor's great speed.

II3. As the month went by, all concerned gained further experience and new equipment began to yield results. Soon the overall performance of the defences, and that of the gunners in particular, surpassed all previous achievements. In the middle of August we reached the stage of being sure that, whatever the weather, we could bring down from one-half to three-quarters of all the bombs that approached this island. Indeed, it has been calculated that during the last three weeks of this phase only one out of every seven bombs that the enemy launched actually reached London. Shortly afterwards the enemy High Command permitted the publication in the German press of the significant pronouncement that the Allies had found a counter-measure to the flying bomb. In the last few days of August only an occasional bomb eluded the defences and got through to its target. Thus it is fair to claim that almost complete ascendancy over this novel and ingenious weapon had been gained when, at the beginning of September, the capture of the launching areas by our Armies ended the main attack.

(f) *Attacks with Bombs launched by Aircraft from Holland (9th July to 5th September).*

II4. Meanwhile, as early as the 8th July, flying bombs had started to approach London from a new direction, namely from the east. No launching sites were known to exist in Belgium; and after a few weeks it was established that these bombs, which came only at night, were being launched by specially equipped He. III in aircraft operating wholly or mainly from bases in Holland.

II5. To meet this new threat I arranged with General Pile that the gun-belt should be supplemented by a gun "box" situated in the quadrilateral Rochester-Whitstable-Clacton-Chelmsford.[18] By the middle of August 208 heavy, I78 40 mm., and 404 20 mm. guns, besides I08 rocket barrels, were deployed in the "box". I also took steps to extend the balloon barrage to Gravesend,[19] and fly standing patrols over the mouth of the Thames.

II6. During July and August I20 flying bombs were seen or detected approaching this country from the east: the number actually despatched from that direction was doubtless much greater, for launching the bombs from aircraft was a tricky business which must have resulted in many premature descents. There followed a lull that lasted until the early hours of the 5th September – four and a half days after the last bomb had come from northern France – when at least another nine bombs approached London from the east. The "battle of the bomb" was not yet over; but these nine missiles were Parthian shafts, which marked the end of one phase rather than the beginning of another. They were a postscript to the main attack.

(g) *Attacks with Bombs launched by Aircraft from Germany* (I6th *September,* I944, *to* I4th *January,* I945).

II7. The further lull that followed the launching of the last bomb by aircraft operating from Holland lasted the best part of a fortnight; and to many it seemed that "the battle of the bomb" was over. Our Armies were advancing rapidly. Before long they had driven the Germans from every part of the Continent where launching ramps within the existing range of London could be built. The German flying unit responsible for launching the bombs from the air was known to be leaving its bases in Holland and moving northeast. Not only the uninformed, but many in positions of authority concluded with relief that London's long ordeal was ended.

II8. This belief was too sanguine. Further attacks with long-range weapons could not be ruled out. Lacking ramps within the existing range of the bomb, and without using their old bases in Holland, the Germans might still send flying-bombs against us. They might increase the range of the bomb and build ramps further back. They might – and certainly could – launch bombs from the air by using airfields in Germany. In the event they were to do both. Moreover, the flying bomb was not their only long-range weapon. They were known to possess a rocket capable of covering more than 200 miles and which was expected to be ready for use against us during the first fortnight in September. Despite some hopeful statements by men in responsible positions, my staff and I felt that, so long as the Germans continued to hold the western provinces of Holland, we ought to be prepared to meet attacks by the rocket.[20]

II9. That the Germans might still launch flying bombs from aircraft was not disputed by the Air Ministry or the Chiefs of Staff; and I secured authority to keep the existing "Diver" defences in being.

I20. By the middle of September the German flying-bomb air-launching unit had completed its move and was installed at bases in western Germany. Towards dawn on the I6th September the attack was resumed. The first bomb fell in Essex at 0549 hours. A few minutes later another came down at Barking. During the next half-hour five more bombs approached this country; one reached Woolwich, one fell at Felsted, and the remaining three were brought down by fighters, one of them into the sea. Two bombs not included in these figures were destroyed at sea by the Royal Navy.

I2I. After a night of inactivity the attack continued on the evening of the I7th September. Only three bombs came within range and two of them were shot down – one by a fighter and one by gunfire. More bombs followed on the succeeding nights.

I22. Countering this phase of the offensive presented special difficulties, because the enemy was no longer tied to fixed ramps. Hitherto he had exploited the mobility of the kind of aerial launching-platform provided by an aircraft only to a limited extent: more than nine-tenths of all the bombs seen or detected up to the beginning of September had come from ramps. Nevertheless the few bombs launched from the air had sufficed to turn the left flank of the defences and compel us to extend it by creating the eastern "box".

I23. The advance of the Allied Armies had now forced the enemy back on bases further to the north and east.[21] Clearly, he intended to make a virtue of necessity by attempting a further turning movement which entailed launching his bombs well out over the North Sea.

I24. To meet this move General Pile and I decided to extend the defences northwards by adding to the "Diver Belt" and "Diver Box" a "Diver Strip" extending from the left flank of the "box" at Clacton up to Great Yarmouth. We had already taken some guns from the "belt" to strengthen the "box". We now carried this process a stage further. Between the I6th and I9th September orders were issued to sixteen heavy and nine light anti-aircraft batteries to move from the "belt" to the coast between Clacton and Harwich. As the month went on further moves were ordered; and by the middle of October no less than 498 heavy and 609 light guns were deployed in the "box" and "strip".[22]

I25. The changed direction of attack brought new problems. For various reasons, of which the chief were the intermittent character of the attacks and the geographical position of our own bomber airfields, I could not give the gunners the same freedom of fire as they had enjoyed in the south-east during the summer. Although I was able to establish the principle that flying over the "box" or "strip" below 6,000 feet should be prohibited in normal circumstances during the hours of darkness, I was forced to defer to the needs of Bomber Command to the extent of permitting their aircraft to fly over the "strip" (though not over the "box") at any height they pleased provided they gave prior warning to my headquarters. This concession entailed a corresponding restriction of gunfire; and I also had to reserve the right to restrict gunfire at any other time in order to safeguard friendly aircraft which, for one reason or another, were unable to avoid flying low over the "strip" to reach their bases.

I26. Another problem for the guns arose out of the fact that, instead of maintaining a height of 2,000 or 3,000 feet during the greater part of their flight, the bombs launched from aircraft often approached the coast as low as I,000 feet. A new type of equipment for controlling low-angle fire was coming into service, but only in small quantities; consequently General Pile had to get over the difficulty by siting the rest of his equipment so as to give the best results against low-flying targets. This meant sacrificing some of its capacity to give early warning.

I27. Despite these limitations, the performance of the gunners was beyond all praise. Out of 576 bombs which approached the coast between the I6th September, I944, and the I4th January, I945, without being shot down into the sea by fighters or the Royal Navy, 32I were brought down by anti-aircraft fire. One hundred and ninety-seven of these fell into the sea and the remaining I24 on land.

I28. For the fighters the chief problem arose out of the fact that all activity was now at night. There was a natural tendency to suppose that interception at night would be easier than in daylight simply because the tongue of flame emitted by the bomb was so conspicuous in the dark. Unfortunately, seeing the bomb was not enough: pilots had also to estimate its range, and this proved extremely difficult, as anyone who has tried to judge his distance from a light on a dark night will understand. Sir Thomas Merton, the distinguished spectroscopist, designed a simple range-finder which eventually proved of great value to pilots; but individual skill and experience remained the biggest factor in overcoming this difficulty. Some pilots showed remarkable aptitude for this work, so baffling to many; for example, one Tempest pilot, Squadron Leader J. Berry, shot down more than 60 bombs at night before being himself shot down while on an offensive sortie.

I29. During this third phase of the attack we used two types of fighters against flying bombs at night: Mosquito night fighters in front of the guns, and Tempest day fighters piloted by specially-trained night-fighter pilots between the guns and London. Although the Mosquito was too slow to catch a flying bomb except in a dive, these aircraft brought down a total of 2I bombs during this phase. The Tempests, which had been outstandingly successful during the main attack in the summer, now operated with the aid of a searchlight belt extending from Saffron Walden and Sudbury in the north to Southend and Brightlingsea in the south.[23] They brought down 50 bombs, most of which fell harmlessly in open country. Thus, throughout the four months of this phase, only 205 bombs eluded the defences out of 608 seen or detected on their way to the capital; and of these only 66 reached Greater London.

I30. To supplement these orthodox measures of defence my staff worked out a scheme whereby Mosquito night fighters were sent to the area from which the He. III aircraft of the German air-launching unit despatched the bombs, in order to shoot these aircraft down. This was not a simple undertaking. The German aircraft flew low, rising to a height of 2,000 feet or so for only a short time while they released their bombs. Thus the night fighters, too, had to fly only a few hundred feet above the sea. For the fighter as for the bomber this was a hazardous proceeding; and at such low altitudes the radar normally employed by night fighters to make contact with their targets was not at its best. Furthermore, the radar stations on land which were used for controlling the fighters were often unable to detect the bombers except when the latter gained height to launch their bombs.

I3I. As a step towards overcoming some of these difficulties we modified the equipment of several radar stations and also tried the experiment of controlling the fighters from the naval frigate H.M.S. Caicos and from an aircraft equipped with A.S.V. Mark VI. But these measures bore little fruit until the air-launched attacks were nearly over. All the more credit is due, therefore, to the skill and perseverance of the night-fighter crews, who claimed the destruction of sixteen launching aircraft, the probable destruction of another four, and damage to four more, between the I6th September, I944, and the I4th January, I945. There is evidence that these losses, coming on top of the natural hazards incurred by heavily laden aircraft operating almost at sea-level, imposed no little strain on the German unit responsible for air launching.

I32. Nevertheless, the Germans seem to have remained unaware how small a proportion of the bombs launched were reaching London, or else to have resigned themselves to receiving a poor return for their efforts so long as some sort of offensive could be continued against this country. For they not only persevered with the operations, but even took steps during the winter to increase their scope. This fact, of which our intelligence service was aware, caused me some anxiety. Although the defences were doing so well, the air-launched flying bomb was still a dangerous weapon because of its mobility. We could not deploy guns everywhere at once; and the bomb might be used against other targets besides London. At that time the country was being bombarded with rockets as well as flying bombs: a simultaneous increase in the scale of attack by both weapons was a contingency against which I felt bound to provide.

I33. On the transfer of the Air Commander-in-Chief's main headquarters to the Continent in the autumn of I944 I had acquired at least a nominal responsibility for directing and coordinating offensive as well as defensive counter-measures against flying bombs and long-range rockets. So many authorities whose interests alternately coincided and conflicted were concerned in this matter that my responsibilities were inevitably somewhat indeterminate. Moreover, I was in an even less favourable position than the Air Commander-in-Chief had been to discharge such a responsibility. Like him, I could not help knowing that our striking forces had many tasks to perform besides that of attacking "crossbow" targets. Unlike him, I could not call at my discretion on the tactical, let alone the strategic, air forces for this work. The area from which rockets were being fired against London was within fighter range, and I was able to send fighters and later fighter-bombers to intervene. But the bases of the flying-bomb air-launching unit in north-west Germany were beyond the reach of all my aircraft except those used for long-range "Intruder" work.

I34. Thus, so far as offensive counter-measures to the flying bomb were concerned the only thing I could do in practice was to make representations. My staff kept a close watch on the activities of the air-launching unit, and as soon as it was plainly seen to be expanding I urged that its bases be attacked. That the response was not more active was perhaps an inevitable consequence of the multiplicity of calls upon the strategic and tactical air forces, and of the very success which the defences had achieved against the flying bomb up to that time. Even so, a number of attacks on the bases were made by our own Bomber Command and the American Eighth Bomber Command.

I35. As a further precaution against a possible extension of the flying bomb campaign General Pile and I took steps to counter any attempt that the Germans might make to turn the northern flank of the defences. A scheme was worked out whereby 59½ batteries of guns could be rapidly deployed between Skegness and Whitby if an attack should develop in that area.

I36. This eventuality was realised, without any specific warning on Christmas Eve, I944. Early on that day about 50 He. IIIs – almost the entire operational strength of the air-launching unit – launched bombs in the direction of Manchester from a position off the coast, between Skegness and Bridlington. Thirty bombs came within range of the reporting system, and all thirty crossed the coast. Only one of them reached Manchester, but six came down within ten miles of the centre of the city and eleven within fifteen miles. Thirty-seven people were killed and 67 seriously injured.

I37. This was one of the few occasions on which the Germans showed resource in exploiting the capacity of the air-launched flying bomb to outflank the defences. Happily for us they were seldom so enterprising; for however carefully our plans were laid, we could not deploy the defences on every part of the East Coast at once, and if more such attacks from novel directions had been tried, they would inevitably have achieved at least a fleeting success, as on this occasion.

I38. Immediately after this attack I ordered that deployment north of the Wash should begin. Shortly afterwards I secured the approval of the Chiefs of Staff to a more comprehensive scheme for the defence of the coast as far north as Flamborough Head. I also arranged that plans should be worked out for the defence of the areas Tees-Tyne and Forth-Clyde. But here again, as in the case of Manchester, I could not afford to order deployment in these areas, at the expense of others, merely on the ground that the enemy might attack them at some future date. Consequently, if he had followed up his attack on Manchester with a series of carefully-spaced attacks at other points north and south of the Wash on succeeding nights, he would undoubtedly have scored some success and set us something of a problem.

I39. However, either this did not occur to the Germans, or such an enterprise was beyond the capabilities of an organisation whose spirit was shaken and which was running short of fuel. No more bombs came from north of the Wash; and three weeks later the air-launching unit ceased operations. The last air-launched flying-bomb to reach this country came down at Hornsey at 0213 hours on the I4th January, I945.

(h) *Attacks from Ramps in Holland (3rd to 29th March,* I945).

I40. This was not the last of the flying bomb. In the meantime the Germans had been working on the problem of increasing the range of the weapon. Fragments of some of the bombs fired from Germany into Belgium in February showed that they were adopting methods of construction which might solve this problem and enable them to attack London from ramps in south-west Holland. Reconnaissance photographs of that area were taken, and showed that two launching sites were being constructed, one at Ypenburg, near the Hague, the other at Vlaardingen, six miles west of Rotterdam. In addition the Germans built a third site near the Delftsche Canal; but of this we were not aware till later.

I4I. To meet this new threat General Pile and I decided to reinforce the gun defences between the Isle of Sheppey and Orfordness by transferring 96 heavy guns from the northerly part of the "strip" and adding a number of batteries then under training to the remaining defences in the latter area. Instructions for the move to begin were given on the 27th February and by the 6th March nine batteries out of twelve had taken up their new positions. In the event, owing to the modest dimensions of the attack, only one further battery was deployed.

142. I also earmarked six Mustang squadrons for operations against the bombs in daylight, and arranged that their engines should be specially boosted. Three of them, together with a squadron of Meteors which I arranged to borrow from the Second Tactical Air Force, were to operate between the guns and London; the other three forward of the guns, over the sea. At night two Mosquito squadrons would patrol over the sea and a squadron of Tempests behind the guns. A direct link with the radar stations of the Second Tactical Air Force in Belgium was set up to assist in giving warning of the approach of flying bombs from the general direction of the Scheldt.

143. The attack began in the early hours of the 3rd March. The first bomb to reach this country got through the defences and fell at Bermondsey at 0301 hours. The next six bombs were all destroyed by anti-aircraft fire: five of them exploded in the air and the sixth fell into the sea. After a lull of nine hours the attack was resumed in the afternoon of the same day and continued intermittently until noon on the 4th, when there was another lull. Ten bombs came over during this second burst of fire: four of them were destroyed by the guns and only two reached London.

144. The second lull came to an end late in the morning of the 5th March. Thereafter, until activity finally ceased on the 29th March, there was spasmodic activity punctuated by intervals of quiet. The performance of the guns during this phase was outstanding. Indeed, it was so good that, in view of the unexpected lightness of the attack, I was able to dispense with the Meteors and five of the six Mustang squadrons, which returned to their former duties. During the whole of this last phase of the flying bomb campaign 125 bombs approached this country. Eighty-six were shot down by anti-aircraft guns alone, one by the Royal Navy and shore guns jointly, and four by fighters. Only thirteen bombs reached London.

145. Typhoon fighter-bombers of the Second Tactical Air Force attacked the launching-site at Vlaardingen on the 23rd March, Spitfire fighter-bombers of my Command that at Ypenburg on the 20th and

again on the 23rd March. At both sites essential components were destroyed. Presumably the missiles launched during the last few days of the attack came from the third site, of whose existence we had not previously been aware.

146. The attacks ended with a bout of intermittent firing between half-past nine on the evening of the 28th March and lunch-time on the 29th. During this period 2I bombs approached this country: 20 were shot down, and the twenty-first came ignominiously to earth at Datchworth, a village of some seven hundred inhabitants twenty-five miles from London Bridge. This was the last bomb of the whole campaign to fall on British soil.

(j) *Summary.*

147. The following table summarises the progress of the campaign and the results achieved by the defences in its various stages:

	Phase I		*Phase 2*	*Phase 3*	*Total*
	(a) I2/6- I5/7/44	(b) I6/7- 5/9/44	I6/9/44- I4/I/45	3/3- 29/3/45	I2/6/44- 29/3/45
(i) No. of bombs reported	2,934	3,79I	638	I25	7,488
(ii) No. of bombs in target area	I,270	I,070	67	I3	2,420
(iii) Percentage of (ii) to (i)	43·3	28·5	I0·5	I0·4	32·3
(iv) No. of bombs brought down					
(a) by fighters	9241/3 [24]	847	71½	4	1,8465/8
(b) by guns	2611/3	1,198½	331½	87	1,8785/8
(c) by balloons	551/3	176½	—	—	2315/8
(d) by all arms	1,24I	2,222	403	9I	3,957
(v) Percentage of (iv)					
(d) to (i)	42·3	58·6	63·2	72·8	52·8

PART III: THE ROCKET CAMPAIGN.

(a) *Intelligence and Countermeasures, I939 to November, I943.*

I48. The German long-range rocket, known to the enemy as the A-4 and to us as "Big Ben," was a rival to the flying bomb. There is no doubt, however, that if circumstances had permitted, the Germans would have conducted simultaneous campaigns with the two weapons from northern France.

I49. The first hint that the enemy intended to use a long-range rocket for military purposes was contained in a report received in this country soon after the outbreak of war. More was heard of the project towards the end of I942, when agents reported that trial shots with such a missile had been fired shortly beforehand on the Baltic coast. Early in 1943 a connection was established between this activity and the German experimental station at Peenemünde.

I50. From that time onwards a stream of intelligence about the rocket reached this country. Not until more than a year later, however, did we receive conclusive evidence about the characteristics and performance of the weapon. During part of the intervening period responsibility for investigating the new threat was taken out of the hands of the intelligence staffs and placed in those of a governmental committee created for the purpose. A number of distinguished scientists and ordnance experts were invited to speculate about the nature of the rocket, and some hypotheses were advanced which ultimately proved wide of the mark. The prevailing impression in responsible quarters during the earlier months of the investigation was that the enemy was forging a titanic weapon which weighed seventy or eighty tons and carried a warhead containing some ten tons of explosive, which would descend upon London with little or no warning. The problem of defending the capital against so disobliging a projectile was naturally a source of some anxiety to my predecessor.

I5I. Towards the end of I943 a fresh approach to the problem was adopted. In November, responsibility for investigating the nature of the rocket and devising counter-measures was transferred to the Air Ministry. Thereafter, as information from intelligence sources accumulated, a conception of the weapon which was based on reports of what the Germans were doing gradually replaced the earlier conception, which had leaned more towards our own ordnance experts' ideas of a suitable rocket. We shall see that ultimately – although only a week or two before the beginning of the campaign – the intelligence staffs were able to show that the alarms of the previous year had been exaggerated as well as premature, and that the rocket was very much smaller than had been supposed.

I52. Meanwhile, by the summer of I943 the authorities who were then responsible for countermeasures had come to the conclusion that, whatever the dimensions of the missile, radar would probably be able to detect its flight. By the time I took up my appointment in the early winter, five radar stations between Ventnor and Dover had been modified to detect rockets fired from northern France, and operators had been trained to identify the characteristic trace which a rocket was expected to produce. As a further precaution, artillery units in Kent were told to look out for visible signs of ascending rockets and a Survey Regiment of the Royal Artillery was deployed there to take care of audible signs.[25]

I53. These measures had a two-fold object. In the first place, if all went well, the radar, backed up by flash-spotting and sound-ranging troops, would tell us when rockets were fired, and perhaps enable us to give the public a few minutes' warning by firing maroons in London or elsewhere by remote control. Secondly, the information obtained by these means might help us to locate the places from which the rockets were coming, so that we could attack the firing sites and the troops who manned them.

I54. To complement these purely defensive countermeasures, an attack, which proved successful, was made by Bomber Command on the experimental station at Peenemünde. Afterwards the Germans transferred part of their activities to Poland. This move somewhat eased the difficult task of our intelligence services in keeping a watch on the rocket trials.

I55. During the summer and autumn of I943 the Germans were observed to be building a number of extraordinary structures in northern France, which we called "large sites".[26] Agents persistently reported that these sites had something to do with "secret weapons". Their impressive dimensions, taken in conjunction with the exaggerated idea of the rocket which prevailed at the time, led to the notion that the sites were intended for the storage and firing of the missile. Ultimately they proved to have little direct connection with the rocket.

I56. At this stage Bomber Command and the American Eighth

Bomber Command made a number of attacks on one of these "large sites" at Watten. Bomber Command also attacked, as part of their normal programme, several production centres in Germany which were suspected of manufacturing components of the rocket or fuel for it.

(b) *Intelligence and Countermeasures, November,* 1943, *to August,* 1944.

157. Thus the situation when I assumed control of the air defences in the middle of November, 1943, was that the Germans were known to be experimenting with some kind of long-range rocket.[27] The intelligence officers on whom the responsibility for establishing the precise nature of this missile would normally have rested had insufficient evidence on which to base any reliable estimate of the date when it might be used against us or the weight of the explosive charge which it would carry. A special investigation had, however, led to much *a priori* speculation about these matters. In consequence the impression had arisen that the Germans were preparing to bombard London with gigantic projectiles each capable of killing hundreds of people and flattening buildings over a wide area. The experimental station at which the weapon was being developed, and where objects some forty feet long which were evidently rockets had been photographed in the summer, had been successfully bombed, as had the first of a series of mysterious constructions in northern France and a number of production centres in Germany. No firm connection between the rocket and the targets in either of these latter classes had, however, been established. Besides taking these offensive countermeasures we had made dispositions which, we hoped, would give us a few minutes' warning of the arrival of individual rockets and also help to tell us where the rockets came from.

158. Soon after I assumed command the discovery of the original flying-bomb launching sites, or "ski sites",[28] in northern France, taken in conjunction with other evidence, convinced us that the pilotless aircraft or flying bomb was a more imminent threat than the rocket. For the time being, therefore, the latter receded into the background. Early in 1944 I received authority to relax the continuous watch for rockets which had been maintained at certain radar stations since the previous summer. I arranged, however, that the operators who had been

trained for this work should remain at the stations and train others, so that the watch could be resumed, if necessary, at short notice. When flying-bomb attacks began next June, I gave orders for the resumption of this watch. Two special radar stations were added to the five whose equipment had been modified.

159. Meanwhile the Allied bomber forces continued to attack the "large sites" as occasion arose and opportunity afforded. At the same time the intelligence staffs at the Air Ministry were gradually piecing together a picture of the enemy's activities at Peenemünde and later also at Blizna, in Poland. Although our ordnance experts continued to believe that anything but an outsize long-range rocket was out of the question, as time went by the evidence began to point more and more clearly to a warhead of relatively modest size.

160. Notwithstanding this evidence, the conception of a huge, earth-shaking projectile persisted. Accordingly much effort was spent on a vain search for the massive launching devices which were believed to be necessary to start so large a missile on its flight.

161. Yet, as the summer of 1944 wore on, the case for the lighter rocket grew stronger. Evidence was obtained that the firing process called for nothing more elaborate than a slab of concrete, on which a portable stand was erected and from which the rocket rose under its own power. By the last week in August all the main characteristics of the A-4 had been established. We knew that it was approximately forty-five feet long and that its all-up weight was less than fourteen tons. We knew that the standard warhead weighed about a ton, but were prepared for the possibility that, by reducing the maximum range from about 200 to 160 miles, the Germans might be able to fit a heavier warhead, weighing up to two tons. We knew that before being fired the rocket was placed upright on the firing platform and there fuelled and serviced – a process which would probably take about two hours. Furthermore, we knew that the Germans had planned at least two methods of storing the missiles, namely in underground pits or tunnels, and in wooden bunkers dispersed in woods. Finally, we had some reason to suspect that active operations would begin during the first half of September.

162. What we did not know was how (if at all) the rocket was externally controlled once it had left the ground. Misleading evidence on this point led to wasted efforts to forestall, detect and hamper non-

existent radio transmissions which were expected to be used for this purpose. Not until some time after rocket attacks had begun was the conclusion reached that control of the rocket under operational conditions was entirely internal and automatic, apart from the use of a "beam" to control the line of shoot in certain instances.[29]

163. The Allied Armies, during their advance through Normandy, discovered a number of sites which the Germans had clearly intended for the firing of rockets. Far from resembling the "large sites", these consisted merely of rough concrete slabs let into the surface of roads. We were bound to assume that similar firing sites existed in areas still in German hands; but their location was unknown to us, and there was not the slightest chance of our detecting them on air reconnaissance photographs.

(c) *The Eve of the Rocket Campaign* (*30th August to 7th September,* 1944).

164. Such, then, was the state of our knowledge towards the end of August, 1944, when we found ourselves faced with the possibility that rocket attacks might begin at almost any moment. For many months past a system for detecting the firing of rockets had existed, and a programme of bombing attacks on the "large sites" and other objectives suspected of a connection with the rocket had been carried out. In addition the Air Staff at the Air Ministry had devised and kept up to date an elaborate scheme of countermeasures which was to be put into effect as soon as the first rocket was fired.

165. One of the provisions of this scheme was that as soon as attacks were seen to be imminent, fighter aircraft should be held ready to fly armed reconnaissance sorties over the firing areas.[30] These operations were to be conducted within the "tactical area"[31] by the Tactical Air Forces, and elsewhere by my Command.

166. Towards the end of the month the stage of imminent attack appeared to have arrived; and the Air Staff decided that we should go a little further than had been contemplated in the paper scheme, by starting to fly the armed reconnaissance sorties without more ado.

167. I had already taken the precaution of authorising my operations and intelligence staffs to issue instructions and memoranda which would enable us to start these operations at short notice; and on the

30th August the sorties began. Since we did not know the location of any firing sites in enemy territory, all we could do was to brief our pilots to recognise anything they might see, and despatch them over the general area from which we expected to be attacked.

I68. A few days later, on the 4th September, the rapid advance of the Allied troops into the Pas de Calais and Flanders obliged us to discontinue the sorties. Thereupon I learned that the Chiefs of Staff considered that, since the whole of the Pas de Calais was or shortly would be ours, the threat to London from the rocket could be regarded as over.

I69. My intelligence staff felt unable to assent to this opinion without a reservation. They pointed put that the rocket, having a range of 200 miles or more, could still be fired at London from western Holland. Western Holland was still in German hands, and part of it would remain so if the Germans stood on the lower Rhine and the Siegfried Line. True, we had no evidence that the Germans had prepared any firing sites on Dutch soil; but the sites could be so quickly built and were so hard to spot that this proved nothing. While recognising that the Chiefs of Staff were better able than ourselves to foresee the effect of future operations, my intelligence officers felt, therefore, that as things stood at the moment we ought to be ready to meet rocket attacks from western Holland within the next ten days.

I70. The logic of this argument was irrefutable; and I was relieved to learn next day that a review of the situation by the Vice-Chiefs of Staff had led to the conclusion that the immediate relaxation of all defensive measures would be precipitate, not because the Vice-Chiefs thought that there was any threat to London, but on the ground that the Germans might still fire rockets at other targets.

I7I. I mention this divergence of opinion, not to claim superior prescience for myself or my staff, but because the factors involved were so delicately balanced as to give the point some interest. The argument for caution was sound so far as it went, and indeed was shortly to be justified by events; yet there was much that might have been urged on the other side. The disorganisation of the enemy's transport services at this stage must have been so great that he might well have shrunk from the task of diverting the rocket-firing organisation from France to Holland. Again, there was a time during those first few days of

September when the possibility that Allied troops might reach Germany in one bound seemed not at all remote; if the Germans had appreciated this, would they have thought an attempt to fire rockets from Holland worth their while? Yet when all this has been said, the fact remains that an area from which rockets could reach London was to remain in German hands for more than seven months to come, and that during this time over a thousand rockets were to fall on British soil.

(d) *The Attacks: First Phase* (*London, 8th to 18th September, 1944*)

172. In the event, only a few days elapsed before brute fact justified the argument for caution. At approximately twenty minutes to seven on the 8th September Londoners on their way home from work or preparing for their evening meal were startled by a sharp report which sounded almost, but not quite, like a peal of thunder. At 1843 hours a rocket fell at Chiswick, killing three people and seriously injuring another ten. Sixteen seconds later another fell near Epping, demolishing some wooden huts but doing no other damage.

173. During the next ten days rockets continued to arrive intermittently at the rate of rather more than two a day. On the 17th September the Allied airborne operation against the lower Rhine at Arnhem was launched. Thereupon the German High Command ordered the rocket firing troops to move eastwards, and on the following day attacks on London ceased for the time being.

174. Up to that time 26 rockets had fallen in this country or close enough to its shores to be observed. Thirteen of them had landed within the London Civil Defence Region. The higher figure does not represent the total fired during the period, which was certainly not less than 29 and probably well over 30; for we know that a substantial proportion of the rockets despatched habitually miscarried.

175. Early in this opening phase two things about the functioning of the technical devices deployed to detect rockets became apparent. One was that radar stations chosen to detect rockets fired from France were not, on the whole, well placed to detect rockets fired from Holland. Accordingly we arranged to increase the number of stations keeping watch between Dover and Lowestoft from three to six, and to deploy additional radar, sound ranging, and flash spotting equipment on the Continent. No. 105 Mobile Air Reporting Unit was formed within my

Command in the middle of September and despatched to Malines, near Brussels, to correlate and transmit the information obtained from technical sources across the Channel. In the meantime the War Cabinet decided that for the moment the public-warning system should not be put into effect. This decision was based on a number of considerations, some of which lay outside my province; but there is no doubt that it was justified on operational grounds alone. If the technical devices had worked perfectly, we could at best have warned the public on any given occasion that the Germans had just launched a rocket which, if it did not miscarry and was not aimed at some other target, would come down somewhere in southern or eastern England in a minute or two. And since at that stage the technical devices were far from working perfectly, our attempts to give even so rudimentary a warning as this would have led, in practice, to many false alarms and the arrival of some rockets unheralded by any warning at all.

176. The other point which emerged during this phase was that, even when the results obtained from the technical devices were good, the calculations based upon them did not, by themselves, enable us to locate the firing points with the accuracy required for the effective briefing of pilots despatched on armed reconnaissance. At best this method told us the position of a site within a mile or two; and until opportunities had arisen of adjusting the assumptions on which the calculations were based by reference to the known location of sites, as established by other means, some of the estimates obtained in this way were manifestly incorrect. Such difficulties were inevitable in the development of a new technique. They did not prevent the radar and sound ranging equipment from giving us useful information from the start. A combination of the data furnished by these two sources confirmed, for example, that the first two rockets to arrive had come from south-west Holland, as our deductions from first principles had led us to suppose they would; and within a few hours "intruder" aircraft of my Command were on their way to that area.

177. After the first day or two, however, we did not depend on technical devices to locate the firing points. One of the first measures taken by the Air Ministry when the attacks began was to brief the Dutch Resistance Movement, through the appropriate channel, to provide intelligence on this subject. A speedy method of getting this information

to the Air Ministry was devised. There it was scrutinized by intelligence officers who passed all reports of probable value to my headquarters with the least possible delay. The information contained in these reports was then correlated by a member of my intelligence staff with that based on the data furnished by the technical equipment, as well as that derived from the observations of pilots on armed reconnaissance and of the many flying personnel in the Royal Air Force and the United States Army Air Forces who reported seeing the trails made by ascending rockets. Within a few days the fruits of this process pointed to a number of fairly well defined areas, all in wooded country in the neighbourhood of the Hague, from which most of the rockets fired at London seemed to becoming.[32] By keeping a close watch on the information pointing to these "suspected areas" and ensuring that it was passed to the Fighter Groups concerned by means of frequent and full reports from my intelligence staff, I was able to satisfy myself that our armed reconnaissance effort was employed to the best advantage. During the ten days which this phase lasted, pilots of my Command carried out approximately I,000 sorties of this kind. They attacked a variety of targets, including road, rail, and water transport vehicles and installations, suspicious constructions, and German troops. On one occasion when Tempests attacked a suspected firing point an explosion occurred so violent as to wreck the leading aircraft. Afterwards a large, shallow crater was seen, such as might have been caused by the detonation of a rocket in the firing position.

I78. At this stage I was made responsible for directing and co-ordinating all operations by air forces based in the United Kingdom against the rocket-firing area as well as the bases of the German flying bomb air-launching unit.[33] This meant that besides using my own aircraft for such tasks as were within their power, I could ask Bomber Command or No. 2 Group, Second Tactical Air Force, to bomb any objectives which seemed to me to call for attack by heavy, medium, or light bombers. But there was nothing mandatory about these requests, and I had no means of ensuring that they were carried out, save that of making representations to higher authority if direct appeals should prove unavailing. My relations with Bomber Command and No. 2 Group left nothing to be desired; but since both had many calls on their resources, mere reiteration on my part and goodwill on theirs were not enough to ensure that my demands should always receive neither more nor less than their due. These difficulties become more intelligible if the requirements for rocket counter measures which preoccupied my attention are fitted into the vast perspective of air operations at that time. In the circumstances it would have been too much to expect a series of firm and favourable decisions on the part of a well-informed and competent higher authority, by means of which alone detailed and adequate response to my special needs could have been ensured. As it was, the Air Commander-in-Chief was busy with the offensive battle, and in any case had no power to direct Bomber Command in matters of this nature; while the Air Staff at the Air Ministry were naturally reluctant to give other than very broad directions to operational commanders.

179. Soon after the rocket attacks had begun, intelligence was received which suggested that the Germans had made preparations to store rockets on three properties situated at Wassenaar, just outside the Hague, and named respectively Terhorst, Eikenhorst, and Raaphorst. At the first two there were comparatively small wooded areas, which for various reasons seemed eminently suitable for the purpose; Raaphorst was a rather extensive property, and we were not sure which part of it was meant. In any case we had no proof that any of the storage shelters which were said to have been constructed on the three properties were actually in use. Nevertheless, I concluded that the Germans must be storing their equipment somewhere, and presumably also supplies of fuel and rockets, unless they were living entirely from hand to mouth. Accordingly, after weighing the probabilities carefully, I invited Bomber Command to bomb given aiming-points at Terhorst and Eikenhorst. Meanwhile, as early as the 14th September, and before receiving my request, they had sent a small force to attack Raaphorst. An aiming point close to the main road bordering the property was chosen. A few days later fresh intelligence gave us the probable location of three supposed storage areas on the Raaphorst estate, one of them close to this aiming point.

180. The first attack carried out by Bomber Command in response to my request was made on the 17th September, when a small force attacked Eikenhorst, dropping 172 tons of bombs. The bombing was well concentrated and a large explosion was seen to occur in the course

of it. No further attacks were made during the first phase of the rocket offensive, which ended on the 18th September.

(e) *The Lull* (19th to 25th September, 1944).

181. During the next week no rockets arrived in this country. Towards the end of that period secret informants reported that the firing troops had received orders on the afternoon of the 17th September to leave the Hague, and been seen departing with their equipment towards Utrecht. We know now that this information was correct; but the arrival of a rocket at Lambeth on the evening of the 18th, coupled with a report that rockets had been fired from Wassenaar on that day and the next, made us a trifle disinclined to give it credence at the time.[34] I decided that for the present armed reconnaissance sorties over the Hague and its neighbourhood should be continued, and the suspected storage sites at Wassenaar be left on the list of "Crossbow" targets which I wished to see attacked by Bomber Command. If no more rockets should come from the Hague or Wassenaar within the next few days, the sites would lose their value as targets and be taken off the list.

182. Accordingly, aircraft of my Command continued to fly armed reconnaissance and "intruder" sorties over the Hague and its environs during the period from the 19th to the 25th September, so far as the weather and the demands of the Arnhem operation allowed. On the 19th, three whole squadrons from No.12 Group – to which I had delegated responsibility for supervising the conduct of air operations a few days previously – were sent to attack objectives in an area south-east of the racecourse at the Hague, from which we believed the Germans had been firing rockets. Troops, transport vehicles, and buildings there were all attacked. On the previous night (as on two other nights about this time) "intruder" aircraft bombed a railway station at Woerden which an agent had mentioned in connection with the supply of rockets to the Hague. Neither Bomber Command nor No. 2 Group attacked any rocket targets during the week. Indeed, the latter were not asked to attack any, for up to this time none suitable for the method of precise bombing in which No. 2 Group specialised had been discovered.

183. All this time aircraft of No. 100 Group, Bomber Command, were flying special patrols with a view to intercepting and jamming any radio

transmissions which might appear to be used to control the rocket. Aircraft of my Command provided fighter escort for these missions both at this stage and subsequently. In addition, thousands of reconnaissance photographs were being taken and interpreted. This procedure was in accordance with the scheme which the Air Staff had prepared before the attacks began.[35] One of the provisions of that scheme was that every area indicated by the radar, sound-ranging, and flash-spotting complex as a suspected firing-point should be photographed as soon as possible. My staff pointed out, however, that since many of the estimates based on these data were manifestly incorrect,[36] and since experience had quickly shown that the firing-points could not be seen on reconnaissance photographs,[37] the procedure served no useful purpose. At our suggestion the Air Ministry agreed to a modification which saved much effort on the part of skilled pilots and interpreters: henceforward only areas in which we expected reconnaissance to reveal something of interest were photographed. We also took advantage of the lull to perfect arrangements for the rapid provision of the "target material" which was used in briefing bomber crews, and to discuss our problems with Bomber Command.

(f) *The Attacks: Second Phase* (*Norwich, 25th September to* I2th *October,* I944).

I84. On the evening of the 25th September the lull came to an end. At I9I0 hours a rocket fell near Diss, in Suffolk. Neither the flash-spotting nor the sound-ranging troops could give us any useful data about its origin, and at first the radar stations were equally reticent. Even the objective which the Germans had meant to hit remained unknown. Hence the rocket might have come from any area in German hands which was within 230 miles of the point of impact – for this, as we had reason to believe, was the maximum range of the A-4. Thus we were reduced to this hypothesis: that if the rocket had been aimed at London, then it must have come from the Hague or somewhere near it; but if at some other target, then it could have come from another part of Holland, from the Frisians, or even from a part of Germany near Cleves.

I85. On the following afternoon another rocket landed in East Anglia – this time about eight miles from Norwich, which subsequently proved to be the target. Once again the technical devices were silent; but five minutes before the rocket fell, chance observers flying over a point about fourteen miles west of Arnhem saw a trail rise, as they supposed, from a wood some twenty miles away, called the Speulder Bosch and adjoining the village of Garderen. Immediately afterwards the wood appeared to catch fire over an area of perhaps two acres and remain alight for about five minutes. The trail, or one like it, was also seen by chance observers who were flying well north of the Frisians, and thought it came from Ameland or Schiermonnikoog.

I86. Now, Garderen lies between Amersfoort and Apeldoorn, in the direction which the firing troops were said to have taken when they left the Hague. Moreover, a secret informant had mentioned Apeldoorn as the apparent destination of a trainload of rockets and fuel which he claimed to have seen a week before. That the rocket which had fallen near Norwich originated from the Speulder Bosch was thus a plausible hypothesis, especially as a trail ascending from that area might well look to observers over the North Sea as if it came from the Frisians.

I87. Meanwhile the films which should have recorded any data obtained by the radar stations about the rocket that fell near Diss had been scrutinized without success. They were scrutinized again; and this time faint traces were found on them. These traces showed that the missile had come from a point more remote from the stations than had the rockets observed during the earlier phase of the attacks. Armed with this evidence, the specialist whose task it was to calculate the location of firing points from such data went to work. After some delay he gave an "estimated position" which coincided with the village of Garderen.

I88. Superficially the case for Garderen as the new firing area now looked stronger than, perhaps, it really was. The specialist, who was frankly giving an estimate and not the result of a purely objective calculation, may have been influenced by the knowledge that the next rocket was supposed to have come from the Speulder Bosch. If so, the whole case really rested on a single item of positive evidence – the trail seen from a distance of twenty miles. Yet one thing was certain from the impartial testimony of the radar traces: the Suffolk rocket had not come from the Hague or Wassenaar but from some more distant spot. Accordingly I authorised the removal of the suspected storage sites at

Terhorst, Eikenhorst, and Raaphorst from the list of "Crossbow" targets which we had furnished to Bomber Command.

189. On the 27th September No. 12 Group sent four Tempest pilots to make an armed reconnaissance of the area between Amersfoort and Apeldoorn. They saw signs of military activity at two points in and adjoining the Speulder Bosch and a third point just south of the neighbouring railway; but there was no proof that this activity had anything to do with rockets. However, on the same day and the two following days six more rockets fell near Norwich and one off the Norfolk coast. In four of these seven cases the information furnished by radar suggested or was consistent with firing from the area between Amersfoort and Apeldoorn. Whether our suspicions of the Speulder Bosch were justified or not evidently the rockets were coming from an area so remote that armed reconnaissance of it could not be performed with maximum efficiency by fighters operating from this country. Unfortunately the airfields on the Continent which had fallen into Allied hands were already so congested that facilities for my aircraft to operate from them could not be provided. I could not resist the conclusion that the task must now be done by a force based on the Continent. Accordingly, at the end of September the Second Tactical Air Force assumed responsibility for armed reconnaissance of the firing areas. Air Marshal Coningham's headquarters in Brussels was not well placed, however, for the detailed work of collating intelligence on this subject, which came from a variety of sources; and we arranged that this should continue to be done at my headquarters, where good communications existed. From the 1st October onwards, therefore, my intelligence staff transmitted to Brussels a daily signal – for which we coined the name "Benrep" – containing a brief appreciation of the most recent information and a note of the areas in which armed reconnaissance seemed most likely to be fruitful.

190. Rockets continued to fall near Norwich during the first half of October, but on the 3rd October, as we shall see, London also became a target once again. Thereafter little evidence of firing from Garderen was forthcoming, and most of the rockets apparently aimed at Norwich seemed to come from northern Holland. The evidence of the radar pointed to the shores of the Zuyder Zee and the islands of Vlieland and

Terschelling; and secret informants confirmed the presence of firing points in wooded country near Rijs, in the former area.

191. Altogether, from the 25th September onwards, some 36 rockets apparently aimed at Norwich fell on land or close enough to the shore to be reported. Not one fell inside the city, although the enemy's shooting against Norwich was actually somewhat better than that against London, inasmuch as the rounds that reached this country were more closely grouped. The last round of this phase fell on a farm in Norfolk soon after half-past seven on the morning of the 12th October.

192. Meanwhile fighters of the Second Tactical Air Force visited a number of suspected firing areas in the course of the operations of wider scope which they were conducting in support of the campaign on land. Apart from a few trails, however, their pilots saw nothing that threw much light on the activities of the firing troops. But by the end of the attack on Norwich a number of fresh factors had combined to produce a new situation, which ultimately led to a further change in the allocation of responsibility for armed reconnaissance.

(g) *The Attacks: Third Phase* (*London, 3rd October to 18th November,* 1944).

193. Among the most important of these factors was the resumption of attacks on London. On the 3rd October an agent reported that the firing troops might be in the process of returning to the Hague. Sure enough, late that evening a rocket fell at Leytonstone – the first in Greater London for a fortnight. More followed on the 4th and 7th. By the middle of the month – when attacks on Norwich ceased – the new phase of activity against the capital seemed to be settling down to a rather unsteady average of two or three rounds a day. The degree of concentration achieved was about the same as in September, but the mean point of impact was further east.

194. So far as we could judge, the Germans were now firing at London from some half dozen wooded parks and open spaces within the built-up area of the Hague and on its southern outskirts. Possibly a few sites elsewhere were being used as well. The firing troops were said to have taken over a lunatic asylum in the suburb of Bloemendaal and to be storing rockets and equipment in the grounds and neighbouring woods. In addition, informants who had usually proved

reliable in the past reported that vehicles and equipment were stored in a wooded park adjoining the Hotel Promenade, in the centre of the town. We were told that supplies were reaching the Hague by way of the goods station at Leiden, and that laden railway trucks were often parked at the main railway station in that town.

195. All this information, and much more besides, we passed to the headquarters of the Second Tactical Air Force by means of the daily "Benreps". Officers from my headquarters visited Brussels to give Air Marshal Coningham's staff the benefit of such experience as we had gained in the first three weeks of the campaign. Both in the "Benreps" and verbally we stressed the desirability of confirming by visual reconnaissance the intelligence obtained from other sources. More than this we could not do. The responsibility for conducting the armed reconnaissance sorties which alone enabled visual observations to be made now rested solely on the Second Tactical Air Force; and according to a recent decision of the Air Commander-in-Chief, this situation was unaffected by the resumption of firing from the Hague.

196. Whatever the merits of this decision, as far as I was concerned the situation to which it led had one grave disadvantage: Air Marshal Coningham, with his many commitments in the battle area, could spare few aircraft for subsidiary tasks. Instead of making sorties over the Hague expressly for the purpose of observing and harassing the firing troops, as my forces had been able to do, the Second Tactical Air Force was obliged to rely on its general programme of armed reconnaissance over the enemy's lines of communication. This method of tackling the problem was probably right in the circumstances; but from my point of view it had several shortcomings. It left us without any means of judging the effect of so indirect a counter-measure; nor did it throw any light on what the enemy was doing at the Hague or meet our demand for visual reconnaissance of suspected areas. Indeed, from the date when the Second Tactical Air Force assumed responsibility for armed reconnaissance up to the 17th October – when this issue came to a head – we were without any report to say that pilots of that Command, while engaged on these duties, had seen or attacked anything on the ground which could be associated with long-range rockets.

197. Another factor which helped to give a new aspect to the problem

created by the A-4 was an increasing scale of attack on Continental cities. By the middle of October well over 100 rockets were known to have fallen on the Continent; and with the capture of Antwerp, whose potential value to the Allies was great, the problem of defending such objectives against both flying bombs and rockets was beginning to exercise the minds of the Supreme Commander and his staff. The likelihood that Antwerp and Brussels would become the main targets for the rocket during the coming winter – possibly to the exclusion of London and Norwich – doubtless contributed to the Air Commander-in-Chief's decision to leave the responsibility for armed reconnaissance with the Second Tactical Air Force even after attacks on London had been resumed.

198. As a result of this quickening of interest in "Crossbow" weapons at Supreme Headquarters, the Supreme Commander directed on the 11th October that the Chief of the Air Defence Division of Supreme Headquarters, who was responsible for co-ordinating terrestrial air defence measures in the north-west European theatre, should also assume responsibility for coordinating countermeasures against flying-bombs and rockets in that theatre.

199. The decision to entrust this task to a staff division of Supreme Headquarters itself, and not to the Allied Expeditionary Air Force, foreshadowed the imminent demise of the subsidiary formation. Now that the Allied Armies were firmly established on the Continent, that body, which had been formed primarily to plan and supervise air operations in support of the assault and build-up, was considered to have fulfilled its purpose. On the 15th October, therefore, the Allied Expeditionary Air Force was formally disbanded. Consequently my Command – re-named Fighter Command – and the Second Tactical Air Force became independent formations. Thereupon the constitutional responsibility for the air defence of the United Kingdom which had hitherto rested on Air Chief Marshal Leigh-Mallory devolved upon me, with this difference: I had no control over the Second Tactical Air Force. A situation in which I was responsible for defending the country against long-range rockets while responsibility for conducting the only countermeasure open to a fighter force was exercised by another Command, not under my control, was no longer merely inconvenient; it was clearly untenable.

200. I therefore negotiated with Air Marshal Coningham and with the Deputy Supreme Commander and the Air Ministry a new arrangement, whereby Fighter Command resumed responsibility for the armed reconnaissance of all known or suspected rocket-firing or storage areas in Holland west of a line running north and south through a point approximately 45 miles east of the Hague. At the same time steps were taken to assist the Air Defence Division of Supreme Headquarters in discharging their responsibility in respect of rockets fired against Continental cities. The Supreme Commander had already asked that the I0th Survey Regiment, Royal Artillery, which had been deployed on the Continent in September to undertake sound-ranging and flash-spotting on my behalf, should return to its normal duties in the field. Meanwhile, experience had suggested the possibility of doing without a Survey Regiment in Kent, where the IIth Survey Regiment, Royal Artillery, was deployed. Accordingly arrangements were now made to move the IIth Survey Regiment to the Continent and place it at the disposal of Supreme Headquarters. No. I05 Mobile Air Reporting Unit, too, was likely to be more useful to Supreme Headquarters than it was to me; and we agreed that this, too, should be handed over. Since the accurate detection and reporting of rockets aimed at Continental targets was of direct as well as indirect benefit to my Command – for without this information we could not be sure of distinguishing the reports that related to rockets aimed at the United Kingdom or assessing their reliability – I readily assented to these changes. I also agreed to lend a number of officers to Supreme Headquarters to assist in setting up the organisation on the Continent.

20I. Under the terms of these new arrangements, during the third week in October No. I2 Group once more assumed the responsibility for operations over the Hague with which I had charged them in September. From the I8th October onwards, No. I2 Group, instead of the Second Tactical Air Force, were the primary recipients of the daily "Benrep"; but we continued to keep in close touch with Air Marshal Coningham's headquarters, and reached an understanding whereby the Second Tactical Air Force undertook to do its best to reconnoitre the Hague on my behalf on any day when the weather made flying possible from Continental airfields but impossible from airfields in this country.

202. In the meantime my staff had been making a close study of the

intelligence bearing on the disposition of the rocket-firing complex, and had selected five objectives at or near the Hague which seemed worth bombing. Three—the goods station and the railway yard of the main station at Leiden, and the suspected store near the Hotel Promenade at the Hague – were small targets situated close to built-up areas in places whose inhabitants were well disposed to us and were, indeed, our Allies. On the information I had at the time, these targets seemed eminently suited to the kind of precise attack in which the Mosquito bombers of No. 2 Group specialised. Accordingly we asked that Group to attack them.[38] The other two – the first consisting of living quarters and storage areas at Bloemendaal, and the second of the storage site at Raaphorst, which was credibly reported to be in use again – were larger and stood in more open situations. We therefore suggested them to Bomber Command as targets for a less precise form of attack. Further enquiry cast some doubt on the validity of our most recent information about Raaphorst, and on the 19th October we withdrew that target from Bomber Command's list, thus leaving them with Bloemendaal as their sole "Big Ben" objective.[39]

203. Urgent as these requests were, the entire attention of Bomber Command at the time was being absorbed by tasks to which greater importance was attached. The proposed targets at Bloemendaal were, therefore, not attacked, and after further discussion with No. 2 Group, the goods station and railway yard at Leiden and the storage site near the Hotel Promenade at the Hague were ruled out as not being suitable as precision targets for low level Mosquito attacks. Consequently the Germans were able to develop their offensive, unhampered save by such punishment as fighter-pilots could inflict in the course of armed reconnaissance sorties over an area heavily defended by anti-aircraft weapons.

204. And in fact, as October gave way to November the scale of the German attack rose sharply. During the first three weeks in October an average of two-and-a-half rounds a day reached this country. The average over the next three weeks was four a day; and the week after that it rose to six a day. Six rockets a day was not an intolerable weight of attack, for an individual rocket was not appreciably more destructive than a flying bomb. Yet I became uneasy about the fact that the scale

of attack was rising and that comparatively little was being done to check it.

205. On the 17th November I expressed my concern to the Air Ministry in a formal letter. I pointed out that armed reconnaissance was clearly not an adequate method of limiting the German offensive unless supplemented by other measures. Yet no bombing attack on any rocket target at the Hague had been made for two months. Since the Tactical and Strategic Air Forces were not, at the moment, in a position to undertake such tasks, I should have to rely on my own resources. Now, the Spitfire aircraft which I was using for armed reconnaissance had recently begun to carry bombs; but their pilots were precluded from dropping their bombs in circumstances which involved any risk at all to Dutch civilian life or property. I suggested that this injunction should be relaxed to the extent of permitting pilots to bomb such targets as could be accurately located and were situated in areas from which the inhabitants were known to have been removed. In these circumstances the risk to civilian life, at least, would be small; and what we had to do was to balance the off chance of injury to life and property at the Hague against its certainty in London. I asked that this question should be carefully considered, in consultation with the Dutch civil authorities if this were thought fit. Such a concession would also apply, of course, to any attacks that the Mosquito aircraft of No. 2 Group might make.

206. Finally, I asked that consideration should also be given to the desirability of allotting a higher degree of priority to the bombing of rocket targets by Bomber Command. At that time an increase in the scale of attack by air-launched flying bombs was also causing me concern; and I took the opportunity of asking that the bases of the air-launching unit should be attacked as well.[40]

207. This letter, as I have said, was signed on the 17th November. On that day four rockets fell in London, killing 14 and seriously injuring 36 people. A gas-holder was set on fire and nine factories were damaged. Only two days earlier ten rockets had landed in this country within 24 hours – six of them in London. Altogether, since the start of the campaign on the 8th September some 200 rockets had arrived in the United Kingdom – an average of three a day.

(h) *The Attacks: Fourth Phase (London, 19th November to 31st December, 1944).*

208. The suggestion made in my letter of the 17th November that the Dutch authorities be consulted was adopted; and on the 21st of the month this point and others raised in my letter were discussed at one of the Deputy Supreme Commander's conferences at Supreme Headquarters. Thereupon, with the concurrence of the Air Staff, I was authorised to undertake fighter-bomber operations on the lines I had laid down. On the other hand, I was given clearly to understand that for some time to come any assistance I could expect to receive from the Second Tactical Air Force would be virtually limited to that provided by their current rail interdiction programme.[41] I was also informed that, unless the enemy increased his scale of attack considerably, the Combined Chiefs of Staff would not be likely to countenance the diversion of any part of the strategic bomber effort from the attack of the German petroleum industry and communications to that of rocket targets. The Air Staff assured me, however, that if the scale of attack by "Crossbow" weapons did increase, the matter would be reconsidered.

209. No time was lost in taking advantage of the concession regarding fighter-bomber operations. My staff drew up a list of storage sites and similar objectives all situated at least 250 yards from the nearest built up area; and from the 21st November onwards the four squadrons in No. 12 Group which were assigned to this duty[42] took every opportunity of attacking them with bombs and machine-gun and cannon fire. The general prevalence of bad weather made these opportunities few, especially in November and the latter half of December. As a result, these squadrons had plenty of time for intensive training in pin point dive-bombing, of which they took full advantage, and during the first half of December, when the weather temporarily improved, more frequent attacks were made. Altogether, between the 21st November and the end of the year No. 12 Group made 470 fighter-bomber sorties against rocket targets and dropped 54 tons of bombs in the course of them. In these operations no effort was spared to ensure that the bombs were dropped with a skill and precision rivalling that displayed by the picked crews of No. 2 Group in some of their spectacular attacks on

buildings used as headquarters by the Germans. A characteristic attack delivered during this phase was one made by Nos. 453, 229 and 602 Squadrons, on Christmas Eve, on a block of flats near the centre of the Hague, which the Germans were using to house the firing troops in that district. The building was so badly damaged that the Germans had to leave it.

2I0. To all appearances the influence of these operations on the rate and quality of the enemy's fire was considerable. The scale of attack declined from an average of nearly seven rockets a day at the end of November to four a day in the middle of December and three-and-a-half at the end of the month. Moreover, the enemy took to doing most of his firing at night, and the apparent accuracy of the shooting decreased. A statistical analysis of the rocket effort and our counter-measures led to the belief that sustained attacks on the firing areas by day and night would exercise a cumulative effect on the enemy and hence on the number of rockets that reached London.

2II. At the time I was not altogether prepared to accept this conclusion. In the light of subsequent experience I feel quite sure that to do so would have been to claim too much for our efforts. The chief factor in limiting the scale of attack was almost certainly the rate at which supplies could be brought to the firing areas; and this in turn must have been mainly determined by the frequency and success of the armed reconnaissance and rail interdiction sorties flown by the Second Tactical Air Force over the enemy's lines of communication. Preparations for the German offensive in the Ardennes – which was accompanied by an increased scale of rocket attack on Antwerp – may also have helped to diminish the attack on London towards the end of I944. The simultaneous decline in accuracy is not so easily accounted for; and its significance in view of the comparative smallness of the figures analysed is open to question.

2I2. On the other hand the enemy's new tendency to fire most of his shots at night was definite and unmistakable. For this change of habit by the Germans our fighter-bombers may perhaps claim the credit, since it cannot readily be explained on any other grounds than a desire to evade their attention. Admittedly the gain was an indirect one, seeing that fire at night was no more inaccurate than by day; in fact, as a general rule a higher proportion of the rounds fired in darkness hit the target than of those fired by day; but casualties were generally lower after dark, when most people were at home, than in the daytime, when they were massed together in factories and offices and in the streets. Thus, from our point of view the preponderance of night firing was definitely favourable.

(j) *The Attacks: Fifth Phase (London, 1st January to 27th March, 1945).*

2I3. However, the respite was short-lived. In the New Year the scale of attack went up again. During the first half of January an average of more than eight rockets a day reached this country. Thereafter the rate of fire declined a little, only to rise again early in February, until an average of ten rockets a day was attained in the middle of the month. Moreover, the Germans again took to doing more than half their firing in daylight, and their accuracy improved. In an average week in January and the first half of February, twice as many people were killed or seriously injured by rockets as in a corresponding period in December.

2I4. Clearly, our fighter-bomber programme was not such an effective deterrent as we had hoped. This was not to say that our methods were wrong: without the fighter-bomber attacks, the rate of fire might have risen still more sharply. But evidently something more was needed if the German offensive was to be kept down.

2I5. What form that something more should take was not so obvious. In December the Air Ministry had asked the Foreign Office and the Ministry of Economic Warfare to investigate the possibility of curtailing supplies of fuel for the A-4 by attacking factories where liquid oxygen was made. The experts reported that there was no means of knowing which of the many factories in German hands or under German control were supplying liquid oxygen for that particular purpose. There were, however, eight factories in Holland, five in western Germany, and five elsewhere in Germany which might fill the bill. As a sequel to this investigation, the Air Ministry invited me to consider attacking three factories in Holland. One of them, at Alblasserdam, near Dordrecht, was successfully attacked by the Second Tactical Air Force on the 22nd January. Another, at Ijmuiden, consisted of two buildings so closely surrounded by other factories that the prospect of a successful attack with the means at my disposal was remote. The third, at Loosduinen, on the outskirts of the Hague, was adjoined on three sides by Dutch civilian property. Hence I was reluctant to attack it, especially as there was no certainty that its destruction would cause the Germans to fire even one less rocket at this country. However, in view of the Air Ministry's request and my desire to leave nothing undone which offered a chance of hampering the enemy, I agreed to do so. In order to reduce the risk to civilian property to a minimum, the pilots chosen for the job were instructed to use methods which can best be described as "trickling their bombs towards the target". This technique necessitated five separate attacks of which all but one were made from the direction in which there were no houses adjoining the factory. Two attacks were made on the 3rd February, two on the 9th February, and one on the 8th. After the last attack on the 9th we judged that the target had suffered enough damage to be left alone in future.

2I6. In January bad weather limited the number of fighter-bomber sorties that we could make to a little more than half the number made in December. In February the weather was better and during the first half of the month we made more fighter-bomber sorties than in the whole of January. Besides delivering the five attacks on the oxygen factory at Loosduinen to which I have alluded, we made six attacks on the Haagsche Bosch, a wooded area in which rockets had been seen on reconnaissance photographs taken in December. The Hotel Promenade was attacked on three occasions, and attacks were also made on other suspected storage areas at the Hague, Wassenaar, and the Hook of Holland, as well as on railway targets. The Second Tactical Air Force continued to attack communications, as hitherto, in the course of their armed reconnaissance and rail interdiction programmes.

2I7. Meanwhile, in consequence of the rise in the scale of rocket attack, towards the end of January the Air Ministry had begun to press me to intensify my efforts against the firing and storage areas. Nevertheless they were still unwilling to see any part of Bomber Command's effort diverted to the attack of such targets. On the 26th of the month, however, the Defence Committee agreed to invite the Air Ministry to ask Supreme Headquarters to sanction the precise attacks on selected targets by the light bombers of No. 2 Group, which I had been urging since the previous autumn. Shortly before this I had arranged to raise the strength of the force earmarked for exclusive use against rocket targets from four squadrons to six, and to equip and use all six squadrons regularly as fighter-bomber squadrons.[43] I now negotiated a new agreement with the Second Tactical Air Force whereby my area of responsibility was extended as far east as Amersfoort. On days when the weather was unsuitable for precise attack on objectives at the Hague, our fighter-bombers were now attacking rail targets; and the inclusion of Amersfoort in our area would enable us to bomb the railway junction there – a bottleneck through which all traffic from Germany to the firing areas in western Holland passed. Under the terms of the new agreement the Second Tactical Air Force would use any light or medium bombers that they could spare from the battle on land to attack rocket targets chosen from lists provided by my staff.

218. The full effect of the expansion of the "Big Ben" fighter-bomber force was seen in the second half of February, when Fighter Command made 548 sorties and dropped 108 tons of bombs – precisely the same weight in two weeks as in the previous six. At the suggestion of my Chief Intelligence Officer, who recommended that we should try the effect of concentrating our efforts on a single target for at least a week, nearly three-quarters of this bomb tonnage was aimed at the Haagsche Bosch, where severe damage was done, particularly on the 22nd February, when a film studio which the Germans used for storage was gutted. An almost complete cessation of rocket fire over a period of more than sixty hours followed this attack; and on the 24th February photographic reconnaissance failed to reveal a single rocket anywhere in the square mile or so of wooded parkland that the Haagsche Bosch comprised. Other evidence strengthened the inference that the Germans had been driven from the Haagsche Bosch, at least for the time being, and suggested that they had been forced to improvise facilities in the racecourse area at Duindigt, further to the north.

219. So far as they went, these results of our new policy of concentrating on one area were encouraging; but events soon showed that no lasting effect on the Germans had been achieved. When firing was resumed (apparently from Duindigt) on the 26th, no appreciable decline in its quality or quantity was apparent. Nor did the first of No.

2 Group's long-awaited bombing attacks, which was delivered on the 3rd March, have any better effect. The attack was delivered by 56 Mitchells, and the target chosen – not without some misgivings since the continued presence of the Germans and their gear was doubtful – was the Haagsche Bosch. Unfortunately the bombing was not sufficiently accurate, in consequence of which casualties occurred among Dutch civilians and their property was damaged. After this unhappy experience, Air Marshal Coningham decided to make no more attacks on targets at the Hague.

220. Another counter-measure considered at this stage was the use of anti-aircraft artillery to fire at approaching rockets and explode them in the air. If only because the rockets travelled many times faster than the fastest bomber and completed their parabolic flight from Holland in less than five minutes, the problems involved seemed formidable. Indeed, proposals in this sense had been carefully considered before the attacks began and found impracticable. General Pile raised the subject again in December, 1944, when he asked permission to make an operational trial of a scheme designed to ensure that the rockets would pass through a curtain of shell-fragments as they approached the earth. An essential requirement of the plan was accurate and timely warning that a rocket was on its way. Although there were still difficulties in the way of disseminating such warnings to the public, for operational purposes reliable information of this kind was now available. There were some obvious drawbacks to the scheme: for example, the expenditure of rounds required to explode even one rocket was likely to be extravagant and possibly alarming to the public. Nevertheless, I was satisfied that it contained the germ of a successful countermeasure, which might become important in the future, and that on purely operational grounds a practical trial was desirable. I made recommendations to this effect when submitting General Pile's proposal to higher authority. The committee before whom the scheme was laid, after taking the opinion of eminent men of science, one of whom put the chances of a successful engagement at one in a hundred and another at one in a thousand, decided that an operational trial would be premature. They invited those concerned to seek ways of improving the scheme, and promised to consider it again in March.

221. Accordingly General Pile repeated his request for an operational

trial towards the end of that month. He pointed out that time was clearly running out: the opportunity of testing the scheme in practice would soon have passed. In response, on the 26th March a panel of scientists were asked to prepare a theoretical estimate of success. They reported on the same day that if 400 rounds were fired against any one rocket the chance of scoring a hit would, at best, be one in thirty. After a further statement by General Pile, who said that he would endeavour to increase the chance of success by trebling the rate of fire, the proposal went before the Chiefs of Staff, who decided on the 30th March that the likelihood of success was too small to outweigh the objections to the scheme. But in any case, by that time the campaign was over.

222. Meanwhile we had been continuing our fighter-bomber offensive against the rocket-firing organisation and its communications. After the 3rd March we made no further attacks on the Haagsche Bosch, but turned our attention to the adjoining racecourse area at Duindigt, along with other storage and firing areas and a group of buildings belonging to the Bataafsche Petroleum Company, which apparently the Germans were using as billets and offices. As before, we selected railway targets for attack when conditions were unsuitable for attacking our primary objectives. During the second week of March alone we dropped some 70 tons of bombs at Duindigt. By the middle of the month we had evidence that the Germans had abandoned the area, which was by that time so pitted with craters that, in the words of a contemporary report, "it looked as if Bomber Command, not Fighter Command, had been attacking it". This success was accompanied by another temporary decrease in the scale of rocket attack on London; and what was, perhaps, more significant was that about this time the Germans took to doing more and more of their firing in the early hours before dawn. We concluded that our efforts had spoilt their arrangements for storing rockets in the forward area and that they were being forced to bring the missiles up at night and fire them off as soon as possible. Accordingly, during the second half of March we paid little attention to storage areas and devoted most of our fighter-bomber effort to communications. Altogether we made more fighter-bomber sorties in March than in the previous four months put together, and dropped more than three times the weight of bombs dropped in February.

223. The German offensive came to an end at I645 hours on the 27th March, when the one thousand, one hundred and fifteenth rocket to fall in this country or within sight of shore fell to earth at Orpington, in Kent. The campaign had lasted seven months. During that time the Germans had fired at least I,300 rockets at London and some 40 or more at Norwich. Of these 5I8 had fallen within the London Civil Defence Region and none at all within the boundaries of the latter city. Altogether, 2,5II people had been killed and 5,869 seriously injured in London, and 2I3 killed and 598 seriously injured elsewhere. These figures would have been substantially smaller but for a number of unlucky incidents, in which rockets chanced to hit crowded buildings. Among the worst of these incidents were three which occurred at New Cross Road, Deptford, on the 25th November, I944, and at Smithfield Market and Hughes Mansions, Stepney, on the 8th and 27th March respectively. Deplorable as these occurrences were, their rarity is a measure of the random quality of the long-range rocket in the stage to which the Germans had developed it.

224. Yet the A-4 rocket cannot be dismissed as a mere freak. Practically, it was a new weapon, which brought new hazards to the lives of millions, and set new problems of defence. Its significance, and that of the flying-bomb, when posed against the wider background of the war as a whole, remain to be considered.

PART IV: A SUMMING UP.

225. In describing our countermeasures to the flying bomb and A-4 rocket, I have been at pains to point out that these measures were only a part of operations of much wider scope, ultimately extending over the greater part of Europe. Perhaps a balanced view is best preserved by remembering that although defence against these two weapons formed the main task of the air defences during a period of nearly ten months, operations directly concerned with the bomb and rocket absorbed only a fraction of the total Allied air effort, offensive and defensive. From the time when attacks on "Crossbow" targets began, in August, I943, until the end of the war with Germany, these operations accounted for about eight per cent. of the total weight of bombs

dropped by the tactical and strategic air forces in the western theatre. On the other hand, the number of guns and balloons concentrated in south-east England that summer as part of our defences against the flying bomb was certainly the greatest ever assembled in a comparable area for the purpose of air defence. The fighter squadrons deployed in this role were limited in number by geographical conditions; but they included some of our fastest aircraft, which had to be withheld from operations in the tactical area.

226. This leads naturally to the question: to what extent did this expenditure of effort prevent the Germans from doing what they set out to do? An answer calls for a few comments on what the German intentions seem to have been. When accelerated development of the A-4 rocket began in 1942, the Germans cannot have known very clearly what they meant to do with it. Not only had the capabilities of the weapon yet to be established, but in any case the formulation of precise strategic aims does not seem to have been the enemy's strong suit. In the OKW[44] the Germans possessed what the Allies sometimes accused themselves of lacking – namely, a permanent and fully equipped organ for the supreme direction of the war. In practice, however, it failed to come up to expectations. For this there seem to have been two reasons. For one thing, Keitel, the head of the OKW, lacked a forceful personality. For another, the selection of his staff was entrusted to the General Staff of the Army, who were not so innocent as to put a rod for their own backs into the hands of men remarkable for their vigour. Hence the OKW worked less as an authoritative body than as a kind of secretariat to the Fuehrer. Hitler was thus the only man in Germany really in a position to settle problems of overall strategy.

227. Hitler, we are told, had little taste or aptitude for long-term planning, though his intuitive judgment of immediate issues was phenomenal. Such qualities as this were not enough to ensure a consistent aim or policy. When firm direction from above was lacking, the three fighting services pursued separate and sometimes divergent courses. "Because of the impotence of the OKW," says Albert Speer, the former Reichsminister of Armaments and War Production, "I had to negotiate and make decisions separately with the three Services."

228. According to the same authority, the development of the flying bomb was begun towards the end of 1942 because the German Air Staff

grew jealous of the success achieved by the Army in developing their own long-range missile, the A-4 rocket. Thus, from the outset the two weapons seem to have been competitors. An attempt to co-ordinate their use at the operational level was, however, made in December, 1943, when a military formation called LXV Army Korps was given overriding control over both weapons. The efficacy of this measure is doubtful, since the staff of LXV Army Korps seem to have had an imperfect understanding of the flying bomb, and were sometimes, at loggerheads with Flakregiment 155 (W), the Luftwaffe formation immediately responsible for its operation. I daresay there was something to be said on both sides.

229. Despite these disagreements and uncertainties, by the spring of 1944 the notion of using the two long-range weapons to remedy the shortcomings of the bomber force seems to have been generally accepted. Outwardly the odds against a German victory had become so great that those in the know could hardly have found the will to go on fighting if they had not been sustained by the mysterious promise of new scientific marvels, reinforced by the hope of driving a wedge between the Allies. Koller, the last Chief of the German Air Staff, has said that "the final role of the flying bomb and the A-4 rocket was to replace the bomber arm of the Luftwaffe entirely." Hitler expressed a similar intention when addressing representatives of Flakregiment 155 (W) at Berchtesgaden soon after the flying bomb campaign had begun. Yet even at that stage inconsistencies of aim and viewpoint were evident. Only a few months earlier the aircraft industry had been directed to continue the production of bomber types; while LXV Army Korps, true to its tradition of conflict with Flakregiment 155(W), envisaged the simultaneous use of flying bombs and bombers. Finally, Goering, who as head of the Air Ministry and Commander-in-Chief of the Luftwaffe was ultimately responsible for the decision to adopt the flying bomb, is said to have had little faith in the weapon; while Speer, who was ultimately responsible for its production, was certainly not unaware of its defects.

230. On one further point, at least, the Germans were agreed: the time to use the long-range weapons was *before* the Allies could set foot in north-west Europe, in order to postpone the day and gain time for dissension to spring up between the United Kingdom, America and

Russia. The A-4 rocket was an ill-favoured monster, slow to reach maturity; but tests of the flying bomb in the summer of I943 were so promising that the commencement of active operations before the end of the year was ordered. Whether attacking London with flying bombs was a good way of upsetting Allied plans for the assault is arguable; but very likely the Germans clung to the hope that opposing views about the diversion of our resources to the defence of the capital would split the western Allies, and the consequent delay in opening the new front detach us both from Russia.

23I. The bombing of the "ski sites" and other factors led to a postponement of this programme. The landings in Normandy on the 6th June, I944, took the Germans tactically by surprise and found them still not ready to use the flying bomb. Thereupon LXV Army Korps, apparently on Hitler's instructions, peremptorily ordered Flakregiment I55 (W) to begin operations on the I2th June. The precise grounds of this decision are never likely to be known. The opportunity to use the long-range weapons to delay the Allied assault had gone, if indeed it had ever existed. But the Germans may still have hoped to gain time by exploiting the harassing effect of the bomb and hampering the flow of reinforcements and supplies. Moreover, it is improbable that we need look very far for the motive that prompted such a natural reaction to events. At moments of crisis the impulse to retaliate against an England which had upset all Hitler's plans by perversely refusing its allotted role was never far below the surface. The Germans quickly publicised the flying bomb as "revenge weapon No. I": and their propaganda may well have contained a hint of their real purpose. With the "west wall" in jeopardy and defeat on the horizon, Hitler may have seen no more than the need to strike back and hope for a miracle.

232. In any case such hopes as the Germans may have entertained were bound to be disappointed. During the next ten months they were to launch well over I0,000 flying bombs at London, thereby squandering about a million and a half gallons of sorely-needed petrol and a productive effort which, according to Speer, would have been better employed in turning out 3,000 fighters. Whether Germany would have gained anything decisive if every one of those peevish darts had found its mark is open to question. But for us the effects would certainly have been embarrassing. As it was, our casualties in the two

V-weapon campaigns included 8,938 persons killed and 24,504 seriously injured, while over 200,000 houses were destroyed or severely damaged and over a million more suffered less important damage. We may therefore be thankful that the number of bombs which reached the London Civil Defence Region was not 10,000 but 2,419.

233. I fancy that Londoners in particular will readily acknowledge their debt to the gunners, fighter crews, balloon crews, and a host of others whose skill, devotion, and unfailing toil brought about the premature descent of far more bombs than reached the target. Nor will they forget the involuntary but cheerful contribution of their neighbours in Kent, Sussex, Surrey, and other counties surrounding London, whose fields and gardens were graveyards for buzz-bombs stricken by the way. Despite the care that we took to bring the bombs down away from houses whenever we could, the path of damaged or defective bombs was sometimes unpredictable. Like their neighbours in London, some of the dwellers in "bomb alley" met their deaths in the front line. It is right that I should record, however, that our efforts were so far successful that the casualties caused by the bombs which failed to reach the target were only a fraction of the total.

234. In this battle the part played by gunners and fighters was so conspicuous and important that it tends to monopolize attention, perhaps unduly. I am conscious that in writing the foregoing account of the flying bomb campaign I have not resisted the natural tendency to bring out those features which make for easy narrative and positive statement. I wish, therefore, in this summing up, to emphasize that victory over the flying bomb was gained by the joint efforts of thousands of men and women of the different Services, working in every variety of unit and at all levels of responsibility. As an example of this co-operation I may cite the mutual trust and unity of purpose that always existed between General Pile's staff and mine. So far as the work of the gunners and fighter crews is concerned, the bare chronicle of their achievements requires no embellishment. Nothing need be added, therefore, except perhaps a word of tribute to those whose work was done outside the limelight. The contribution of Balloon Command, too, speaks for itself, although perhaps in too modest a tone for its true value to be apparent. Every one of the 232 bombs brought down by the balloons was one which had eluded the

other defences and would almost inevitably have hit the target if it had been allowed to continue on its way. To the administrative skill and practical efficiency which enabled the deployment of the initial barrage to be completed in less than a third of the time originally forecast, I can give no higher praise than by comparing this feat with those performed by Anti-Aircraft Command at the same time and in July. The part played by the Royal Observer Corps – the Silent Service of the air defences – was an epic in itself. Together Anti-Aircraft Command, Fighter Command, Balloon Command and the Royal Observer Corps made up a team in whose play I am proud to have had a share.

235. Of the helping hand extended by many who were not members of the team, limitations of space forbid that I should say much. A hint has already been given of the technical advice and assistance rendered by distinguished men of science. Acknowledgement must also be made of the important part played by the Royal Navy and the Admiralty, especially in connection with the problems of obtaining and utilising early warning of the approach of flying bombs over the sea, and also that of helping pilots to "pinpoint" their position off the coast. In particular, the heroism of those who sailed in the small craft which operated off the French coast, under the noses of the Germans and exposed to attack by land, sea, and air, deserves to be remembered.

236. Teamwork, aided by such help as this, won the "battle of the bomb". Indeed, it is not too much to claim that the flying bomb was prevented from achieving even a secondary purpose; for although we suffered casualties and damage, the flow of supplies to the Allied Armies across the Channel went on unimpeded by the worst the flying bomb could do.

237. Such, then is the answer to our question, so far as it concerns the flying bomb.

238. I turn now to the A-4 rocket. This was in some ways a more disturbing menace than the flying bomb. Not that it was more destructive; but it was difficult to counter, and fore-shadowed further developments which still loom ahead of us. Albert Speer, one of the ablest and most far-seeing of our enemies, remarked soon after the German surrender that, whereas the flying bomb had had its day, the rocket must be considered the long-range weapon of the future. On the

other side of the scale must be set the complication and high cost of such missiles. Delivering approximately the same explosive charge as a flying bomb, the A-4 rocket required twenty times the productive effort, or as much as six or seven fighters.

239. That the German rocket attacks of 1944 and 1945 were conceived with a well-defined military object in view is open to doubt. I fancy that if the situation had been less desperate the Germans might have postponed active operations until further trials enabled them to attain a higher standard of accuracy. Their plight was such, however, that in September, 1944, they found themselves constrained to improvise a rocket offensive from Holland in order to cushion the shock resulting from the obvious failure of the flying bomb. This does not mean that if northern France had remained in their hands, and our countermeasures to the flying bomb been less successful, they would not have used both weapons together; but that in such circumstances the use of the rocket would have been equally premature. The standard of accuracy attained, the many misfires, and the inconsistency of method adopted by different firing units, all point in the same direction.

240. To an even greater extent than the flying bomb campaign, then, the rocket offensive must be regarded merely as a harassing attack. In the outcome it was not particularly successful in that capacity. Why was this? The contribution of the defences, as I have related, was practically limited to tracking the missiles, trying to locate the firing points, and attacking these and other targets more or less frequently and more or less effectively with fighters and fighter-bombers. As I urged at the time, these measures were not, by themselves, enough to interfere seriously with the rate or quality of the enemy's fire. The ineffectiveness of the A-4 rocket was due rather to the inaccuracy of the weapon and to the restricted scale of attack, reduced as it was by the enemy's insistence on dividing his efforts between Antwerp and London, probably from propagandist motives. But to say this does not imply that no effective countermeasure to the rocket would have been possible in any circumstances. In one sense its very lack of weight was what made the attack so hard to counter. For if the enemy had begun to fire at a much greater rate, he could no longer have lived from hand to mouth. He would have been obliged to store rockets and fuel in bulk near the firing area. Valuable bombing targets would then have been

offered to us; and in such a case the Chiefs of Staff would doubtless have considered lifting their virtual ban on the use of the strategic bomber forces against rocket targets. I have little doubt that if this had been done and the diversion of part of our bomber effort been accepted, we should soon have been able to restore the scale of rocket attack to its original proportions.

241. Accordingly, so far as the rocket was concerned the answer to our question is that, although in the circumstances the effect of the defences was small, potentially we had the means of keeping the situation in hand if the scale of attack had risen.

242. On the broader issue of the extent to which the Germans were right, in the military sense, to develop their two long-range weapons and put them into operation, a number of questions naturally arise. Would several thousand fighters have been worth more to the enemy than the 20,000 flying bombs and 3,000 rockets, or thereabouts, which he aimed at England and Continental cities? Put thus, the issue is misleadingly simple; the fighters would have been no use without pilots, ground crews, bases, and supplies of aviation spirit greater than the Germans could command. If this effort had been put into the production of bombers instead, the Germans would still have been no better off: the crews and the aviation spirit would not have been forthcoming. And indeed, since by the time the most important decisions were taken the Luftwaffe had lost much of its striking power, the devotion of so much skill and manpower to the flying bomb and the A-4 is at least understandable. The former was an ingenious weapon, which we might not have overcome if we had been less well prepared; the latter a notable advance on anything that had gone before, and a source of problems with which the nations are still grappling. The sponsors of these engines of destruction may be pardoned for a certain lack of judgment if they fancied themselves on the brink of changes comparable to those which followed the rifled barrel and the machine-gun.

243. Whatever the pros and cons of the German policy which lay behind the operation of the flying bomb and the A-4 rocket, it is probable that, as the end approached, the German measures to stave off general defeat became less well co-ordinated and more involuntary. I have tried to show why I think it more than doubtful whether Hitler

could have developed a decisive attack with the flying bomb and the rocket in 1944, whatever targets had been chosen. I have suggested that in fact he was confronted with the peremptory need of a sign which would show his followers that England was being attacked, and so mitigate to some degree the terror that was coming upon them. Where action is taken under forces of overwhelming compulsion there can hardly be a question of fastidious strategic judgment. None the less, in the complex and often tangled web of German strategy one important thread was missing. Though hidden at first by reason of the great number of aircraft deployed to lead off the German land campaigns, its absence became more obvious as operations went on. I refer to the German failure to think consistently in terms of airpower. The Luftwaffe was allowed to run down, and no big enough measures were set in train for its continuous replenishment, especially in respect of competent bomber crews. The result of this neglect was a progressive loss of air superiority, at first over the occupied territories and finally over the "living space" of Germany.

244. If, as Koller had said, the flying bomb and the A-4 rocket were to be regarded as a substitute for the strategic bomber force, the cardinal mistake was to suppose that these novel weapons could be used effectively in the absence of air superiority, which alone could have provided reasonable immunity from air attack. Only air superiority could ensure that the places where the missiles were stored, serviced, and fired, the crews who fired them, and the vehicles which carried them by road and rail would not be subject to systematic interference.

245. By the time the flying bomb and rocket campaigns were got under way, the Allies had gained a high degree of air superiority over all the areas from which the weapons could be fired. Hence we were in a position to conduct a counter-offensive at will, and without serious hindrance from enemy aircraft, wherever targets might present themselves and whenever the scale of attack by the Germans was sufficient to warrant the diversion of Allied bombers from their main task. Sometimes – as with the rail interdiction programme of the tactical air forces – operations conceived with the main task in view served a dual purpose, and no diversion was involved.

246. Moreover, this vital condition of air superiority, for which we had fought without respite since the Battle of Britain, enabled us

constantly to improve the system of air defence whose application to new threats I have endeavoured to describe. Because we had air superiority we found ourselves free to adapt the system to novel circumstances and keep it in action day and night, with scarcely a rap from the German bombers not an hour's flying away.

247. The problems of air defence which have been described will not remain static. They may recur in new forms in the future. The scientific advances which the Germans used so spectacularly, if unsuccessfully, gave us a foretaste of hazards against which it is our business to provide. As science goes forward, and fresh discoveries lead to changes in the apparatus and methods of air defence, fertility in research and skill in engineering will provide better tools and weapons; but these are only raw materials of progress. What we need to do, above all, is to give rein to the qualities of mind and imagination which can take the growing mass of technical knowledge and mould what it brings forth to fit the shape of things to come.

Footnotes

1 They were so called because on each site stood a number of buildings shaped like a ski laid on its side. The buildings seem to have been meant to provide blast-proof shelter for the missiles while they were being stored and serviced.

2 At that time we believed that the missile could be made to turn in the air. In point of fact this effect was limited to the first few moments of flight, during which it had to be directed on to its calculated course by an adjustment of the automatic control mechanism made beforehand.

3 Later it was established that the missiles were not controlled by radio. To divert them by means of an electro-magnetic field was theoretically possible, but would have needed so much copper and electric power that it was quite impracticable. Thus neither investigation produced any positive result.

4 "Overlord" was the code-name for the European operations and "Diver" that for pilotless aircraft.

5 All these assumptions proved correct.

6 At that stage lack of communications and manning difficulties were expected to make the usual system of control impracticable.

7 The weapons actually deployed in the middle of August, I944, when the campaign was in full swing, comprised 800 H.A.A. and I,I00 40 mm.

L.A.A. guns, over 700 rocket barrels, and some 600 light guns (mostly 20 mm.) manned by the R.A.F. Regiment and the Royal Armoured Corps.

8 On the IIth June, however, the Air Ministry received a report which stated that a train loaded with missiles had passed westwards through Belgium two days earlier. On the same day photographic reconnaissance revealed unusual activity at six of the "modified sites". This information did not reach my headquarters until after the German offensive had begun; but little or nothing would have been gained if I had received it earlier, for the defence plan had been ready since March, and I should not have ordered deployment merely on the strength of these two reports.

9 The figures were:

	Brought down outside London	Brought down inside London
By fighters alone	7	-
By guns alone	14	11
By fighters and guns jointly	1	-
Totals	22	11

I0 Originally the Germans meant the bombs to fly higher, doubtless so as to minimize the effect of light A.A. fire. This proved impracticable, and without the knowledge of the Air Ministry they changed their plans.

II This figure does not include "abortive" bombs which fell in France or into the sea on the French side of the Channel. It seems that the Germans launched five flying bombs for every four that came within the compass of the defences.

I2 Most of the bombs seem to have left the launching sites at about 200 m.p.h. Their speed increased throughout their flight, reaching about 340 m.p.h. at the English coast and 400 m.p.h. or thereabouts over London.

I3 During the first six weeks of the attacks alone, eighteen fighters were substantially damaged and five pilots and one Navigator/Radio Operator killed in this way. Even though the flying bomb could not hit back deliberately, "Diver" patrols were by no means unattended by risk.

I4 The "double parachute link" was a device whereby, as soon as a balloon cable was struck, it was automatically severed near the top and bottom, so that the aircraft which struck it carried away the central portion. Parachutes then opened at each end of this portion and exercised a drag intended to make the aircraft stall.

I5 It is true that by D-Day at the latest we knew that heavy damage had been done to the German transmitters. But until experience had shown that in consequence the Germans were manifestly unable to jam, General Pile and

I would not have been justified in departing from the plan on that account.

16 This figure was made up as follows:

Bombs brought down by

Guns alone	23
Fighters alone	19
Guns and fighters jointly	1
The balloon barrage	17
	60

17 This figure was made up as follows:

Shot down by fighters

over sea	13
over land	10
=	23

Shot down by A.A. guns

over sea	46
over land	19
=	65
Brought down by balloons	2
	90

18 An alternative deployment envisaging the mounting of guns on ships moored in the mouth of the Thames, as well as on land, was considered, but rejected because General Pile preferred a deployment that would allow of continuous engagement of bombs by cross fire as they flew up the river, and also because, in any case, not enough ships could have been found to make the plan fully effective. Nevertheless, a few guns mounted on forts and small vessels were eventually included in the eastern "Diver" defences.

19 In addition, 1,250 possible balloon-sites north of the Thames were reconnoitred; but I decided not to fly any balloons in that area unless it became essential to do so, since General Pile feared that their cables would hamper the defence of London against orthodox air attack by interfering with the radar sets belonging to the guns.

20 For an account of the rocket campaign, which was to start on the 8th September, 1944, see Part III.

21 There were airfields in northern and central Holland which he might still have used; but tactically they would have been no more convenient than bases in Western Germany, and to supply them with bombs and fuel would have been no easy matter.

22 The permanent defences of towns like Harwich and Lowestoft were incorporated in the "strip" and are included in these figures.

23 At first these searchlights were deployed at intervals of 3,000 yards. Experience showed that so thick a spacing tended to dazzle pilots and we altered the interval to the normal 6,000 yards.

24 The fractions relate to claims shared between different arms of the defence.

25 These activities, which were an extension of those normally conducted in respect of artillery fire, were accordingly known as "flash spotting" and "sound ranging" respectively.

26 They were at Watten, Wizernes, Mimoyecques (near Marquise), Siracourt, and Lottinghem in the Pas de Calais, and at Martinvast and Sottevast near Cherbourg. The constructions had few features in common apart from their great size.

27 There were, however, some distinguished disbelievers in the rocket, who continued long after this to argue that the story was a hoax.

28 See paragraphs 16-18, above.

29 In the later stages of the campaign the Germans did, however, use radio for control of range in certain cases. They do not seem to have perfected this technique, which gave less accurate results than their usual methods.

30 "Armed reconnaissance" is defined as "air reconnaissance carried out by offensively-armed aircraft with the intention of locating and attacking suitable enemy targets".

31 This was an area, defined from time to time by the Air Commander-in-Chief, in which the conduct of all air operations devolved upon the Tactical Air Forces.

32 During the first phase a few rockets were fired at London from the Island of Walcheren as well.

33 See paras. 133-134, above.

34 The rocket fired on the 18th must have been a parting shot from a rear detachment of the departing troops. The report that firing occurred on the 19th was doubtless a mistaken one; or perhaps the message was misconstrued.

35 See paragraph 165, above.

36 On several occasions areas under water or otherwise unsuitable for rocket-firing were indicated.

37 During the previous few weeks nearly 100,000 photographs of western Holland had been examined by interpreters. Not a single firing point had been found.

38 Air Marshal Coningham, of whose Command No. 2 Group formed part, had agreed to my making such requests direct to the headquarters of the Group in England.

39 Strictly speaking, there were two objectives at Bloemendaal, with separate target names and numbers. The storage area round Bloemendaal church was known as "The Hague/Bloemendaal"; the neighbouring lunatic asylum in which firing troops were quartered and whose grounds were said to be used for storing and possibly for firing rockets was known as "The Hague/Ockenburg Klinier". Our suggestion was that the two should be regarded as a single complex, whose internal and external communications could be disrupted at the same time as the living quarters and equipment were destroyed, by bombing two given aiming points.

40 See paragraph I34, above.

4I This programme included attacks on railway bridges at Deventer, Zwolle, and Zutphen, which some competent judges considered the most promising form of countermeasure to the rocket offensive from western Holland.

42 The squadrons were:

No. 453 Squadron Spitfire XVI
No. 229 Squadron Spitfire XVI
No. 602 Squadron Spitfire XVI
No. 303 Squadron Spitfire IX

The Spitfires XVI were each capable of carrying two 250 lb. bombs and an overload tank which enabled them to fly to and from their bases in England without refuelling on the Continent. By refuelling in Belgium – which became possible on a strictly limited scale at the end of November – they could dispense with the tank and carry twice the load of bombs. The Spitfire IX could carry at most one 500 lb. bomb and that only by refuelling in Belgium. At this stage, therefore, we did not normally use No. 303 Squadron to carry bombs.

43 The additional squadrons selected were Nos. 45I (Spitfire XVI) and I24 (Spitfire IX, modified for bombing).

44 Oberkommando der Wehrmacht, or Supreme Command of the Armed Forces.

ABBREVIATIONS

AA	Anti-aircraft
AALMG	Anti-Aircraft Light Machine-Gun
A/C	Aircraft
ADC	Aide-De-Camp
ADGB	Air Defence of Great Britain
AFC	Air Force Cross
AI	Airborne Intercept (radar)
AOC-in-C	Air Officer Commanding-in-Chief
ASV	Aircraft to Surface Vessel
ATS	Auxiliary Territorial Service
AVM	Air Vice-Marshal
BBC	British Broadcasting Corporation
CAM	Catapult Aircraft Merchant (ship(s))
CB	Companion of the Most Honourable Order of the Bath
CBE	Commander of the Order of the British Empire
CH	Chain Home
CHL	Chain Home Low
C-in-C	Commander-in-Chief
CMG	Companion of The Most Distinguished Order of Saint Michael and Saint George
CVO	Commander of the Royal Victorian Order
D/F	Direction Finder/Direction Finding
DEMS	Defensively Equipped Merchant Ship(s)

DFC	Distinguished Flying Cross
DSO	Distinguished Service Order
FAS	Forward Area Sight
GCB	Knight Grand Cross of the Most Honourable Order of the Bath
GCI	Ground Controlled Intercept/Ground Control of Interception
GCVO	Knight Grand Cross of The Royal Victorian Order
GDA	Gun Defended Area
GL	Gun Laying
GOC	General Officer Commanding
GOR	Gun Operations Room
GPO	Gun Position Officer/General Post Office
HAA	Heavy Anti-Aircraft
HE	High Explosive
HF	High Frequency
Hp	Horse power
HQ	Headquarters
KBE	Knight Commander of the Most Excellent Order of the British Empire
KCB	Knight Commander of the Most Honourable Order of the Bath
LAA	Light Anti-Aircraft
MBE	Member of the Most Excellent Order of the British Empire
MC	Military Cross
MM	Military Medal
mph	miles per hour
MVO	Member of the Royal Victorian Order
NCO	Non Commissioned Officer
OBE	Officer of the Most Excellent Order of the British Empire

OC	Officer Commanding
OIC	Officer-in-Charge
OTU	Officer Training Unit
R/T	Receiver-Transmitter/Radio Transmitter
RAF	Royal Air Force
RAFVR	Royal Air Force Volunteer Reserve
RAOC	Royal Army Ordnance Corps
RASC	Royal Army Service Corps
RCAF	Royal Canadian Air Force
RDF	Radio Direction Finding (Radar)
REME	Royal Electrical and Mechanical Engineers
SLC	Search Light Control
SOR	Sector Operator's Room
UP	Unrotated Projectile
US	United States
VHF	Very High Frequency
VIE	Visual Indicator Equipment
VP	Vulnerable Point
WAAF	Women's Auxiliary Air Force
W/T	Wireless Telegraphy/Wireless

INDEX OF NAVAL, MILITARY AND AIR FORCE UNITS

INDEX OF PERSONS